本书受到了三峡大学发展规划与学科建设办公室、
外国语学院以及三峡大学尼泊尔研究中心的资助，
在此表示感谢！

IRHRM

劳动关系和人力资源管理

跨国公司在华企业的跨文化障碍对比研究

# Industrial Relations and Human Resources Management:

a Comparative Analysis of Cultural
Barriers in Chinese Companies

席敬 / 著

中国社会科学出版社
CHINA SOCIAL SCIENCES PRESS

## 图书在版编目（CIP）数据

劳动关系和人力资源管理：跨国公司在华企业的跨文化障碍对比研究：英文 /
席敬著. —北京：中国社会科学出版社，2020.9
ISBN 978－7－5203－7175－9

Ⅰ.①劳…　Ⅱ.①席…　Ⅲ.①跨国公司－企业管理－人力资源管理－
研究－中国－英文　Ⅳ.①F279.247

中国版本图书馆 CIP 数据核字（2020）第 169056 号

出 版 人　赵剑英
责任编辑　刘凯琳
责任校对　孙砚文
责任印制　王　超

出　　　版　中国社会科学出版社
社　　　址　北京鼓楼西大街甲158号
邮　　　编　100720
网　　　址　http：//www.csspw.cn
发 行 部　010-84083685
门 市 部　010-84029450
经　　　销　新华书店及其他书店

印　　　刷　北京明恒达印务有限公司
装　　　订　廊坊市广阳区广增装订厂
版　　　次　2020年9月第1版
印　　　次　2020年9月第1次印刷

开　　　本　710×1000　1/16
印　　　张　18.5
字　　　数　342千字
定　　　价　108.00元

At first mankind

Is kind at heart,

With natures alike

But habits apart

——Mencius

# ACKNOWLEDGMENTS

When the curtains fall down, the actors come to salute, I would like to thank my supervisor: Prof. Karl Koch, who has given me more assistance than I thought was possible, who has taught me more than I realised was knowable, and who has shown more kindness than I believed possible. I appreciate Mr. Colin Knapp and Ms Avril Platt helping my PhD study as a second, and third supervisor and giving me advice all the way along.

I also would like to express my thanks to Dr. Lynn Xiao, my PhD colleagues and friends for her hospitality and encouragement for the whole time of my studies. I thank Faculty of Business for providing my PhD scholarship.

My thanks go to my family, my wife, Ms Cao Hongping who has offered me endless love, and my son, Xi Yiru, who has accompanied with me in London in unforgettable experience, and offered lots of help in statistics. Thanks to my colleague, Ms Libby Liu in China Three Gorges University who helped me take care of our career in the international cooperation, and my post-graduates students, Miss Xi Chunlian, Mr Wan Zhongchi, and Miss Li Yanjiao who assisted my administrative work when I was out for the research.

Last, my mother: hi, mum, thanks for bringing me to this world. All is well and ends well!

# PREFACE

Over the past decade the economic and political rise of China as a leading country in the global environment has been spectacular; the significance of China as a global force has given it an exceptional position in the determination of the development of economies on almost all continents. In economic terms China has achieved to create a manufacturing economy and exporter of goods which occupies a leading global position. Since China's entrance to the World Trade Organisation in 2001 it has rapidly established itself as one of the most significant trading nation in the world playing a crucial role in international trade. In addition to this solid economic base in the international environment China's investment strategies, both in internal and external markets, had a marked expansion.

The consequences of these developments in China have resulted in a rapid, and all-embracing internalisation, inclusive of the vast industrial sector; this has opened an ever growing territory which necessitates deeper knowledge and perceptions by the actors involved in these areas. As outward Foreign Direct Investment (FDI), in particular where Chinese companies invested in developing and developed countries, expanded significantly from 2015, and indeed was strengthened in 2019 by a Foreign Investment Law, passed by China's National People's Congress, awareness and detailed knowledge of specific areas, such as industry for example, became progressively imperative.

It is in this context that the author of this book has provided a crucial analysis of part of the socioeconomic infrastructure pertinent for a deeper understanding of the structure, organisation, and understanding required by managers active in the internationalised environment that companies are required to operate in. The book, therefore, focuses on the broad area of Industrial Relations (IR) and Human Resource Management (HRM), and specifically in evaluating and explaining the under researched area of cultural barriers in Chinese companies. The cultural perceptions, practices and underlying socio-economic behavioural patterns are individualistic to nations and as the book reveals this impacts on the efficacy of companies and ultimately on their profitability.

Central then for any study investigating cultural barriers in the framework of multinational corporations (MNC) is constructing a conceptual model that clarifies the nature and meaning of 'culture'. The literature dealing with culture is vast, and is frequently determined by both the genesis of the research focus and the discipline, and this is reflected in the present book. Thus the review and discussion of culture in terms of definition and application for the empirical research is embedded in the industrial relations and human resource issues being considered. A unique feature of the approach is that culture and language are merged and consequently there is a direct practical value from the company case studies on which the empirical research is based. This can be illustrated by the expression 'industrial relations', which has deep historical roots in the English-speaking world and linguistically embraces a system describing a particular set of factors shaping the relationship between employees and management. It is, therefore, a phrase which cannot be translated easily into other languages. The author has summarised these idiosyncratic aspects of employment relations under the umbrella term, Anglo-Saxon. This allows an emphasis in comparative employment relation analysis which is distinctive from both European and USA systems and distinctly relates to the context of those MNRC's influenced by those Anglo-Saxon systems.

This provides a pragmatic understanding of how cultural barriers can be bridged by comprehension of how Chinese interpretations of industrial relations, and the human resource issues arising from these, in MNC's differ. Thus the concept of industrial relations in the Anglo-Saxon framework has an original historical meaning based on the ideological concept of the stark differences between employees and employers; the process of collective bargaining, for example, is regarded as conflictual. In contrast many European industrial relations systems have an approach which is consensual or, as in the case of Germany, based on a partnership model. China's conception of employee and employer relations are based on profoundly different historical origins and for those from other cultures it is crucial to understand the Chinese cultural predispositions as they apply to the term industrial relations. Predominant is the influence of Confucianism, which is extremely complex, but a principal idea is the role of harmony through the subordination of all other goals; the creation and maintenance of a Chinese economy for a 'harmonious society' of which, of course, industrial relations systems are a part.

The author has succeeded in analysing and describing these interrelated aspects which form part of national cultures and explain the values, behavioural patterns and beliefs of different national cultures and which are challenges that MNC's have to overcome when based in a variety of different cultures. In essence these different components shape the comprehension of industrial sectors and the larger business environment, including the actors and HRM strategies, and individual interpretations are based on specific contextual paradigms. So the ability to communicate in the increasingly interconnectivity of the global business environment through correct translations becomes of paramount importance.

However, comparative research focusing on the multifaceted variable as those pertinent to cultural barriers demands not only a rigorous, but also a wide-ranging methodology. This was fulfilled by the research described in the book by adopting a mix of questionnaires, inclusive of the internet, surveys, and selected semi-structured interviews, and encompassing a range of areas and enterprises, for example manufacturing, international trade, textiles, pharmaceuticals, and the automobile industry. The combination of qualitative and quantitative data permitted clear conclusions of extend, complications, problems and significance of cultural barriers in the selected industries and enterprises. Amongst the findings is the clear evidence that the recognition of cultural and language synthesis, and hence language structure and expression, derived from it, create obstacles for HRM management. It indicates that cultural intelligence is a positive skill that allows industrial relations actors to exercise a constructive role, and thereby increase the efficiency of companies.

The author suggests a conceptual model which can be applied as a tool by researchers and the relevant actors in IR and HRM, it has the virtue of addressing the macro level of culture and language, that is the national and organisational level of companies, as well as the micro level, where intrapersonal and interpersonal communication is so vital in overcoming cultural barriers. In this respect the author has produced a valuable and unique book which will be an enormous asset for Chinese scholars and IR and HRM actors, as well as adding a significant factor to the impetus of China's dynamic economic development.

**Professor Emeritus Karl Koch, Fellow of the Royal Society of Arts (FRSA), Business School, London South Bank University, UK**

# CONTENTS

# LIST OF FIGURES

# LIST OF PIE CHART

# LIST OF TABLES

# LIST OF DIAGRAMS

# LIST OF HISTOGRAMS

# LIST OF MAPS

# ABBREVIATIONS

ACFTU: All China Federation of Trade Union
ASC : Anglo-Saxon Culture
BRI: Belt and Road Initiative
CFCRS: China-Foreign Cooperation in Running Schools
CET: College English Test
CCC: Cross-Cultural Competence
CCT: Cross-cultural training
CPC: Communist Party of China
EAIEs : East Asian-owned firms
FDI: Foreign Direct Investment
FICs: Foreign Invested Corporations
GDP: gross domestic product
GLOBE: Global Leadership and Organizational Behaviour Effectiveness
HRM : Human Resources Management
IRs: Industrial Relations
IMF: International Monetary Fund
ILO: the International Labour Organization
JVEs: Joint-Venture Enterprises
LLLIRs: Linguistics of Labour Law and Industrial Relations
MNCs : Multinational Corporations
MIR: Modern Paradigm
NVC :Non-verbal Communication
NVA: Non-verbal action
NBSC: National Bureau of Statistics of China
OIR: Original Paradigm
PPP; Purchasing Power Parity
RGT : Repertory Grid Interview
SPSS: Statistical Package for Social Science
SOEs: State Owned Emprises
TEDA: Tianjin Economic Technological Development Area

TOEs, VOEs : Township and Village Owned Enterprises
UNCTAD: United Nations Conference on Trade and Development
YICT: Yantian International Container Terminals

# Chapter One
# Introduction-Research Objectives and Framework

The world seems very big and some countries are so far away. But with advances in technology and transportation, the world seems to be shrinking. It has become smaller in the sense that we can now communicate instantly, anywhere around the globe. We can also mobilize and physically be anywhere in the world in a matter of hours. This has created an avenue for companies to both share and compete with each other even though they may be on different continents. This is something that is referred to as "internationalization". This chapter is trying to place the research into context and explain the research questions and focuses. Furthermore, this chapter will discuss how research questions shall be answered by offering an outline and references.

## 1.1. Internationalization

**Contour of Internationalization: Convergence or Divergence**

It seems that internationalization has been the trend of the world's economy for years, as it has obvious advantages in extending one nation's competitiveness. Trade between nations brings competition, while 'competition in many industries has internationalized, not only in manufacturing industries but increasingly in services (Porter, 1990). In 2000, the International Monetary Fund (IMF) identified four basic aspects of globalization: trade and transactions, capital and investment movements, migration and movement of people, and the dissemination of knowledge. Thus, a number of questions could be raised, such as the following:

Is it possible for one nation to develop without stepping into the internationalized economic structure? And if this is unavoidable, are there convergent patterns of internationalization for every nation?

For the first question, the answer is negative: in the course of one nation promoting its competitiveness in the world market, it is necessary for the nation to search and extend its strength in a certain area, such as low-cost labour, abundant natural resources, or capital flows. Differences in nations' strengths and products will trigger trade, making it valuable, while conflicts come into being along with the imbalances of trade between nations.

To improve the competence of competitiveness, companies are thinking of various ways to improve quality and achieve lower costs and more harmonious employment relations. For example, the post-Fordist pattern for employment relations (Piore and Sabel, 1984) offers a more flexible and innovative way to meet challenges by offering diverse and customized products. Internationalization is a gateway to release a nation's competitive advantage.

International trade is one of the most effective ways of strengthening companies' competitive advantage, which ultimately forms a nation's prosperity. This is the reason why almost every nation issues policies encouraging varieties of internationalized strategies to stimulate products, labour and technological exports. It can be said that the ocean of internationalization floods all the people of the world who wish to keep their independent and preserved realm. Facing the coming twenty-first century,"immensely powerful currents of capital, labour and information turn and shape the world, with a growing disregard for the borders and opinions of states." (Harari, 2014:232) We are living in a global village.

A nation's international strategy could be analyzed from three aspects: economic systems, cultural patterns, and political systems. As for the second question, researchers have focused on national advantages (Porter, 1990), culture (Hofstede, 1998, 2000; Trompenaars and Hampden-Turner, 1998), and political systems (Caramani, 2008), arguing that only when one nation develops its strength in a certain area can people earn their seats in the tide of internationalization. Porter (1990) pointed out that the divergent advantage of a national strategy creates the multi-dimensional beneficial relationships between nations: therefore, a divergent internationalized pattern for the nations is a dominant situation in today's world.

## Internationalisation or globalisation

The words 'internationalization' and 'globalization' have been quoted in many scenarios, which make it necessary to distinguish them and their relations. Although these words do not mean the same thing, many people mix them up, thinking they are interchangeable. When analyzing these two words, discrepancies can be identified, as summarized below.

First of all, judging from the definitions, subtle differences can be found between the lines. From the Oxford Advanced Learner's English-Chinese Dictionary, internationalization is defined as "to bring something under the control or protection of many nations; to make something international, connected with or involving two or more countries". However, the depiction of globalization from Wikipedia (2014) is that if something – for example, a business company – globalizes or is globalized, it operates all around the world. Additionally, from the website, "elimination of barriers to trade, communications and cultural exchange" are also defined as globalization.

Some subtleties will still be lost in these definitions due to the relatively abstract nature of these concepts. Hereon, more examples will be given. Internationalization means that firms extend their products and services to overseas markets, usually from their home country. In other words, the behaviour of exporting could be called internationalization. As to globalization, it can be understood as the process by which businesses create value by leveraging their resources and capabilities across borders, and includes the coordination of cross-border manufacturing and marketing strategies. Thus, globalization is actually at a higher level than internationalization, as globalization starts from a strategic perspective.

Secondly, distinguishing from their correlation, internationalization could be regarded as the first stage in the globalization process. A company firstly exports its goods to other countries, starting its internationalization, and then goes on to extend its scale and influence: hereafter, the process of globalization begins. There is no doubt that internationalization and globalization are inseparable, but internationalization could be treated as the prerequisite to globalization. Without internationalization, globalization cannot function well.

Furthermore, internationalization could appear to be a simpler process. The way to judge this is to check whether the products or even other abstract objects are exported to other countries. However, globalization is a much more complex process throughout the world's development. The quantization of globalization (Bridges, 2002) could be the proportions of foreign investments with respect to the total volume: for example, foreign assets with respect to total assets, foreign sales with respect to total sales and foreign employment with respect to total employment.

Scholars gave different conceptualized interpretation, for example, Knight and De Wit (1997:6) argued that globalization shall be defined as the "flow of technology, economy, knowledge, people, value, ideas... ... across borders", while internationalization emphasises the link between local and global and includes diversity and intercultural communications(Ainsworth,2013:30).

To sum up, internationalization and globalization will extend successful home market products and strategies, taking advantage of factor resources available in the worldwide marketplace. Distinguishing them in a more subtle way will make our world function better.

## 1.2. Importance of Multinational Corporations (MNCs)

Multinational corporations (MNCs), sometimes also named trans-national corporations or global corporations (Harrod, 2000), can be traced back as early as the 15th century during the major colonising and imperialist ventures from Western Europe. But earlier trans-national corporations, such as Britain's East India Trading Company, were focused on helping their home countries' territorial acquisitions or extending the trade business.

The achievements of the industrial revolution in the 19th century were remarkable: factory systems changed, modern technology was widely adopted, and faster means of transportation shortened the distance between people in different continents. These developments laid the foundation for new types of MNCs as they are known today.

There has been some debate surrounding the terms 'trans-national', 'multinational' and 'global' corporations. Harrod (2000) argues that 'multinational' implies administrating in several countries, and says nothing about the relationship of the companies with national boundaries or with the structure of the global economy. 'Trans-national' transcends nations and borders, and 'global' implies global operation. He later explained:

*"...Many multinationals only operate in a select number of countries and have a core objective of using international production to service a single national market. However, the inclusion of financial corporations and banks in the multinational*

*discussion permits the use of both transnational and/or global in relation to banks and non-bank financial corporations as their production assets are not necessarily fixed or established in a national state". (Harrod, 2000)*

For the convenience of research, this paper uses the term 'multinational', which refers to those corporations that have set up subsidiaries in China, which may include all types of corporations that Harrod defined as trans-national and global. In the year 2000, there were 63,000 MNCs controlling about 690,000 subsidiaries in almost all countries, industrial areas and economic institutes of the world (Aid, 2000). In China, the number of foreign invested corporations (FICs) reached 122,288 in 2015, according to China Buereau of Statistics. In 2007, 27% of value-added production was from FICs and more than 24 million Chinese workers were hired in FICs (US-China Business Council 2007). Statistics from the China Ministry of Commerce showed that in 2011, FDI had taken 49.6% of gross export value, and 52.4% of gross import value, which took one-third of the nation's gross export and import value (Ministry of Commerce 2011). MNCs in China are playing an increasingly important role from a range of aspects, such as employment relations, economic systems, local culture and government policies.

## 1.3. Impetus on Global Strategy

After the Second World War, MNCs became prosperous. The first sign of MNCs expanding worldwide was in the 1950s, when corporations in the US, Europe and Japan, with the help of banks' investment with vast sums of money in stocks and capital flows, rapidly expanded their market shares. By the 1970s, one-third of the 300 MNCs owned assets of 1 billion US dollars or more, and controlled 70-80 percent of world trade outside the centrally planned economies (Greer and Singh, 2000).

There are two different opinions towards MNCs' expansion in the global market. The positive group argues that MNCs have brought new technology, advanced management and capital to many countries, which generally are developing countries that expect financial input and high technology support. People from these countries gain more employment opportunities, and their life quality also improves. Conversely, another group contends that MNCs have a purely profit-oriented motivation, which impacts the MNCs' policymaking, such as exploiting the cheap labour of developing countries, investing in polluted industries and controlling the political system of the governments.

Even worse, the media, one of the most important forces today, is most likely controlled by MNCs, and information relating to them is often biased, lacking in objectivity.

No matter what arguments they may cause, MNCs have been thriving worldwide, especially in developing countries and newly reviving economic regions. MNCs have earned welcome by the governments. UNCTAD has defined three ratios to measure the scale of MNCs, namely foreign sales to total sales, foreign assets to total assets, and foreign employment to total employment (UNCTAD:1995). The achievements and the problems associated with MNCs' success have drawn the attention and interest of both academia and government officials.

## 1.4. Developing Trend for MNCs

Even though there have been different comments on MNCs function, no matter it is good or not, certain types of trends for MNCs' development are more clear thanks to the new technology in internet information and large data revolution, which could be concluded as:

(1). More globalized marketing. Groups of MNCs changed their strategy from selling their products worldwide to taking part in global competition by managing global resources.

(2). More emphasis on servicing. In the process of the whole industry chain, MNCs have concentrated their main power into certain core sections with the aim of expanding the global market, becoming stronger competitors and earning competitive advantages. With

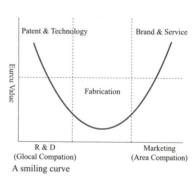

**Figure1.1. A smiling curve**

*Source: netmba.com. 2006*

the development of technology, products could be fragmented into different modules which make possible cheap large-scale modular manufacture: thus, MNCs set these correspondent sections abroad, and devote more interest to the two ends of the 'Smiling Curve' (See Figure 1.1.): that is, the patent and technology, and brand and service.

(3). Outsourcing strategy. MNCs, due to the needs of the global industrial chain, generally outsource their manufacturing sections, and more recently this outsourcing has expanded to the service section. Today, MNCs undertake outsourcing cooperation not just in traditional manufacturing, but also in finance, information management and product design (See Figure 1.2.).

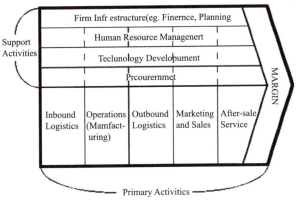

**Figure 1.2. MNCs' outsourcing contents**

*Source: netmba.com. 2006*

(4). Integrated strategy. MNCs sometime voluntarily withdraw from certain areas in order to earn competitive advantage. To strengthen some of their core business, MNCs adopt the strategy of integrating with other MNCs in the form of amalgamation, reconciliation, or strategic alliance.

(5). Networking management structure. A new managerial structure has been formed with the characteristics of multi-functional, regional and business-oriented management, which has created a network of multi-centred conjuncture. MNCs set their regional sub-divisions and business agencies in different nations and territories (See Figure 1.3.).

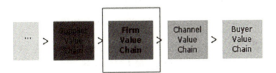

**Figure 1.3. The value system**

*Source: netmba.com. 2006*

(6). Informatics management platform. As MNCs adapt their strategy to a more global-oriented market and outsourcing, information technology such as large data and cloud computing, is a supporting platform to help make those strategies happen.

(7). Internationalized employability. In the course of MNCs' global strategic adjustment processing, employees with global competitive competence require MNCs with a more efficient mixed module. A high-end talent for MNCs should have global perspective, strategic thinking and be capable of international and cross-cultural competence in management.

(8). Accelerating capitalization in source distribution. It has been demonstrated that amalgamation of international enterprises is an important channel for MNCs to absorb and optimise global resources, whereas most of the amalgamation has occurred in the international capital market: that is to say, MNCs' resource distribution has been capitalized for the first time.

(9). MNCs accountability. It has been taken as the mainstream for MNCs' accountability to be directly underpinned by the United Nation, especially since the economic recession in 2008, as low carbon emission and new energy industries have become a new economic driving force for all countries. Accountability has been the priority for MNCs' international management.

(10). Multi-structure of corporate governance. Corresponding with corporate accountability, the structure for corporate governance has evolved into a more diverse pattern, from the traditional stakeholder management to current shareholders' participation: the shareholders could be stakeholders, corporative partners, employees, or society.

## 1.5. Research Area and Research Objective

### 1.5.1. Culture /Language and its Connection with MNCs

With the expansion of MNCs in the global market, high-end talents with cross-cultural competence are one of the key factors to earn competitive advantages. On the other hand, the low-end parts of the industry chain are generally located in the developing countries, where their prosperity is generated by mass cheap labour, and issues relating to industrial relations, which were not previously considered in western countries, are becoming an important phenomenon, while culture, language and international industrial relations (IIR) all contribute to a more complex and culturally nuanced situation.

To understand and manage the IIR in the respective countries, culture and language barriers are the first factors to consider. The barriers of culture and language on IIR are not only a one-way process, but a long series of conflicts and negotiations. Managing the IIR is actually a process of cross-cultural communications: for this reason, this study takes the perspective of cross-cultural theories and international language (See Figure 1.4.).

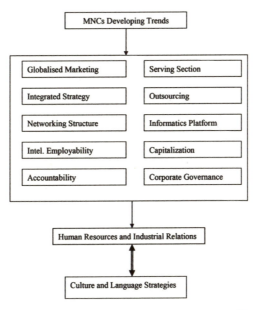

**Figure 1. 4. MNCs and its connection with culture and language**

As for the factor of language, English is becoming a global *lingua franca*. More than one billion people speak English around the world, of whom 400 million are native English speakers and 600 million are non-native speakers (Bolton, 2002). In light of this, it has been argued that English no longer exclusively represents the culture and nationality of native English-speaking countries (Sung, 2013), but reflects the culture of any nation where English is spoken. For instance, research from the Chinese university English curriculum suggests that it is necessary to make amendments for required and optional courses for Chinese English-major college students (Hu and Xi, 2013). In the Chinese *Gaokao*, a national college entrance test which is described as once-in-a-lifetime fight for young people's destiny, the score for the English component is as important as that for the Chinese component.

When talking about the role of English, Chinese government has asked for English language education from elementary school level since the 1970s, shortly after the Cultural Revolution, but English is still spoken only by a few educated people due to its ineffective and low quality language pedagogy, as well as the wide range of dialects in China, and Mandarin Chinese is still not well spoken among the migrant workers, bringing further problems and interfering with MNCs' language strategy. Generally speaking, there are seven dialect groups in China, creating communicative barriers for people from different regions and easily creating in-group organization, which possibly defies the trade union administration policies.

Cultural diversity presents another challenge for MNCs merging into the local society and market, especially anything relating to people. The management of IR and HRM is, of course, managing people. The uniqueness of China's cultural features and language situation creates different IR and HRM management characteristics.

English today is no longer just what people thought years ago. Its diversity and characteristics as a global *lingua franca* create a more complex phenomenon of English language learning, not just American English and British English, but also Indian English and *Chinglish* – Chinese English: that is to say, language learning is accompanied by a certain type of cultural acquisition. As for the MNCs, although English could be defined as the official language for internal communications, the cultural background varies in the different nations: this is one of the reasons forcing MNCs to set respective global language strategies.

Culture, as the anthropologist Taylor (cited in Murphy, 1986, p. xx) said, is "a complex of whole", and caught the attention of scholars from different areas early in the 19th century. Thanks to modern technology, transportation and communication innovations, MNCs came to prosperity after 1988 (Greer and Singh, 2000). Since then, scholars have noticed the cultural barriers faced by MNCs in the course of their expanding business. Hofstede (1980, 1988, 2001, and 2015) was one of the pioneers in this field and was assigned to investigate cultural interference in IBM, which at the time was the biggest MNC in the world in 1980s. Hofstede's four cultural dimensions, a theoretical innovation absorbing the achievements from management, sociology and psychology, give a convincing interpretation of cross-cultural encounters in MNCs. Since Hofstede, scholars have contributed more theories on guiding cross-cultural management (Trompenaars and Turner, 1997, 2004; Triandis et al., 1990; Patel and Taran, 2014)

Language strategy has been one of the unavoidable challenges for MNCs entering into guest countries or regions. Research has proved that certain types of language strategies have been considered in MNCs (Marschan, 1996; Harzing and Feely, 2003, 2008; Buckley et al., 2005; Wang and Zhu, 2013).

Marschan (1996) explored the control mechanisms in MNCs in formal and informal ways, and argued that language could be either a facilitation or impediment in inter-communication and the multinational's operations. In her case study of a Finnish multinational elevator company, she found that "language policies are clearly linked with the HRM process with respect to selection, training, and staff transfers as a way of building language competence" (1997). Marschan explored the language impact from the perspective of communication control mechanisms, which was a feasible and innovative method in culture and language studies, and offered many constructive clues for successors. Unlike Cyr (1995), who insists on a divergent strategy by setting up corporate culture in multinationals, Marschan argues that "a shared company language does not necessarily ensure that meaningful communication occurs". This could be quite contentious in the context of different MNCs' management.

Harzing and Feely (2003, 2008) have undertaken research into the language issues in management domains and presented some constructive suggestions and patterns for further study. Harzing (2008) extended the social identity theory by absorbing active components from sociolinguistics and social psychology. Social identity, an essential component of Harzing's communication patterns, is defined on the basis of Tajfel's (1978) research, as:

*"That part of an individual's self-concept which derives from his [or her] knowledge of [his or her] membership in a social group (or groups) together with the values and emotional significance attached to that membership."*

Harzing then explained that contemporary sociolinguistics has shown that language is one of the major factors to categorize one person from another and to provide a more powerful indication of a person's identity (Giles and Johnson 1981), thus setting up the linkage between language and social identity. Harzing and Feely (2003) advanced a model that attempts to address the language barrier and its impact on communication. In a recent reseaerch on how a host country language acquisition may or may not improve the relatiosnhip between expatriates and local employees in MNC subsidiaries (Zhang & Harzing: 2016), language and cultural were proved to be pivtal in creating harmonious relationship. If expatriate willing to learn and can speak host country language, home employees may feel to be respected and prefer a harmounious relationship; if expatriate willing to learn, but cannot or does not feel confident speaking local language, a certain distant relationship shall be likely formed, and even worse, the research found that if expatriate not willing to learn, nor to speak local language, it may easily come to a segregated relationship (see Figure 1.5).

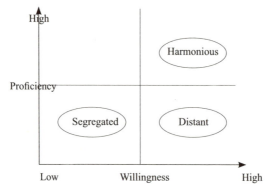

**Figure 1. 5.   Impact on expatriate and home country employees**

*Source: Zhang, E.L., & Harzing, A.W. 2016. From dilemmatic struggle to legitimized indifference: expatriates' host country language learning and its impact on the expatriates - HCE relationship*

Park (1996) demonstrated, in his study of American MNCs in South Korea, that Korean staff who possessed limited English proficiency encountered more problems in dealing with their American counterparts. He suggests that "foreign language training should become a key aspect of expatriate training in order to facilitate more effective communication within foreign subsidiaries".

Language as a barrier in international business has attracted considerable attention from scholars, but there has been little research in the context of MNCs in China and joint venture practice. Buckley et al. (2005) explored how social knowledge is transferred to the Chinese subsidiaries from the parent companies. To find out how social knowledge, along with language, promotes communication and the transfer of knowledge across borders, their study investigated MNCs located in Beijing and Shanghai and tried to find out the technology transfer, management skills and language strategy for each subsidiary. Buckley et al. argued that "technical competence and management skills are normally the key to success in transferring knowledge, but in doing it across borders, language competence is equally important" (2005:55). The research found that different language strategies brought distinctive gaps in technology transfer and company achievement.

Buckley's research explained the role of language strategy for MNCs in managing their subsidiaries. It exposed meagre research in China's transition period and argued that, in terms of HRM and IRs operations, language strategy plays the same role as Buckley's technology transfer, but further empirical studies are required to reveal what exactly is the objective of this research.

## 1.5.2. Research Objective

China has, therefore, evolved a complex socio-economic system which needs analysis of many aspects, including an in depth understanding of cultural barriers. Previous research from scholars and practitioners proved that, in the course of internationalization, the expansion of MNCs in the global market, management relating to culture barriers has been one of serious obstacles preventing the MNCs from further development.

Looking at the influence of MNCs, JVCs and FDI on China's economy, the recent increasing factory actions, and clashes provoke a series of questions relating to industrial relations and cultural barriers.

This research is trying, under the guidance of previous theoretical findings and a model invented by the author, to find out cultural barriers and its functions in managing the IR and HRM issues in China's MNCs, JVCs and FDI enterprises.

## Why Using Anglo-Saxon Culture (ASC) Term

This research is based on the background that China has been developing rapidly with large overseas investment coming in. Thinking of a large number of above mentioned enterprises coming from different cultural background and, more importantly, enterprises derived from the Anglo-Saxon cultural took a big proportion in China, and owned quite distinctive cultural features with local tradition, this research, thus, is focusing on the cultural encounters between the Anglo-Saxon and Chinese cultural characteristics. More explanations for the reasons of selecting and defining Anglo-Saxon culture will be given in the next chapter. Among these overseas-funded enterprises, those which are Anglo-Saxon culture based account for a remarkable proportion. According to the statistics of Fortune 500 enterprises, by the end of year 2016, there have been 13 British enterprises engaged in the industry of finance, food, pharmaceuticals and energy in China; 55 American enterprises in food, pharmaceuticals, finance, IT, mechanical and electrical engineering, automobile, retail, energy and chemical engineering; 3 Australian enterprises in agriculture, mining and finance. These enterprises, with a large number of Chinese employees, exert huge influence on them through their unique Anglo-Saxon culture. Compared with Japanese and Korean enterprises which are culturally similar to Chinese ones, there are larger cultural and language differences and more intense conflicts in the enterprises mentioned before. Besides, considering the predominant role and economic power of Anglo-Saxon culture in the West, comparison research between it and Chinese culture could prove to be meaningful.

The comparison research between two cultures and languages is conducted within IR framework, since industrial relations is one of the basic social relations among people. The harmony of IR is closely related to the enterprise's survival and development potential. Thus this research is trying to: find out the cultural and language barriers in IR of Anglo-Saxon culture based enterprises in China; look for approaches to these cultural and language barriers from the perspective of industrial relations; whether the approaches are effective or not; find out whether these enterprises will make exact language strategy to counter differences; find out whether if there is a ready-made model for enterprise operators to counter differences and realize effective cross-cultural communication in order to achieve the harmony of industrial relations.

By and large, this research is trying to explore some aspects in relating to the IR and HRM, for example, what are the cultural features of China's industrial relations and human resources management in the context of transition economic period?

Industrial relations (IR) are both an old and a young topic in the analysis of the management of companies. It is old because IR was so crucial in the early days of the industrial revolution. But the situation has changed considerably along with the development of human society, advanced technology and our understanding of human relations. IR, traditionally defined as "the institutions of job regulation", is a set of phenomena, both inside and outside the workplace, concerned with determining and regulating the employment relationship (Flanders, 1965:4; Salamon, 2000:3). Stanton et al. (2009) concluded, after an explicit study of MNCs management in the past, that there are four key research areas for IR, namely (1) what levels of discretion do subsidiaries have over decision making? (2) What are the factors influencing levels of control, and how are HR operations structured, organized and supported? (3) What are the host country effects, and (4) how are the differences of employment relations applied to local employees?

The IR of MNCs in different countries varies with the local culture, political system, religion and economic structure. Scholars from different countries have analysed the characteristics of the localized IR application in MNCs (Stanton et al., 2009; Hall and Soskice, 2001; Whitley, 2001; Oliver and Wilknson, 1998; Almond et al., 2005; Fenton O'Creevy et al., 2007; McGraw, 2004). This research has proved that industrial relations are one of the key factors in MNCs' investment. Harmonious and effective IRs have paved the way for the success of MNCs' business, not just in the guest countries, but also in the global community.

China, as one of the newly reviving economic markets, has attracted many MNCs' investment. Subsidiaries from the world's top MNCs have been widely distributed in China's economic developing zones, such as the Yangtze Delta Economic Zone near the city of Shanghai, the Pearl River Delta Economic Zone near the city of Canton and the Tianjin Economic-Technological Development Area (TEDA). Industrial relations caused governments in the 1910s to pay more attention on it impact to economic construction. After Dengxiaoping's new economic reform in 1978, the IRs in China developed into a new era. In recently year, industrial conflicts, along with the development of China's economy, have increased dramatically according to a report from the economists comparing with the year 2011 to 2016. (See Figure 1.6.).

As for the factors of Anglo-Saxon culture impact, what are the most distinctive and influential factors of Anglo-Saxon and Chinese culture, and how those differences impact enterprises operation in terms of industrial relations and HRM? IRs is a kind of relationship between people, while gaps between people exist partly because of culture and language differences. Therefore, a study of IRs is to some extent unavoidable because of the factors in culture and language. Given the MNCs developing trends and the reason of China as key market for international investment, this study is trying to contribute an appropriate strategy for constructing harmonious industrial relation and HR module by analyzing the cultural and language barriers.

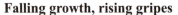

**Falling growth, rising gripes**

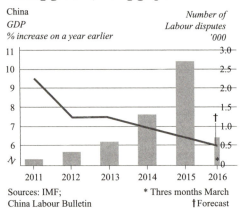

China
GDP
% increase on a year earlier

Number of
Labour disputes
'000

Sources: IMF;
China Labour Bulletin

\* Thres months March
† Forecast

**Figure 1.6.   China's rising industrial conflicts**

*Source: the Economist, March 19th - 25th, 2016*

This study presumed that there were big different cultural features and national characteristics between ASC and China, even somehow, according to the western researchers' findings, that those cultural features are sometimes contradictory, for example, individualism vs collectivism (Hofstede, 1980), past orientation vs future orientation (Kluckhohn,1951). So what if applied those different cultural values into ASC based MNCs practices, remarkably, its industrial relations and human resources management? This study is planning to find out above differences by exerting some research methods, for example, distributing survey among special group of people, making interviews among those who working in the relevant enterprises, etc. , sorting out the specific points of gaps and finding out effective way to manage the barriers and conflicts for MNCs administration.

Following the above question, this study also focuses on what role of trade union is playing in the ASC based enterprises, and how to understand the tripartite relationship between TU, government and management at the enterprises level? Chinese labour law has obligated the settings of trade union organization at the enterprises level, but it performed diversely due to different situation. Research showed (Harzing, et al., 2011,2013; Holden,2001; Lockett,1988) that MNCs from different cultural background may encounter different conflicts and barriers which require correspondent strategies.

Trade Union from the traditional view of points has been interpreted into different roles and functions in the operation in different cultural context. This study, following up the previous findings, is to pay more attention to the trade union practice at the enterprises level, and explore how it work effectively with the managerial team and government, more importantly, to discuss if this type of structure is effective and acceptable for involved people.

Following the theme of efficiency, this paper continues to explore into more micro way if culture and language differences create the barriers for intra-personnel communications, employee promotion, and team work efficiency? If so, how to overcome it? In the history of human society, culture was initially the characteristic of ethnic groups and tribes; later, nations and countries, symbols of human society in higher stages, came into being, and culture played an important role. Culture seems to play a multifunctional role in human evolution, both a positive one, perceiving "more intimate and subordinate social behaviours as likely towards their in-group members", and a negative one, that is, "more disassociate and super-ordinate behaviours towards members of their out-groups" (Triandis et al., 1990). There has been explicit research in culture from the perspectives of anthropology, psychology, sociology and linguistics, which have elaborated on its features and applications in their respective fields. Since culture has an impact on so many disciplines, deriving from interactive theories and viewpoints, it may easily cause confusion to researchers in terms of categorization, application and analysis. The wide nature of culture makes it difficult to create a cultural framework for research.

Linguists observed the cohesive connections between culture and language, and found that communication is the medium from which culture is transmitted via the oral articulation of language. Bright (1976) categorized culture into 'big-C' and 'small-c' forms. The big-C Culture, achievement culture, refers to such things as education, history and geography; while small c-culture, behavioural culture, means the way of life for people, including values, beliefs and perceptions. It is obvious that small-c culture explains the total way of life of a group of people, and encompasses everything within this total way of life, while big-C Culture refers to refinement or sophistication within a society, part of small-C culture.

Interviews and survey being designed and applied in this study, it is expected to find out how language and culture influence the daily intra-personnel communications, furthermore, to analysis its position on the success of MNCs operation in China.

Looking at China government policies, one of its traditional philosophical concept "harmony" (*he xie* 和谐) has a high frequency word in dealing with public management, so how does the Chinese style of "harmony industrial relations" take effect on trade union's collective bargaining and clampdown the resentments at the work floor level?

Social stability, for being a long time, has been taken as priority in Chinese social administration, Mr. Wen Jiabao, then China Prime Minister said in his government Gazette in 2010 that "all we are doing is for letting people have a happier life with more dignity, for letting our society more fair and harmonious". Even the word harmony can approach consensus with Chinese native citizen, it is somehow a kind of contradictory with traditional ASC understanding. This study presumed that concept of harmony may cause some wrong interpretations and inappropriate actions among the MNCs expatriates and policy makers, thus, may create some barriers in the collective bargaining which is one policy advocated by the ACFTU. Besides, this research, mainly based on the aspects of language and culture and the researcher's model, is conducted from macro and micro level in order to achieve the harmony of industrial relations within enterprises.

Before applying the theories of cross-cultural and language comparisons into TU and HRM practices, it is necessary to pay attention on the issues of language strategy MNCs have taken, thus focuses on if there are language strategies for MNCs in China at the macro level? If yes, how the strategies work? Empirical research (Lincoln et al.,1995;Smircich,1983; Cyr,1996; Verburg,1999; Gamble,2000; Choi,2008; Manzella,2012; Li et Nesbit,2013; Zhang et Peltokorpi,2016) from other scholars have once proved the importance of effective language strategy for MNCs, but the questions is how a certain type of language strategy can meet the enterprises demand in industrial relations, especially in a more complex situation in China where most of working staff are migrant workers (*nong min gong*) who have owned comparatively strong township association, an organization different from the official trade union.

Continuing the exploration of language strategy, this study is trying to find out how the different language expressions in MNCs cause the barriers in management at the semantics, syntax, pragmatics and discourse level? Linguists have noticed the cross-cultural barriers at different linguistics level. For example, in terms of semantics, the word dog, in Chinese *gou* (狗), can be interpreted into two quite different meanings.

The connotation of dog in ASC may refer to loyal, lovely, and smart, while in Chinese traditional cultural connotation, dog can be described as flunkyism. As for syntax, both cultures have quite different ways to form sentences or phrases as well as the rules of grammar. Some of typical Chinese syntax ways have gradually stabilized and became acceptable English expression, for example, "long time no see", "people mountain people see". In pragmatics way, more misunderstandings occur, for example, in when people greet in their meeting, Chinese do not say "hello, how are you", but " have you got a meal". ASC people take a person's salary and income as privacy, while Chinese people regard the question of "how much do you earn every month" as a kind normal chatting way. In terms of discourse analysis, Chinese people have obvious different way to organize the structure which sometimes is quite out of the accepted degree by ASC people (Scollon et Wong, 1995). This study tries to explore more details of the above barriers, to search for a solution in approaching communicative understanding for both practitioners and researchers.

Non-verbal action (NVA) is another important factor hindering the smooth communication. This paper intends to find out if non-verbal actions matter in the management? If so, how does it work and how to manage it? NVA is hidden dimensions of human communication (Hall, 1959), but it is not easy to sort out in details on how it works in the IR and HRM practice. Qualitative research method, such as interview, observation is presumed as an effective way in this study.

The final research result is trying to improve cross-cultural competence (CCC) and find out if it can bring effective management for IR and HRM practice. So the questions are how to improve the cross-cultural competence (CCC) in the context of ASC and Chinese cultural environment? and if the CCC training programme work effectively in IR and HRM management? If so, how to operate it and make it adaptive to China's cultural environment?

Predicted research achievement of this study shall contribute with a new perspective in connection with the culture, language barriers in the IR and HRM research domains, especially in the context of ASC background with China culture characteristics.

Even though, there have been some of studies, according to the findings from literature reviews, involving the language strategies, cross-cultural management, and cultural impact on human resources management, few studies has paid attention on the culture and languages barriers in the management of IR and HRM context, nor did any studies focus on the clashes between Anglo-Saxon and Chinese culture.

This research, inspired by the previous studies respectively in the culture, language, industrial relations and HRM, has proposed a new model in analyzing the barriers and its functions at the macro and micro level, which has a contribution to the knowledge in culture/language and IR/HRM studies.

## 1.6. Conclusion

In the course of globalization, multinational corporations, after more than a century of evolution, have changed many of their strategies along with the innovation of communication, technology and development of humanity and management philosophies. At the beginning of the 21st century, the so-called 'golden BRICS' countries (O'Neil, 2001), namely Brazil, Russia, India, China and South Africa, became newly revived economic giants and started to attract MNCs' investments. The strategy of human resources management and industrial relations are the initial factors for the effective management of MNCs' subsidiaries, within which culture and language can either hinder or promote the smooth flow of HRM/IR practices.

This research focuses on the culture and language barriers in MNCs' employment relations in the context of the economic boom in China, a country with 5000 years of history, accumulating strong cultural features and an unique language structure. By capturing some typical examples of the barriers of culture and language on internal and external IRs and HRM practice, this research expects to find an efficient and pragmatic solution for harmonious employment relations in MNCs.

Chapter One is a general introduction to the research, which aims to illustrate the objective of the research in three dimensions: a framework for the research, the research focus, and the research strategy.

Chapter Two states that Anglo-Saxon Culture (ASC) is one important concept being adopted in this study. To an avoidance of too much ambiguity, this research analyses the differences of Anglo-Saxons and Anglo-Saxon culture, and explained why choose ASC as comparative research subject. It has significance for the research perspective moving from Euro-centric or USA - centric interpretation to an indigenous Chinese interpretation.

Chapter Three is the research rationale, which includes two parts: culture/language and industrial relations/human resources management. This chapter is the core part of the research, not just giving the definition and characteristics of items relating to culture, language, IR and HRM, but also explaining its internal connections, the significance of the research and the conceptual models for further research.

In Chapter Four and Chapter Five,a series of empirical cases are collected and discussed in an effort to illustrate the following research achievements: first, how culture and language function in multi-national companies in the developed countries, and how they function in companies in developing countries as well. Second, what valuable findings from previous empirical studies can offer some help in this research? Third, are there some shortcomings or uncertainties in these empirical studies? This chapter

## Structure of the Book

| 1. General Introduction and Research Objective |
| --- |

| 2. Chinese Economy in Transition and Anglo-Saxon Culture in the Chinese Context | 3. Literature Review: Culture and language Studies |
| --- | --- |

| 4. Literature Review: IRs and HRM Studies |
| --- |

| 5. Literature Review of Empirical Studies |
| --- |

| 6. Industrial Relations in Contemporary China |
| --- |

| 7. Research Design and Methodology |
| --- |

| 8. Data Analysis of Empirical Research |
| --- |

| 9. Chinese Culture and its Characteristics |
| --- |

| 10. Findings and Conclusions |
| --- |

ends by explaining that few previous studies have focused on the cultural and language barriers in the fields of industrial relations and HRM in developing countries, such as China.

Chapter Six profiles industrial relations in China from the early 1920s, the eve of the collapse of China's last emperor, to the contemporary period dominated by the communist government. It explores the functional changes of three actors – government, management and trade unions – in different economic systems, and the challenges they faced in the transitional period from the planned economy to the current marketing system.

Following the models from the literature review and findings from the empirical studies, Chapter Seven presents details of the research design and methodology. A hypothesis created with reference to the classical research findings is set as the base for further qualitative and quantitative studies. The approach to data collection is given in detail.

Chapters Eight present and discuss the research findings by analyzing the data obtained from questionnaires, interviews and other sources. The SPSS statistical software was used to compare the opinions from hypothesis in the previous chapter with the information from two hundred questionnaires. Furthermore, the second part of Chapter Eight focuses on the qualitative findings from the interviews with people in the relevant industries. More specific discussion of the researcher's contribution to the models on cultural/ language functioning in IR/HRM is provided in this chapter, which verifies the standpoint proclaimed in Chapter One.

Chapter Nine continues the discussion from previous chapters and finalizes the outlines for Chinese cultural features which come from previous in-depth research. It points out that contemporary Chinese culture has three main resources: traditional value which affected by Confucianism, Taoism and Buddhism, communist ideology, and impact of western culture after Open Policy in 1980. More importantly, the research analyzed the relevance and irrelevance factors with Anglo-Saxon culture resources.

Findings and conclusions from this research are presented in Chapter Ten. Apart from the general review of MNCs in China, and the impacts of culture and language on IR/HRM, further and continuous research relating to non-verbal actions, migrant workers in Chinese MNCs, and the problems faced by Chinese MNCs in other countries are discussed in this chapter. It also addresses the implications and limitations of this research and provides recommendations for further studies.

## 2

# Chapter Two
# Chinese Economy in Transition and Anglo-Saxon
# Culture in the Chinese Context

In the past three decades, the dramatic changes of China economy have caused attention and interests by both academians and MNCs practitioners. It is necessary to illutrate the significance of China's rise and its role for world economy. Furthermore, MNCs is a linkage to set up China economy with world economic development. Anglo-Saxon Culture (ASC) is one important concept being adopted in this study. To an avoidance of too much ambiguity, this research analyses the differences of Anglo-Saxons and Anglo-Saxon culture, and explained why choose ASC as comparative research subject. It has significance for the research perspective moving from Euro-centric or USA - centric interpretation to an indigenous Chinese interpretation.

## 2.1. China's Rise

One of the dramatic changes in this world in the past decades has been the change of China, and most notably, the changes in its economy. China's economic growth started in 1978 when Mr. Deng Xiaoping launched the "Openning-up" and "Four Modernizations" policies in 1978. Since then, China has stepped into a rapidly developing trajectory in economic reforms.

China is assuming a central role in the world economy. Between 1980 and 2003, China's growth rate (of GDP as a whole and of manufacturing) was the highest in the world, with annual average growth rates of around 10% (Dickens, 2007). China is either an ermrged or emerging market in many sector, for example, it is world's largest market for cars, air conditioners and LCD-TVs (the Economist, 2011). Since 2001, export has been taken as a driving force for China's economy, with the value added increasing from 19 to 27 percent of GDP between 2001 and 2007. The employment growth added 70 million jobs between 2002 and 2007. Data from China National Bureau of Statistics proved that 14,46million people working in 122,288 foreign invested companies in 2016. (NBSC, 2016)

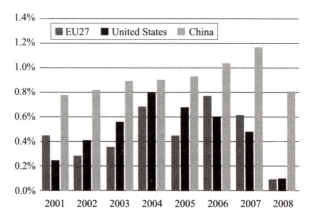

**Figure 2.1.  Contributions of the EU, the US and China to world growth, 2001-2008**
*Source: IMF, national accounts, Bruegel calculations Weighted by share of world GDP in 2005, PPP*

In 2014, China owned the world's longest highway and the longest high speed train, had the biggest port handling capacity, and overtook the US as the world's biggest economy (See Figure 2.2.).

### Gross domestic product in 2014 $bn at PPP

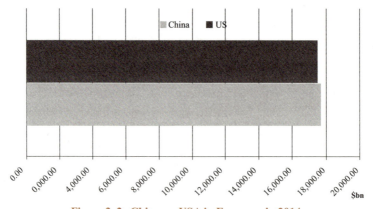

**Figure 2. 2.  China vs. USA in Economy in 2014**
*Source: Financial Times (2014)  http://blogs.ft.com/ftdata/2014/10/08*

In the transition period for China, a country with 5000 years of tradition, contemporary concepts of international management are likely to take a certain time to assimilate. Currently, Chinese management approaches, based on traditional

Confucian values, operate side-by-side with collectivist and institutionalized bureaucratic management approaches, along with more recently introduced international managerial philosophy (Chatterjee & Nankervis, 2007). Previous research (e.g. Child, 1981, 2003; Warner, 1993, 2003; Cooke, 2008) has offered evidence for the important role of culture in Chinese management: it is essential, therefore, to understand the importance of culture.

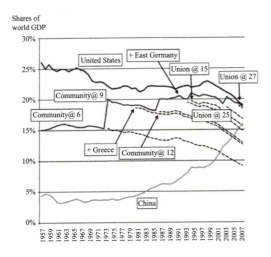

**Figure 2.3.  Shares of China, the EU and the US in the world economy (1957-2007)**
*Source: GGDC, Total Economy Database, Purchasing Power Parity GDPs*

China, as a newly rising economic entity, has been attracting MNCs' interest in consecutive investments, thanks to its large numbers of cheap labour resources. Each year, there are more than 100 million migrant workers (nong min gong) from all areas of the Chinese countryside available to work in the factories (Figure 2.4.), as well as educated young people (Figure 2.5.). Official statistics reveal that there are more than a million college students graduating from higher institutions each year, offering continuous qualified and less expensive labour resources for the MNCs, which are facing labour shortages in the developed countries.

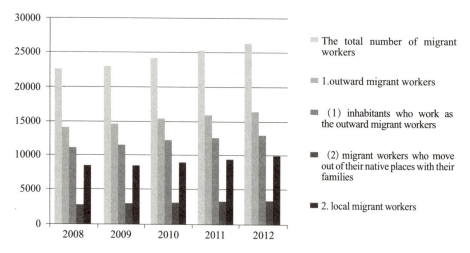

**Figure 2.4. Migrant workers from 2008 to 2012**
*Source: NBS:2013. http://www.stats.gov.cn/tjsj/zxfb/201305/t20130527_12978.html*

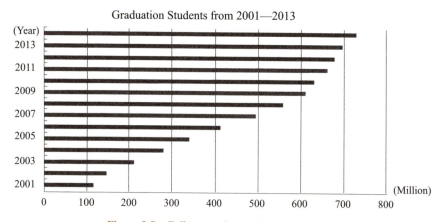

**Figure 2.5. College graduates from 2001 to 2013**
*Source: http://career.eol.cn/kuai_xun_4343/20131210/t20131210_1050496.shtml*

Another reason for China's attraction is its completed infrastructure facilities. In 2013, China constructed more 100 thousand kilometres of highway to overtake the US as the country with the longest highway in the world. China also has the longest high-speed train service, with rails of more than ten thousand kilometres in 2013, taking 46% of the high-speed rail business in the world. For the past six years, China has also had the world's biggest port handling capability (NSB, 2014).

Despite its rapid growth in the early 21st century, China has been recently experiencing a slowdown in economic growth. According to National Bureau of Statistics of China, after reaching the peak in 2007, China's nominal GDP growth rate has been declining from 14.2% to 7.3% in 2014 (See Figure 2.6.). Accordingly, the unemployment rate, as recorded by The World Bank, the nation's unemployment rate has risen from 3.8% in 2007 to 4.7% in 2014, which confirms the worsening GDP growth data.

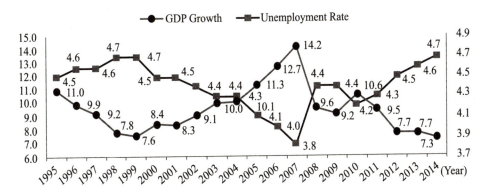

**Figure 2.6. China GDP Growth Rate & Unemployment Rate**

*Source: National Bureau of Statistics Database, retrieved from http://data.stats.gov.cn/adv. htm?m=advquery&cn=C01*

*The World Bank, retrieved from http://data.worldbank.org/indicator/SL.UEM.TOTL.ZS*

The current situation is itself a significant challenge for the Chinese policy makers. In year 2015-2016, despite measures taken to boost the economy, industries still possess unoptimistic view towards the future. As suggested by the Markit, the general manufacturing sector's Purchase Managers' Index (PMI) statistics have been recorded below 50 since January 2015, which indicates that the sector's performers lack confidence in the future businesses (Markit, 2015); the service sector, though slightly more optimistic than its manufacturer counterpart, still views the future as uncertain as suggested by its highly volatile PMI around 50.

Foreign investors are obviously concerned. Statistics provided by the World Bank indicates that foreign capitals have been invested more cautiously in China in 2015 as the foreign direct investment (FDI) net inflows in 2015 was 289 billion US dollar compared to 290 billion in year 2014 (World Bank, 2014); the latest data announced by the Ministry of Commerce in People's Republic of China also confirms the trend as the newly approved foreign-invested enterprises amounted to 2008 is down by 11.4% year on year. Nevertheless, significant amount of foreign enterprises are still operating in China and are significant to the nation's development. According to the Ministry of Commerce (2016), till March 2016, among the 2.168 million enterprises that are required to publish their annual report, 478 thousand, which is 2% of them, are foreign enterprises. In face of the challenging economic climate, there is an unprecedented urgency to research the cross-cultural relationships within the foreign enterprises in China as well as their interactions with the policy makers, local operators etc.

Even though China is still the most important key market that MNCs would like to invest (PWC: 2013). For example, statistics from NBSC proved that China has attracted 1074.63 billion yuan (equal with 158.03 billion US dollars) foreign investment in 2015 with which more than 60% of investment was mainly located in the TEDA area in 70.57 billion yuan, Yangtze Economic Zone ( include Shanghai city, Zhe Jiang Province and Jiang Sua Province) area in 359.75 billion yuan. Pearl River Economic

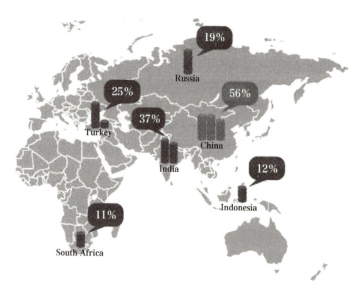

**Figure 2.7.  China, the most important invest market for MNCs in 2013**

*Source: The Pwc Global CEO Panel (227 respondents)*

*Note: the results exceed 100% because each respndent chose more than one destination for investment*

Zone in 139.8 billion yuan and Shangdong province in 80.59 billion yuan.

On the other hand, in 2015, there were 99,693 companies with the share controlled by foreign capitals in China (NBSC, 2015). A further study showed that more than 90% companies came from the above four areas, where are the core areas for MNCs' contribution to China's economic prosperity. Most of samples and case studies subjects have been set from the above areas.

## 2.2. Different Opinions on China-rise

There are two typical different opinions regarding China's rise. Examples were given by a conversation between then state secretary of the US, Madame Hilary Clinton, and then Australia foreign minister, Mr. Kevin Rudd in 2010. When talking about the challenge of China's rise, Clinton asked Rudd how to deal with the relationship with the US's biggest debt owner. Mr. Rudd's answer was to let China take more responsibility for international affairs by putting it into the international community effectively.

Some negative comments followed the phenomenon of China's rise. In the course of becoming the world's manufacturing centre, China's appetite for consuming natural resources has boomed: for instance, China has consumed 5% of the world's raw mineral material, including 20% of the world's alumina and copper, 30% of its steel and coal, and 45% of its concrete. Pollution caused by manufacturing has had a damaging influence not just on Chinese people, but also on its neighbouring countries. Carbon emissions have also caused conflicts in China's relations with the European Union. It was difficult to approach consensus in the intentional climate conference.

Nonetheless, the positive opinons on China-rise have argued that in spite of the problems mentioned above, people should be clearly aware of some points. As one of the strongest power engines for the world economy, China has successfully solved the crises of labour surplus. Each year, China has moved 25 million people out of unemployment into new jobs, which generated value as a middle sized industrial country. More than that, China is now the centre of the world in most product manufacture at the low end of the industrial chain, while hi-tech product research and some very specialized products have moved to developed regions such as the US, Europe and Japan. China's labour market has profoundly changed the patterns of global trade.

On the other hand, China's consumption of mineral resources has brought economic prosperity for many countries. For example, although the global economic recession had an impact on many people in 2008, countries like Chile, Brazil and Argentina were not hit too badly. China's policy of investment in Africa has focused more on constructing roads, building power plants and new harbours, and less on political interference, which has made African countries feel more secure and cooperative. In October 2013, China unveiled Belt and Road Initiative (BRI) strategy in focusing on a bigger role in global affaris, and need for prority capacity cooperation in the relevant industrial areas. The BRI plan encompasses around 60 countries with a wide range from Oceania to East Africa. To strenghten the cooperation and offer financial surpport, China proposed a development bank, the Asian Infrastructure Investment Bank, and announced that over one trillion yuan (160 billion US dollars) of infrastructure projects were in planning or construction (Wikipedia, 2017)

Furthermore, there is a view that when talking about the development of MNCs in China, some people complain of being exploited and of hardly seeing any benefit from it. The world economy is becoming increasingly integrated, and China's rise can bring benefits to anyone taking part in the new world economic order.

China's central role in the world economy and its contribution in the globalization process make it essential to the world that its business environment and practices are understood. A crucial aspect is the understanding of HRM and industrial relations (IRs), which the present research addresses.

Barriers to understanding include those of culture and language, these being the essential focus of this research. Given the special cultural characteristics in China, such as the concept of face and *guanxi* (personal networking) as well as the strong hierarchical bureaucracy, it is predictable that this study may encounter some difficulties in these respects.

## 2.3. The Challenge of Multinational Corporation in China

In the late 1970s, several internationally famous brands were introduced to mainland China under the policy of reform and opening, among which the Japanese electronics producer Panasonic and the American beverage manufacturer Coca-Cola took the lead and made their name locally. Since then, multinational corporations have been flooding into the country, thriving in this booming market, which currently carries the largest economy worldwide.

However, the success of those enterprises is not unprecedented, since Google's departure from China and the exposure of Glaxo Smith Kline's bribery scandal in the 2010s. Multinational corporations, which used to play a condescending role due to their efficient management and sophisticated mechanisms, now have to bear the brunt of the threats coming from the rising clout of China and its ever-diminishing demographic dividend. In other words, they are now being challenged not only economically and technologically, but also politically and culturally.

When it comes to the economy and technology, westerners are still sanguine about their edge, which they consider to be overwhelming. People still believe Goldman Sachs makes the smartest financial strategy and Apple Inc produces the finest electronic products. Even regarding political issues, an increasing number of firms could now easily come to terms with the regulations and requirements. Speaking of culture and language, however, westerners tend to hold that it is these two elements that would constantly and subconsciously challenge or even undermine their businesses in China. Some aspects will be described below.

Moving on to the first aspect, the different value systems in different cultures contribute to the characteristics of different industrial relation systems. Most westerners are admittedly characterized by their linear ways of thinking, while people from China prefer to bypass the complexity and seek shortcuts (Faite, 2004). Different ways of thinking stem from their languages and in turn facilitate cultural discrepancies in their own directions. In the early days, employees of different races were commonplace in a multinational corporation. People had to spend much time learning and adjusting to their colleagues' cultural backgrounds and religious beliefs, making it less efficient and more time-consuming to run a company, and most importantly, creating mounting overheads to cover. Localization was a solution to this problem and more local employees were assigned to higher positions, leading to a remarkable reduction of costs. Nowadays, it is more common for foreign employees only to take the helm of a multinational corporation. Surrounded by a group of domestic staff, these expatriate bosses should be expert in handling localization complications, not only being familiar with Chinese culture and language, but also knowing how to think in a Chinese way. Unfortunately, suitable persons seem always hard to find.

The second aspect is that traditional ideas will affect the recruiting and appointing systems in multinational corporations. Chinese people have been taught for thousands of years that fidelity overrides everything and dedication decides everything. Moreover, the traditional idea of "Slow Promotion and Lifelong Employment" was further entrenched by the socialist state-run companies in the 20th century. Thus, Chinese people usually value stability more than ability, two characteristics which, ironically, are regarded the other way around by foreign companies (Scott, 2009). Furthermore, Chinese people, and even Korean or Japanese people who belong to the same cultural cycle, are inclined to accept that position is often decided by seniority, or less mature managers would have their hands full with refractory subordinates. But the situation is different in western companies, especially in American ones, where it is never rare to see a fresh face skipping several rungs and appearing in a key place on an organization chart. Therefore it is unadvisable for enterprise managers to mechanically apply their own theories to practical operations in China, regardless of totally different cultural backgrounds.

Thus, whether or not the expectations of a job and position are fulfilled will influence the development of the multinational corporations (Muchlinski, 2011). Western enterprisers should pay more heed to residence, individual development, career ceilings and pension after retirement, which have been frustrating their local employees most. Shackled by these problems, multinational corporations, which used to be ideal occupational choices, are now losing their lustre. And numbers of graduates are more willing to apply for vacancies in state-owned companies in monopoly industries such as State Grid or Sinopec, whose welfare system proves to be more alluring and career promotion more secure. Meanwhile, the glamour of multinational corporations has also been weakened by burgeoning enterprises controlled by nongovernmental capital, among which IT giants like Alibaba and Tencent (Tenxun in Chinese), or real estate tycoons like Vanke (Wanke in Chinese) and Wanda, are becoming people's most desirable options. And with more and more accessible start-up loans sponsored by government or private investment, people who are young and vibrant are easily galvanized to set up their own businesses, from which they could probably reap more benefits on running business and interpersonal skills compared with other careers. The decreasing competitiveness of multinational corporations is surely and mainly triggered by their unwillingness to fully embrace the Chinese culture and language. Without good knowledge of these aspects, they often fail to know what local staff want and what local markets need.

Last but not the least, language is an essential tool to transmit information and ideas. When people communicate, various channels are needed to convey their ideas, and language is regarded as the main medium of communication. Verbal communication is divided into high and low correlation patterns (Fan, 2006). In high correlation mode, the speaker and listener are dependent on a common understanding of context to communicate. In the low correlation model, most of the information is conveyed plainly through the language (Yang, 2010). To compare the United States and Japan, for example, Japan is a high correlation model country, while the United States has a low correlation model. In business letters between Japanese and American companies, the Japanese will firstly describe a lot of things that are not directly related to the business, such as greetings, care, wishes and old friendships, and 200 tons of cargo will eventually be mentioned later in the letter. However, Americans find the Japanese too vague and unclear; thereafter, when Americans read Japanese letters, they often turn directly to the end, looking for the specific business demands. Conversely, the Japanese feel uncomfortable about the Americans talking about setting 200 tons of cargo in the first place, regarding this as insolent and insensitive to Japanese ways. Therefore, similarly, the Japanese will also turn to the last page, reading greetings, care and good wishes as a warm up, and then look at the beginning for the business aspirations (Scollon, 1995).

## 2.4. Anglo-Saxons Origin

The Anglo-Saxons were a group of people who lived in the eastern and northern regions of Great Britain from the 5th century to the Norman Conquest. It is believed by some historians that they are the descendants of the Angles and Jutes from the Jutland Peninsula and of the Saxons from the Lower Saxony Region, which explains why they spoke similar Germanic dialects. In 449, the Jutes, a Germanic tribe from Denmark, invaded Briton, and later, in the 11thcentury, William I the Conqueror, and a French speaking dynasty, created Anglo-Saxons culture. The English nation was established during the Anglo-Saxons period between the years 450 and 1066 (Keynes, 2001). The history and language which they adopted and developed is called the Anglo-Saxons culture, which can be reflected in its architecture, arts, language, kinship, law, literature, religion, and symbolism.

As a modern term, Anglo-Saxons before the 20th century often stood for people who have English descent and sometimes more generally for people whose native language is English. Before the term White Anglo-Saxon Protestant (WASP) came into being in the 1960s, the term 'Anglo-Saxon' conveyed the same meaning (Shay, 2008). Then the term 'Anglosphere' came into use to describe a set of English-speaking nations with a similar cultural heritage. The populations among the Anglosphere usually originated from the British Isles and today have close political and military ties with each other. In its most restricted sense, the Anglosphere includes the United Kingdom, the United States, Ireland, Canada, Australia and New Zealand (see Map 2.1). Undoubtedly, the major culture in these countries is often regarded as the Anglo-Saxon culture, from which they maintain a close affinity of language, literature, science, politics and economics.

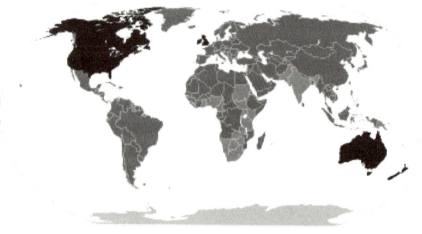

**Map 2.1. The Nations of Anglo-Saxon Culture**

*Source: Shay, Scott . 2008. The history of English: a linguistic introduction. Wardja Press. p. 86.*

## 2.5. Anglo-Saxon Culture

The history of the Anglo-Saxons is the history of a cultural identity (Wikipedia,2017). As one of the most brilliant cultures in the world, Anglo-Saxon cultural heritage was abundant in many aspects, including architecture, arts, language, kinship, law, literature, religion, and symbolism.

**Architecture.** Anglo-Saxons were often reluctant to live in old Roman cities but preferred to stay in simple buildings made of timber and thatch. They built small towns around the agricultural centres, usually constructing a main hall the centre of each town.

**Language.** Anglo-Saxon, also Old English, became the common language of England in the age of Alfred the Great. Later, under the influence of the Norman Conquest, the Anglo-Norman language evolved from Old English into Middle English between 1150 and 1500.

**Kinship.** The concept of "local and extended kin groups" has been regarded by some historians as the key element of Anglo-Saxon culture. Without this kind of kinship, nothing could foster the development of its culture as well as its freedom and relationships.

**Law.** The legal system was far more affected by the Roman Law than by the Anglo-Saxon one. People often attribute the legal development to the Norman Conquest as well as the contribution in the Anglo-Saxon age.

**Literature.** The history of Anglo-Saxon literature is also the development of Old English, ranging from epics, hagiography, sermons and Bible translations to legal works, chronicles and riddles (Milsom, 1981). Fortunately, there are still 400 surviving manuscripts from that period, which contribute a great deal to research into Anglo-Saxon languages.

White Anglo-Saxon Protestants played an essential role in the foundations of the American culture. It is widely accepted that the Anglo-Saxon culture is the dominant part of American culture which serves as the touchstone for equality. Generally speaking, the Anglo-Saxon culture has two ideas to its credit: one is the love of liberty and the other is pure spiritual Christianity. The religious tenet was similar to Puritanism, which can be described as follows: ① the basic sinfulness of mankind, ② the belief of God determining people ③ the highlight of individual responsibility, ④ the advocating of diligence, thrift, self-discipline and readiness to endure hardships (Godden, 1994).

The concept of humanity is of great importance to the development of economy and society. Humanity refers to human nature, which is embodied by consumerism, contributing to its economic development. The second feature is individualism. Its development, originating from Anglo-Saxon Culture, is outlined below.

Over time, Anglo-Saxon culture became dominated by certain other features, such as its value system. While individualism is at the centre and core of all values, at the same time society is the means of the realization of personal goals in which individualism is the only purpose (Fleming, 2004). This can be traced back to the early years of its history, when the first American immigrants came to the North American continent; this resulted in a new culture putting more emphasis on the individual, since consumerism and the development of industrial capitalism depended on individual needs and desires.

There is no doubt that individualism plays an ever more important role in modern society, which could be described as follows. Together with individualism, the democratic system is another feature of the Anglo-Saxon culture, which can be concluded as a social contract and natural rights as well as popular sovereignty and a limited government. Last but not least, the guiding principle and goal of Anglo-Saxon Culture is pursuit of freedom and equality culture. Most of the history of the United States has put this basis into practice. For example, freedom and equality is an engaging examination of who we are as ethical beings and an explanation of why we behave the way we do when confronted with value conflicts. A more detailed explanation will be given in this thesis.

Anglo-Saxon culture has long affected the American and British culture. As the author has mentioned before, Anglo-Saxon culture possesses several features that are of great influence to the development of the society. First of all, its impacts on humanity – that is to say, myriads of people – highlight human nature increasing. This can be demonstrated in the process of development of law and democracy. Taking the Period of William the Conqueror for example, the Common Law was established in the name of the basic rule of Phil English (Higham, 2013), regarding the customs and rules of Anglo-Saxon people as the solid foundation of new governance. William the Conqueror announced that all the British should adapt the old Anglo-Saxon customs into their daily lives, together with the new law, out of a desire to bring people close together. Furthermore, the Laws of William the Conqueror also preserve the old Anglo-Saxon customs. In contemporary society, many rules are still deeply affected by the Anglo-Saxon culture, as *the law is the guiding principal*. Secondly, its value system, especially the focus on individuals and independence, has played an important role in all social activities, mainly in the areas of work and finance. In the history of America, people put these values into practice and several wars broke out as they fought for them. In modern society, it plays an increasing part in the economy, called Anglo-Saxon Mode, which initially began in England and helped both Britain and America to overcome economic crisis and gradually conduct economic reform. This economy mode has three key features. The first is that the market determines resource allocation and social activities, the second is the emphasis on individualism, freedom and innovation, and the third is that profit comes first. Under the guidance of the Anglo-Saxon mode, America gained 2.7 trillion dollars from 1991 to 2000, creating 25 million new occupations, bringing it into a period of *long boom*. After this, the economy did not continue to increase; this is how a healthy economy should be, sometime increasing and at other times remaining stable. However, to date, the Anglo-Saxon mode is still evident in many economic and social activities, which serve as the best demonstration of its profound influence on the development of human civilization.

The concept of industrial relations originated in the industrial revolution, which was led and advocated by the Anglo-Saxon nation Britain. During the revolution, the modern employment relationship was created under the influence of Anglo-Saxon culture and people, bringing in massive economic and social changes as well as labour problems. Gradually, as the importance of non-industrial employment relationships is being highlighted, industrial relations is increasingly being called employment relations and is becoming more closely related with human resource management. Applicants' abilities, length of working experience and previous achievements are regarded as more important than social relations among people from Anglo-Saxon backgrounds (Merkle, 2010). Therefore, individuals are becoming increasingly important during Human Resources Management (HRM). People controlling human resources systems should be aware of the impacts of Anglo-Saxon culture on management methods. To be specific, two techniques can be used in management to take full advantage of Anglo-Saxon culture. One is to pay more attention to employees' self-development, including career training before employment, occupations, career plans and overseas training. All these factors could stimulate workers to fulfill their potential and improve their careers (Wright, 2011). The other is to establish an improved democratic system, accepting the good points of employees' suggestions in working operations. Democracy has long been an essential part of Anglo-Saxon culture, influencing the whole development of human civilization. As regards the situation in China, trade unions should play an increasing role in democratic discussions, while in western countries, decision-making meetings could be highlighted.

In summary, Anglo–Saxon culture is a mixture of local Celts, Celtic-speaking Christianized Britons, Picts and Scots in the north (Mursell, 1997). which can being outlined as,

A strong value acquisition of Christianity;

Adventurous characteristics due to its geographical location and maritime experiences;

## 2.6. Conclusion

It seems that China for quite a long time has played a role as strong engine for world economy, and this situation quite possible will last for a while. MNCs as media linking up this economic chains have special function. A study in exploring its IR and HRM structure in the context of cross-culture environment is predicted to give more help and references for academia and practitioners. But regarding to the cross-culture research, for quite a long time, when researchers facing the Chinese project, most of time, the Euro-centric or USA -Centric ideas and theories will guide them for the rest of studies. This paper argued that an indigenous Chinese interpretation of cultural differences may open a new window and have different findings in terms of cultural and language impacts. It has no doubt that, in Western countries, scholars may have different interpretation on the concept and usage of Anglo-Saxon culture, but from Chinese traditional cultural awareness, ASC has stood for western civilizations which once brought too much historical memories for them. Defining ASC as comparative research subject may give this study more clear and direct framework.

# Chapter Three
# Literature Review: Culture/language Studies

This chapter sets out to establish a link between general studies of culture and language in the context of industrial relations and human resource management. Previous research into culture and languages has been categorized into a number of conceptual patterns corresponding with their internal connections with IRs and HRM.

## 3.1. Culture

### 3.1.1. Definition and Evolution of Culture Theories

Various definitions of culture have been proposed in recognition of the varied functions of human society and the environment. Anthropologists were the first to study the impact of cultural differences. Early in the 1870s, anthropologist E.B. Tyler gave a first definition of culture:

> "..... [culture is a] complex whole which includes knowledge, belief, art, morals, law, customs, and many other capabilities and habits acquired by ... [members] of society."
>
> (Encyclopaedia Britannica, 2000)

According to Taylor's explanation, one can find that, first, culture is a 'complex whole', and research in culture should focus on the group – the collective entity at the macro level. The abstract cultural ideas stem from substantial components of life, such as human artefacts, certain types of social structure and religion, which are from micro dimensions shaped by culture.

Since then, scholars from their respective research fields have proposed a variety of definitions of culture. For example, Herskovits (1948) took culture as "the man-made part of the human environment", Kroeber and Kluckhohn (1952) insisted that culture is the "transmitted patterns of values, ideas and other symbolic systems that shape behaviour", and Schwartz and Jordon (1980) extended these patterns to encompass "… beliefs and expectations shared by members that produce norms shaping behaviour". Some scholars (Beker and Geer, 1970) argued that culture is "the set of common understandings expressed in language", emphasising the intimate connection between culture and language, while others (Harries and Moran, 1987) said that culture is "a distinctly human capacity for adapting to circumstances and transmitting this coping skill and knowledge to subsequent generations". Furthermore, Louis (1983) argued that there are three aspects of culture, referring to content (meaning and interpretation), to a group, or peculiar to something.

### 3.1.2. Features of Culture

When analysing the concepts and findings of culture from previous anthropologists, socialists, psychologists, and managers, it is not hard to find certain features that provide a better understanding of culture in multiple dimensions.

**Culture is shared.** Hofstede (1991) once argued that culture was a 'mental programming' lying between universal nature and unique personalities. This mental programming is shared by the members of particular groups. Figure 3.1, below, illustrates the function of culture as shared mental programming. The society may be regarded as the composition of three levels. At the first level, everyone has almost the same

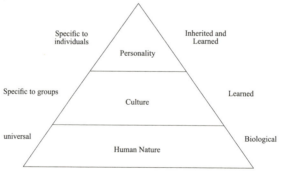

**Figure 3.1. Three levels of Mental Programming**
*Source: Adapted from Hofstede (1980)*

biological structure and the same reaction towards nature: for example, we cry when we feel pain, and we eat when we are hungry. Meanwhile, at the second level, people obtain shared experience from a particular society and these cultural understandings acquired by individuals are not shared by outsiders. Within a particular group, values and understandings are epitomized by its heroes or representatives: for example, people in the US take the story of George Washington's life as a symbol of honesty because he accepted the consequence of a childhood misdeed by confessing it (Peterson & Thomas, 2014). In China, young people know to honour senior citizens because of the Confucian tradition. At the third level, the personality possesses unique characteristics specific to individuals, who might differ quite widely in what they personally like and dislike about the cultural characteristics of their society. But individuals cannot avoid awareness of the cultural impact of the particular group.

**Culture is learned.** Another important feature of culture is that culture is obtained by learning and interacting with a particular social environment after one's birth. Thus, some patterns, such as language, systems of government, forms of marriage and religion, etc., are acquired as one grows up. The social institutions may change with the times, but their functions are transmitted to the new generations, as they have to learn a certain type of response in a cultural environment. This cultural transmission is usually written in the stories that parents deliver to their children (Howard, 1991). Although children might sometimes encounter cultures from other societies, the new generation is usually likely to accept their familiar cultural patterns, which gradually undertake a slow evolution in adaptation to new environments. This can be likened to an adult learning a new language but speaking it with a strong accent.

**Culture is systematic and organized.** The study of culture is an interesting area in international management, but most of time, it refers to something "soft, human, unquantifiable and difficult to account for in rational terms" (Holden, 2002). This soft part of culture is systemically organized and is composed of values, attitudes, beliefs and behavioural meanings under the umbrella of a particular physical environment. In the area of cross-cultural management, scholars have been trying to sort out those soft components, analyze the cultural variable and measure its impacts on managers' performance in an effort to present a more effective way to guide practitioners. For example, Darlington (1996) analysed the different dimensions of culture given by Kluckholn (1961), while a number of other scholars, such as Hall (1960), Hofstede

(1980), Trampenaars et al. (1984) and Mazneski (1994), have similar thinking on those dimensions. They have tried to generate lists and rankings to compare cultural differences, although Holden (2002) has noted that culture being categorized as the periodic table of chemistry elements. When one culture (C1) encounters another culture (C2), Holden (2002) argued that the exaggerated attitude from some researchers is the consequence of culture shock, friction or misunderstanding, which could be illustrated as,

$$C1 + C2 = Culture\ Shock,\ Friction,\ Misunderstanding$$

This misunderstanding is something unpleasant, unwanted or uncontrollable. However, after an empirical study of cultural fusion from Japanese and American cultures, Beecher and Bird (1999) claim that a 'new substance', C3, is created by the C1 and C2 cultures. This process could be illustrated as,

$$C1 + C2 = C3\ (a\ new\ cultural\ hybrid)$$

The C3 cultural patterns offered a new perspective for culture studies.

**Culture is dynamic and integrated.** Once a culture being formed, it shall remain relatively stable over time, but meanwhile, it is constantly changing. Heraclitus, the ancient Greek philosopher, once declared, 'Man could not step into the same river twice time, for the waters are continually flowing.' So as to culture which is changeable and it is not a vacuum, but in an endless 'process of reinvention (Ethington 1996:348). Factors making culture changes involve technological breakthroughs, cultural contact, disasters and environmental changes etc. Each time, culture contact endows each culture wish a chance to borrow new things from the outside. All cultures in the process of contact are being bombarded with outside new information which implies huge potential to drive cultural changes. Culture, as a complex and integrated system, consists of numerous sub-cultural systems covering all dimensions of life, for example, kinship, law, education, religion, medical treatment. Those aspects, seemingly discrete, are actually closely interrelated and interaction in essence.

**Culture is a way of life.** It is the context in which we exist, think, feel, and relate to others. It is the "glue" that binds a group of people together. Several centuries ago, John Donne (1624) described his feeling about culture:

*"No man is an island, entire of itself, every man is a piece of the continent, a part of the main;...any man's death diminishes me, because I am involved in mankind; and therefore*

*never send to know for whom the bell tolls; it tolls for thee." (John Donne, 1624)*

Richard Porter (1972) said, "when I use the word 'culture' I am referring to the cumulative deposit of knowledge, experience, meanings, beliefs, values, attitudes, religions, concepts of self, the universe, and self-universe relationships, hierarchies of status, role expectations, spatial relations, and time concepts acquired by a large group of people in the course of generations through individual and group striving."

**Culture is our continent, our collective identity.** Larson and Smallery, describes culture as a "blueprint" (1972:169) that guides the behaviour of people in a community and is incubated in family life. It governs our behaviour in groups, makes us sensitive to matters of status, and helps us know what other expect of us and what will happen if we do not live up to their expectations. Culture helps us to know how far we can go as individuals and what our responsibility is to the group.

Culture might also be defined as the ideas, customs, skills, arts, and tools that characterize a given group of people in a given period of time. But culture is more than the sum of its parts:

*"It is a system of integrated patterns, most of which remain below the threshold of consciousness, yet all of which govern human behaviour just as surely as the manipulated strings of a puppet control its motion."*

(Condon 1973:4).

The fact that no society exists without a culture reflects the need for culture to fulfil certain biological and psychological needs in human beings. Considering the bewildering host of confusing and contradictory facts, propositions and ideas that present themselves every day to any human being, some organization of these facts is necessary to bring some order to potential chaos, and therefore conceptual networks of reality evolve within a group of people for such organization. The mental construction that enables us thus to survive are a way of life that we call "culture".

### 3.1.3. Different levels of culture

To facilitate comparative cultural research, scholars have attempted to develop quantitative or categorized methods to analyse the impact of culture. Generally speaking, culture could be examined at five levels, namely the universal level, national level, the regional/organizational level, the interpersonal level and the intrapersonal level.

We have to recognize that the subject itself has broadened as a result of the influences described above. "Big C" (achievement culture) remains as it was, but little c (behaviour culture) has been broadened to include culturally-influenced beliefs and perceptions, especially as expressed through language, but also through cultural behaviour that affects acceptability in the host community. Gail Robinson (1985), an American researcher in the area of cross-cultural education, reports that when teachers are asked, "What does culture mean to you?" the most common response falls into three interrelated categories: products, ideas, and behaviours.

Big C culture has benefited from a clearly identified curriculum of topics to be covered, and textbooks which deal with them. The culturally-influenced behaviour which constitutes 'little c' culture has tended to be treated as peripheral or supplementary, depending on the interest and awareness of teachers and students.

Another popular way of classifying culture is to group it into three categories: **high culture, popular culture and deep culture**. This is a classification based on anthropological theories. According to Hu (1993), high culture refers to philosophy, literature, arts and religion. This is culture understood in a narrower sense. Popular culture, which is understood in a broader sense, includes customs and habits, rites and rituals, ways of living (such as housing and dressing, eating and drinking) and all interpersonal behaviours. Deep culture refers to the conception of beauty and ugliness, definition of sin, notions of modesty, ordering of time, tempo of work, patterns of groups, criteria of good and bad, decision-making, approaches to problem-solving, roles in relation to status, age, sex, social classes, occupation, kinship, body language and so on. High culture, popular culture and deep culture are not separate, watertight compartments but closely related. High culture and popular culture are deeply rooted in deep culture, while in turn, deep culture is reflected in popular culture by customs and habits or ways of living, and in high culture by art works or literature subjects. For foreign language education, the main attention should be paid to popular culture and deep culture rather than high culture, because high culture is probably not relevant to every individual. Many native speakers may not know much about literature, history or philosophy, but this does not hinder them from conducting daily communication activities and building up normal personal relationships with others (Hu, 1993).

Culture has become a significant issue for anthropologists. Kluckhohn (1951) found that human beings, no matter where and when they live, face a limited number of problems requiring solutions. To solve these problems, humans weight values differently. Kluckhohn (1951) then pointed out that value is one factor dominant in human culture, and presented five value orientations from which the profiles of certain cultural groups may be identified in accordance with the different answers to the questions derived from these orientations. They are: human nature (people seen as intrinsically good, evil, or mixed), man-nature relationship (the view that humans should be subordinate to nature, dominant over nature, or live in harmony with nature), time (primary value placed on past/tradition, present/enjoyment, or future/posterity/ delayed gratification), activity (being, becoming/inner development, or doing/striving/ industriousness) and social relations (hierarchical, collateral/collective-egalitarian, or individualistic). In addition, she analysed how people from different value trends performed differently in respect to the five orientations.

The question of human values attracted more researchers after Kluckhohn (Braithwaite & Law, 1985; Jones, Sensening, & Ashmore, 1978). It seems that anthropologists place more emphasis on the macro level of culture study, trying to work out the general features of a certain cultural group, while research on values has extended into more detail in the field of psychology. Schwartz and Bilshy (1987) tried to establish human values as criteria, and constructed a theory of universal types of standard values in three dimensions: (1) biological needs; (2) inter-action requirements for interpersonal coordination, and (3) societal demands for group welfare and survival.

An outstanding contribution from psychologists is their research achievement in group identification and individualism vs. collectivism (Triandis, 1990; Triandis, et al. 1990; Kim et al, 1994), which was pioneered by Hofstede (1980) in his model of national culture patterns. Unlike Hofstede's polarized pattern, many psychologists regard individualism and collectivism as interactive facets influencing a certain cultural group. Kim (1994) gave three types of collectivism, and Triandis (1995) suggested two dimensions, vertical and horizontal, to analyse individualism and collectivism, thus offering new perspectives for the study of human cultural characteristics.

### 3.1.4. Hall's low- and high-context patterns
In his book "Beyond Culture" (1976), Hall classified culture into low context and high

context patterns in accordance with the way human communication is undertaken:

*A high context (HC) communication or message is one in which most of the information is already in the person, while very little is in the coded, explicit, transmitted part of the message. A low context (LC) communication is just the opposite; High context transactions feature pre-programmed information that is in the receiver and in the setting, with only minimal information in the transmitted message; Low context transactions are the reverse. Most of the information must be in the transmitted message in order to make up for what is missing in the context, i.e. the mass of information is rested in the explicit code. Twins who have grown up together can and do communicate more economically (HC) than two lawyers in a courtroom during a trail (LC), a mathematician programming a computer, two politicians drafting legislation, two administrators writing a regulation.*

(Hall and Hall 1976:79:101)

Another concept proposed by Hall is the polychronic versus monochronic time orientation. For cultures with a monochronic time orientation, people are used to the idea of doing one thing at a time; while in the polychronic orientation, people handle multiple tasks all at one time, the latter being subordinated to interpersonal relations.

*Monochronic time means paying attention to and doing only one thing at a time. Polychronic time means being involved with many things at once ... In monochronic cultures, time is experienced and used in a linear way - comparable to a road extending from the past into the future. Monochronic time is divided quite naturally into segments; it is scheduled and compartmentalized, making it possible for a person to concentrate on one thing at a time. Polychronic time is characterized by the simultaneous occurrence of many things and by a great involvement with people. There is more emphasis on completing human transactions than on holding to schedules.*

(Hall 1990:13-14)

Hall's findings in high/low context culture and polychronic/monochronic orientation were verified and applied in the research later carried out by scholars and managerial practitioners (Bloom, 1981; Bond, 1986; Adler, 1989; Victor, 1992; Scollon, 1995). They may well explain some of the cultural problems encountered in business actions as, for example, when people from the USA, a low context culture background, do business with people from China, a high context cultural milieu, they may find obvious cultural barriers in negotiation and decision making. Alder (1989) drew the conclusion from one of his failed empirical studies that the managerial questions used to measure Western managers did not fit their counterparts in China. As for the analysis in verbal level, the high-context cultures take word-level-only message as "unsophisticated, childish, and rude" (Beamer & Varner,2001), so people seems more interested in taking allusion to classical texts, parables and proverbs, understatement, and antipharxis, that is to say something in terms of what it is not. Therefore, misunderstanding occurred with the communicators who is from the low-context cultures.

There are some arguments against Hall's classification, saying that little statistical data is given to identify the given countries in respect of the high/low context dimensions. As with his monochronic/polychronic distinction, critics say there is a lack of empirical support.

## 3.2. Culture shock and cross-cultural management
### 3.2.1. Culture Shock

The word 'Shock' initially refers to a biological phenomenon of plants which shall wither in several days after being transplanted and then recover vitality slowly. Kalvero Oberg (1960), the American anthropologist first proposed the term of culture shock in describing the state of anxiety occurred while people started living in new cultural environment which has unfamiliar behaviours and symbols. Xu(2004) pointed out that cultural shock exists in the course of intercultural communications in every dimensions, such as how to greet people, how to dealing with others, how to perform properly at table, how to accept and refuse the invitations, and even when and how to take statement seriously and when not.

Different types of cultural shock have been described by scholars. Smalley (1963) proposed the term of *language shock* referring those who encountered into a new environment of human languages. Along with the changes of language, Higbee (1969) discussed the *role shock* to express the state that people had emotional changes while transferred into a perplexing new environment. Bennett (1977) continued Higbee's role shock, and argued that it is a *"transition shock"*, remarkably when people face the challenge of transit into a new culture, similar situation occurred when people experienced the state of geographic resettlement, divorce, or loss of a close relative or family member.

Scholars studied the cultural shock from different perspective. Guthrie (1975) presented "cultural fatigue" from the research of psychology and physical treatment, since then, more research continuing the questions on what is the process of cultural adaptation while people encounter cultural impacts (Y.Y. Kim, 1991;Barna, 1997).

Earlier in 1960s, the American anthropologist, Kalvero Oberg, illustrated the symptoms of culture shock in different stages, and suggested a U-curve model which was later developed by some other scholars in the relevant fields. Generally speaking, there are four stages concretely for people experiencing the culture shock: honeymoon stage, crisis stage, recovery stage and biculturalism stage (see figure 3.2 )

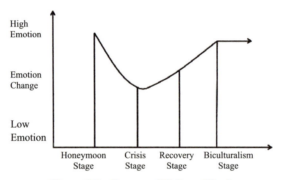

**Figure 3.2. Process of Culture Shock**

*Adopted from Oberg.1960. Culture shock: adjustment to new cultural environment. Practical Anthropology. pp.177-182.*

The honeymoon stage, also called initial euphoria stage, occurred when people have just move into a new culture and fascinated by the new environment, people, scenery and fresh things encountered, but they still treat those from their original cultural perspective. In this stage, sojourners may easily neglect the cultural differences and focuses more on the similarities of two cultures.

While in the crisis stage, some researchers also named frustration stage or hostility stage, people have to face the challenges coming from the differences of lifestyles, beliefs, behaviours and habits between two cultures, especially the conflicts of values. Many things taken for granted suddenly become insurmountable problems. Sometimes, too much emotion like ethnocentrism may be provoked and confuse people's identity.

In the recovery stage, also named gradual improvement or gradual adjustment, people have gradually adapted to the new cultural environment, achieved great development of personal flexibility and lived in the new environment without any assistance of their own culture cues.

When come to the biculturalism stage, or full adjustment stage or mastery stage, people come to a stable state of mind. In this stage, people basically accept and adapt to the new environment taking the host culture as part of their life. In daily performance, they treat people and events with a positive and friendly attitude, thus, there is no distinct boundaries between outsides and insiders. Mansell (1981) pointed out that people in this stage have owned freedom and capacity for both cultural identities, obtained the awareness of being in control of creative enjoyment, appreciation for the contrasts of cultures, developed a satisfactory interpersonal relationships and a high level of commitment towards both cultural contexts.

### 3.2.2. Models of Culture Shock

Two major kinds of culture shock being discussed by scholars. The first is disease model, a disease arousing psychological and physiological disorder and discomfort but could be cured with proper medical treatment and psychological therapy. When people in a new culture environment, different behaviour patterns such as dress, preferences of food, non-verbal behaviour, sense of time, may be mentally disturbed. Thus, Gudykunst and Hammer (1988) argued that uncertainty reduction is one of effective method for the cultural adaptation. For example, a number of actions like positive stereotypes, favourable contact, shared networks, inter-group attitudes, a secure culture identity, subsequent cultural similarity, developing a second language competence, knowing about the host culture, display of nonverbal affiliative expressiveness, attraction and intimacy, etc., can reduce the uncertainty.

Anxiety is closely related to the disease model of culture shock, Stephen and Brigham (1985) suggest that anxiety is associated with the contact hypotheses of inter-group relationships. Four factors can be considered as effective way reducing anxiety which are: cooperative interdependence, equal status, supported by authority and interacting with other group members as individuals outside their stereotypes.

Unlike the disease model which take more emphasis on the negative effects of culture shock, the growth model analyse the positive and impetus way of intercultural adaptive stresses for the people (Adler,1975; Xu,2004; Ruben et Kealey,1979, Furnham et Bochner,1986 Juffer,1987). The researchers believed that culture shock may somehow encourage, stimulate, propel and strengthen people's intercultural communicative competence and long-term adaptation. If handled well, culture shock can lead to profound self-awareness and growth.

A part from the above two models of culture shock and its consequences, some scholars also worried about the lose of identity, for example, Weaver (2000) argued that culture shock " allows people to give up an inadequate perceptual and problem-solving system to allow another more expanded and adequate system to be born" and "it is somewhat of a death-rebirth cycle).

As to the employees and employers in the MNCs and FDI companies, it is assumed that culture shock exists both in those expatriates and workers, and it, thus, becomes a big challenge for them to learn the host language, customs, behaviours, manners, values and communicating ways. Studying of culture shock phenomenon in MNCs and FDI companies can bring some valuable reference for the management in terms of trade union and human resource management. It may also help the people be more tactful in coping with ambiguous situation, more empathetic, and be more competent in playing different social roles required by the cooperate culture. Given the contents of theories in culture shock, hypothesis following the four stages can be presented as follows,

- Culture shock is an inevitable experience for people working in JVCs and FDI companies.
- Culture shock brings people stress both psychologically and physically, which greatly hamper their life and communication with people form different cultural background.
- According to Stephen and Brigham's (1985) anxiety reduction analysis, while the migrant workers in the JVCs and FDI organize the underground Townsmen Association replacing the trade union is functioning as a way to reduce their anxiety.
- According to Furnham et Bochner's research, corporate culture may play an

important and positive role in guiding the employees adaptation into new culture.

## 3.3. Hofstede's four cultural dimensions

Hofstede's four cultural dimensions, derived from his earlier investigation of what was at that time the only multinational company, IBM, during the 1970s, are the most famous and most cited works in the area of cross-cultural communication and management. By collecting data through examining work-related values in employees from 40 countries, "a number extended to 50, plus 3 multi-country regions", he presented four cultural dimensions: power distance, individualism/collectivism, masculinity/femininity, and uncertainty avoidance (see Table 3.1.). Later he added a fifth dimension: short/long term orientation (Confucian dynamism).

Table 3.1.    The four cultural dimensions proposed by Geert Hofstede

| | |
|---|---|
| High-versus low- power distance | Power distance is the extent to which inequality is seen by the people of a country as an irreducible fact of life. |
| Masculinity versus femininity | Masculinity/ Femininity concerns the extent of emphasis on work goals (earnings, advancement) and assertiveness, as opposed to personal goals (friendly atmosphere, getting along with the boss and others) and nurturance. |
| Individualism versus collectivism | individualism is a concern for yourself as an individual as opposed to concern for the priorities and rules of the group to which you belong. |
| Uncertainty avoidance versus risk-taking | Uncertainty avoidance is the lack of tolerance for ambiguity and the need for formal rules. This dimension measures the extant to which people in a society feel threatened by and try to avoid ambiguous situations. |

*Source: Hofstede 1984*

Hofstede's typology comes from the previous achievements in the fields of anthropology and psychology, which promoted the development of the subject. He writes in the foreword of Kim's (1994) work:

*"Out of the five dimensions, Individualism/collectivism was the one that most directly appealed to psychologists. Other dimensions were more immediately relevant to other academic fields. Power distance and uncertainty avoidance become favourite dimensions in comparative management and organization theory; masculinity versus femininity is crucial for a number of political science and comparative religion issues; Confucian dynamism has consequences for economics." (1994: x)*

51

Robock and Simmonds (1989) supported this, stating that the cultural dimensions provide global managers with a checklist for understanding particular business problems, enabling them "to predict how and why people behave as they do" (Chiang, 2005). Sondergaard (1994) concluded that there are four distinct ways in which the four cultural dimensions can be applied, namely: 1) nominal quotations; 2) substantively interesting citations for reviews and criticisms; 3) empirical usages; and 4) beyond citations.

Inspired from Kluckhohn and Strodtbeck's (1961) time dimension in culture analysis, Hofstede then developed a new time orientation dimension named Confucian Work Dynamism, and later renamed long-term orientation Chinese Culture Connection, 1987). This long-term orientation supported the value of hierarchy, thrift, persistence, and as sense of shame which were similar with the traditional Confucius value, but in some way against it , for example, it rejected the value of steadiness, face, tradition, personal net-work which were part of the core cultural values of Confucius tradition. Finally, this cultural dimension did not receive much attention due to its research resources, the examples just came from undergraduates in Hong Kong.

Even though, Hosftede (Minkov & Hofstede,2012) continued his research by collecting data from 38 countries in the late 1990s, and found that the long-term orientation put a low importance on service to others and high importance on thrift and perseverance, which is highly correlated with economic growth.

Hofstede then, following his design of World Values Survey (SVS), proposed the sixth cultural dimension: indulgence vs. restraint (Hofstede & Minkov, 2010). It is said that people in a society with indulgent culture are happy with life, believe that they control their own lives, take care of leisure time and have high performance of friendship.

### 3.3.1. Comments of Hofstede's contribution

Scholars assessed Hofstede's work has shaped the basic themes, structure and controversies for over three decades in the field of cross-culture studies. (Bond, 2002; Peterson,2003). and

*"... it has only boosted the development of cross-cultural analysis in a number of academic discipline, such as cross-cultural psychology and international*

*management, but has also unintentionally inspired a significant amount of work based*
*on misunderstandings, misrepresentations and misuse of some of its main elements. "*

*(Minkov & Hofstede,2011:11)*

The culture theory showed how culture can be unpacked into independent
dimensions, and was the first empirical confirmations that all societies have to deal
with a theoretical model of universal problems. His research proved that national
culture did "constrain rationality in organizational behaviour and management
philosophies and practices, and in society at large". Today, no one denies the fact that
culture matters in international business.

### 3.3.2. Critiques on Hofstede's National Culture Models

It is true that arguments for Hofstede's cultural dimensions are also contradictory,
mainly from the perspective of methods and classifications (McSweeney, 2002).
Concerning the methodology, it has been argued that data collected only from
questionnaires is insufficient for drawing conclusions. Others argue (Black, 2005) that
Hofstede's dimensions ignore the importance of language, since cross-culture is the
study of communication, while "culture is communication" (Hall, 1959). There have
also been criticisms of the ambiguity of the fifth dimension, which is difficult to apply
and seems contradictory (Fang, 2003). As to the empirical study, Chiang (2005) argued
that culture is not the only factor that influences management, as a multiplicity of other
contextual factors also come into play.

Magala (2005) argued that there were three influential theories so far in
conceptualization of culture: Huntington's (1996) Clash of Civilization, Ritzer's (2011)
McDonaldization thesis, and Hofstede's cultural dimension. Following Hofstede's
theory, there have been some continuing discoveries, and the most well-known
contribution were Trompenaars' value dimensions and the Global Leadership and
Organizational Behaviour Effectiveness Research Programme, founded in 1991 by the
late Robert J. House which were "Trio" of cross-cultural management contributions.
(McSweeney,2015). But criticism ranges from different perspectives, for example,
Ailon (2008) argued the epistemology assumption of Hosfstede's work, and some
(Gerhart & Fang,2005) questioned the research methodology and data analysis,
challenged his associated cultural value dimensions. Touburg (2016) identified seven

interrelated premises questioning Hofstede's national culture and value dimension as follow,

- Hofstede appears to see culture and values as coherent, self-sustaining, and subjective which denies human actors agency;
- Hofstede ignored the possible influence of non-culture factors, e.g. legal or economic characteristics of a nation;
- Hofstede's view of culture as "software of mind" is a pitfall of reification;
- Hofstede disregards the internal diversity within one nation and constructs uniform of national dimension;
- Hofstede assumes that cultures endure for centuries, are static and conservative;
- Hofstede arbitrarily uses the nation-state as the preferred locus for culture (Magala,2005:83), but the question is "whether the uniform and causal culture is that of a nation, a nation-state, or a multi-nation-state" (McSweeney,2012:155);
- Hofstede's framework of theoretical model has an in-built Western bias, a few non-western countries have been included in the data from the start.

Instead, Kuipers (2013) proposed concept of "national habitus" to replace Hofstede's national culture of which being defined as,

" to learn practices and standards that have become so much part of ourselves that they feel self-evident and natural. Habitus is our culturally- and socially-shaped "second nature". What we learn as member of a society, in a specific social position, is literally incorporated - absorbed into our bodies- and becomes our self." (Kuipers,2013:20)

While some scholars (Brewer & Venaik, 2012) pointed out that Hofstede and GLOBE national culture can not form a valid and reliable scale at the level of individuals or organizations, and thus cannot be used to analysis individuals or sub-groups within countries.

### 3.3.3. Trompenaars' and Turner's seven value dimensions

Trompenaars and Hampden-Turner (1997) identified seven value orientations (see Table 2) in a bid to offer consultancy for organizational management. The seven value dimensions were: universalism vs. particularism; analyzing vs. integrating; communitarianism vs. individualism; inner-directed vs. outer-directed; time as sequence vs. time as synchronisation; achieved status vs. ascribed status; and equality vs. hierarchy (See Appendix 1) .

By collecting data through mailing questionnaires to a large number of executives, Trompenaars attempted to offer a practical manual for organizational operation in a cross-cultural paradigm. Connections of the seven dimensions with Kluckhohn's, Hall's and Hofstede's dimensions could be detected. Two dimensions conform to Hosftede's collectivism vs. individualism, while the time and nature relationship is related to Hall's time perception and Kluckhohn's value orientation.

McSweeney (2016) concluded that GLOBE, Hofstede, and Trompenaars as the "Trio" were assertive and supportive in understanding the national culture with seven features:

(1) internalized values: defined as invariant transituational preferences;

(2) share by the population of a country;

(3) coherent (contradiction free);

(4) the exclusive or dominant cause of behaviour;

(5) enduring;

(6) identifiable from answers to self-response questions; and

(7) depictable and rankable as dimensions derived from the mean scores and ranking of those answers. (McSweeney, 2016:70)

By and large, McSweeney finally suggested, after a critique of Trio's national culture concentration, that it is necessary to follow guidance for cross-culture research: "acknowledge definition/conceptual variety; engage with and be open to findings outside management; avoid the ecological fallacy; do not treat everything as a cultural consequence; recognize the causal power of /with non-cultural factors; be open to recognizing translational influence and internal diversity; avoid confirmatory bias; do not confuse correlation / coincidence with causality; test causal claims historically / longitudinally; and do not confuse national identity/ patriotism with collective programming." (McSweeney, 2016:75)

The GLOBE (Global Leadership and Organizational Behaviour Effectiveness) research program was carried out by 170 researchers working together for ten years. This research involved about 17000 managers in 951 organizations covering a range of industries such as food processing, finance and telecommunications (House, 1993; House et al., 1995; GLOBE, 1996; Hartog et al., 1997). Although the rationale for the GLOBE research was to investigate "global leadership characteristics, competences, antecedents, and developmental strategies" (Morrison, 2000), it makes a valuable contribution to cross-culture studies thanks to its nine cultural attributes, which were developed from the works of Strodtbeck, Kluckhohn, Hofstede, and Trompenaars (see Table 3.1). Unlike Hofstede's framework, which studied culture at the level of nations, and Trompennars' at the level of societies, GLOBE categorized the cultural dimensions into homogenous regions (Patel, 2014).

These nine cultural dimensions were correlated with each other, and ten regional clusters that share similar cultural characteristics were given, which offered "a convenient way of summarizing intercultural similarities as well as intercultural differences" (Gupta and Hanges, 2004). For example, the regions with Anglo culture were Australia, Canada, England, Ireland, New Zealand and South Africa (white sample), while the culture of Confucian Asia included China, Hong Kong, Japan, Singapore, South Korea and Taiwan (House, et al., 2010)

There has been criticism of the GLOBE study. It ignored the fact that variations of cultural behaviours may exist in the same cultural clusters, exposing the shortcoming of these geo-ethnic parameters in culture definition. The other obvious omission made by GLOBE is the lack of description of language competence, which is one of the most important characteristics of leadership. Even so, it is still a beneficial reference for further comparative culture studies.

## 3.4. Language: a Linguistics Perspective

Culture could not exist without language, for language itself is part of culture. Over millions of years, human beings have evolved the anatomy necessary to produce and receive sounds; in a much shorter span of time, we have created a cultural system in which those sounds have taken on meaning by representing things, feelings, and ideas. This combination of evolution and culture has led to the development that enables us to share our internal states with other human beings (Samovar 1998: 120). Culture, on the other hand, influences our oral expressions, while in reverse, language will also format our cultural directions, as summed up a hypothesis by Whorf (1958). The background linguistic system (in other words, the grammar) of each language is not merely a reproducing instrument for voicing ideas but rather is itself the shaper of ideas, the program and guide for the individual's mental activity, for his analysis of impressions, for his synthesis of his mental stock in trade. Formulation of ideas is not an independent process and strictly rational in the old sense, but is part of a particular grammar and differs, to varying degrees, between different grammars. We dissect nature along the lines laid down by our native language. The categories and types that we isolate from the world of phenomena are not found out because they stare every observer in the face; on the contrary, the world is presented in a kaleidoscopic flux of impressions which has to be organized by our minds, and this means largely by the linguistic system in our minds. We cut nature up, organize it into concepts, and ascribe significance as we do so, largely because we are parties of an agreement to organize it in this way, an agreement that holds through our speech community and is codified in the one, patterns of our language. The agreement is, of course, implicit and unstated, but its terms are obligatory: we cannot talk at all except by subscribing to the organization and classification of data which the agreement decrees.

It is apparent that culture, as an ingrained set of behaviours and modes of perception, becomes highly important in the learning of a second language. In an era in which globalisation ties people together more and more closely, explicit understanding of different cultures reveals its importance to us. The author cannot help remembering an excerpt from an issue on "Chinese literature" in the "New Standard Encyclopaedia" published in 1940, which is an incredible example of a cultural misunderstanding by western people as a result of a stereotype:

> The Chinese language is monosyllabic and uninflectional. ...With a language so incapable of variation, a literature cannot be produced which possesses the qualities we look for and admire in literary works. Elegance, variety, beauty of imagery, these must all be lacking. A monotonous and wearisome language must give rise to a forced and formal literature lacking in originality and interesting in its subject matter only. Moreover, a conservative people...profoundly reverencing all that is old and formal, and hating innovation, must leave the impressions of its own character upon its literature.
>
> (Volume VI)

The study of culture has been a traditional part of school curricula in western countries. Sometimes it has taken the form of special courses, such as Civilisation in France, Landeskunde in Germany, and Civilta in Italy (Tomalin et Stempleski, 1993). These courses emphasize the big "C" elements of British and American culture, history, geography, institutions, literature, art, music, and the way of life.

Language, a small Culture component, awakened the interest of linguists in the research of culture in the micro paradigm. It gave rise to the famous Sapir-Whorf Hypothesis:

> "*Human beings do not live in the objective world alone, nor alone in the world of social activity as ordinarily understood, but are very much at the mercy of the particular language which has become the medium of expression in their society...We see and hear and otherwise experience very largely as we do because the language habits of our community predispose certain choices of interpretation*" (Sapir, 1958:69)
>
> "*...the world is presented in a kaleidoscopic flux of impressions which has to be organized by our minds – and this means largely by the linguistic system in our minds.*"

(Whorf 1940:213)

If the hypothesis reflects a true phenomenon for human society, one conclusion we may reach is that language is playing an important role in cultural communication, and that this fact should be put into consideration in culture-related study.

Grice (1989) placed his cultural interests in the context of pragmatics, from which he argued that human conversations should follow the cooperative principle with four essential maxims in order to approach successful verbal communication. These maxims are the maxim of quantity, i.e. the individual shall make the contribution to the conversation as informative as necessary and not make the contribution more informative than necessary; the maxim of quality, i.e. people shall not say what they believe to be false, shall tell the truth and not say that for which they lack adequate evidence; the maxim of relevance, i.e. one should say things related to their conversation; and the maxim of manner, i.e. in conversation people shall avoid obscurity of expression and ambiguity.

Critics have argued that Grice's four maxims do not fall within high context culture, but low context culture. There is even some doubt as to whether the four maxims cover all purposes for human conversation.

Leech (1983: 80) developed Grice's cooperative principle (CP), and pointed out that:

*The CP in itself cannot explain a) why people are often so indirect in conveying what they mean, and b) what is the relation between sense and force when non-declarative types of sentences are being considered.*

Thus, he suggested a Politeness Principle for human conversation, as follows:

Minimize (other things being equal) the expression of impolite beliefs.

Maximize (other things being equal) the expression of polite beliefs.

To meet the above principle, Leech (1983) gave six maxims to support his theory, namely the tact maxim, the generosity maxim, the approbation maxim, the modesty maxim, the agreement maxim and the sympathy maxim.

Sociolinguists like Grice and Leech presented a new paradigm in terms of language and culture. The cooperative principle illustrates a universal internal construct in human communication, such as the maxim of manner and certain social restraints. Leech's theory emphasised the social function of language, saying that human speakers use language according to rules of politeness. Since then, other linguists (Brown & Levinson, 1978) have been trying to set up their theories in respect of his politeness study. One controversial point is that even human politeness is confined within corresponding social patterns; Leech and Brown seemed to ignore the cultural impact when one language, e.g. English, is used in different cultural circumstances. Thus the politeness principle may not be applied to all situations, for which some scholars (Hill et al, 1986) have argued and presented their empirical evidence. For example, one researcher into Japanese politeness suggested that Leech's Tact and Generosity Maxims did not meet the Japanese politeness criteria.

## 3.5. Non-verbal Actions (NVA)

Non-verbal actions are regarded as 'hidden dimensions of human communication' (Hall, 1959), playing the same role as language. Pragmatic Failures in Non-verbal takes majority as for the sources of failures in cross-cultural communication, mainly including the pragmatic failures in body language, paralanguage, object Language as well as the environmental language. Body Language is a kind of non-verbal Lingua Franca which is most frequently used, widest various and deepest linked to non-verbal communications. With the increasingly frequent cross-cultural communication activities, linguistic scholars have already paid high attention to the phenomena of the pragmatic failures in cross-cultural communication, as for the direct activities of communication, 30% information transmitted by language, and the rest 70% relied on non-verbal means, whereas, 90% information carried-out by non-verbal means, （Birdwhistell,1970） promoted by other scholars. These statistics are sufficient to illustrate the importance of non-verbal communication; therefore, the researches upon the Pragmatic Failures in non-verbal communication have been moved to the front burner accordingly. Non-verbal communication refers to all other communications or behaviours outside linguistic performance, to be specific, which means the process of the interactive transitional information through body, gesture, facial expressions, Eye Contact, the distance when talking, Pronunciation & intonation, dressing, environment and so on, both silent and Non-semantic language unit. Therefore, broadly defined, non-verbal communication which is certain kinds of information-transferring means outside language that will cause misunderstandings between communicating parties because of misemploy in the process of cross-cultural communication, mainly including the pragmatic failures in body language, in paralanguage, in object Language and in environmental language. Body language is a kind of non-verbal Lingua Franca which are most frequently-used, widest various as well as deepest linked to Non-verbal communications.

### 3.5.1. Definition

Speaking of "Body Language" in a broad sense, there are in English such expressions as body language, body movement, gesture, body behaviour, etc. Body language refers to facial expression and body actions used for carrying communicative information. Body language is defined by Foss D. as a reflex or non-reflex action by a part or the whole of the human body applied for exchanging emotions with the external world. Kinesics is a word created by R. Birdwhistell after 1952, referring to the study of body language. Since then, a series of research working on body language have been developed in succession." New Webster College Dictionary "defines" kinesics" as a discipline systematically studying nonverbal body gestures (such as blush, eye contacts etc.) and interpersonal relationship as well. Samovar (1981) said, "Kinesics is the systematic study of body actions by which these actions or behaviours are formalized and coded."

### 3.5.2. The Characteristics of Body Language and its pragmatic failure

Demond Morris (1981), after the analysis of gestures, summed up the characteristics of gesture language, which can be widely used in the characteristics of body language. The following 6 aspects could be summarized according to his analysis:

(1) A great number of the body behaviours are of multi-meaning. Taking gestures for example, most gestures have more than one meaning in different cultures.

(2) Most of the body behaviours are cross cultures, cross countries, and cross regions. It may have one meaning in this culture, while have the other meanings in another culture.

(3) Only few if the body language is belonging to only one culture, one country, or one region.

(4) Some body behaviours may have different meanings in the same culture. Taking tapping the temple for example, it not only means cleverness, but also means an idiot.

(5) The geographical distribution of body language is of a regular way. There are a number if language regions, each of which has its own characteristics.

(6) Some of the body language, which is of special use, will be given wide popularity by the radio or TV. After that, these signs will be used by the people all over the world, such as the "V" sign (Jia, 1997).

Regarded as one of cultural carriers, Body Language is the same as the semantic or verbal language unit, including all parts of actions conducted by human body showing communicative information, such as handshake, stamp, hug, smile, stare, nod and so on. During the process of communication, if one communicator's actions of one or some parts are regarded by the other as inappropriate or ill-timed, or even being deep misunderstood, here comes the pragmatic failures in body language. For example, as for male from middle class in North America, "handshake" usually means "friendly", furthermore, to grab the other communicator's right arm with left hand when handshaking refers to "extremely friendly". Once, one businessman from North America went to visit Middle East, who tried to express the extreme friendship to his Saudi Arabia partner by his own way, however, the latter was unhappy or even angry, cause he thought his American friend was impolite or even rude(Bi,1999). In real time communications, these kinds of cultural diversity examples are countless as for the pragmatic failures in body language, for example, in China, "stamp" means angry or worry, while in US, which refers to impatient, whereas in Deutschland, that is compliment; in China, when finishing speech, the Speaker will always clap together with audience, which means appreciate and friendship, whereas American usually regard this behaviour as less modest; in China, accepting & sending gifts with two hands means respect, whereas, American will usually ignore it(Bi,1999).

### 3.5.3. Facial Expression

On most occasions, facial expression can show one's joy, fear, boredom, anger and some other emotions. According to Birdwhistell's research, middle class American displays about 33 communicative behaviours are in the face area.

Although some facial expression suggest differently across the culture, many of them have the same indication in different cultures. Smiling is for praise, encouragement, or friendliness; while frowning is for anger, pain, or dissatisfaction, etc. are the same meaning both in Chinese and American culture.

However, when the Chinese are in America, what the Chinese really need to take care of is the same facial expression may convey quite different indications, for example, as for making apologies; the Chinese often use a smile as a display of embarrassment. However, Americans do not accept apologies with a smile and expect to have far different facial reaction. To Americans, making apologies with a smile conveys less apologetic intention, which are we should bear in mind to avoid misunderstanding of our facial expressions.

### 3.5.4. Posture

Posture, as the term itself suggest, is the way in which a person holds himself as he stands, walks or sits. As well as facial expression, of course American posture has its own particular style.

Talking about posture, there is one thing the Chinese should pay great attention to when we communicate with Americans, which is American people prefer standing to sitting(Morris,1988). They stand to chat, to meet, and to have a meal, etc, because they think this will make it more comfortable. Therefore, the Chinese who do not like this kind of culture should take care of it. For example, in the National Party of America, there will be all kinds of people, from low class to high class; from young to old; in politics or in business, but you cannot find even one chair in the yard. So does in social party or family party. It's Chinese traditional custom that sitting to a big party or some celebrations, so for the Chinese people, this may be considered impolite; while for Americans, this is not impolite because it's convenient for people to chat with each other. In a word, when we are in USA, we must respect standing to communication and get used to this kind of posture culture

### 3.5.5. Gesture

Gestures refer to the movement of hands, or arms to reinforce a verbal message. Leger Brosnahan states that gesture is actually the core of body language.(Bi, Jiewan, 1995) Gestures are able to communicate a great deal of meanings. Some gestures may indicate general emotional arousal, which produces diffuse bodily activity, while others appear to be expressions of particular emotional states.

When gestures interpreted by Americans and the Chinese are the same, there is not likely to be a problem. For example, both Americans and the Chinese nod for "yes", and shake for "no"; applaud to show approval of a performance; move hands from side to side to signal goodbye. However, when gestures interpreted by Americans and the Chinese differ, misunderstandings may arise.

Just as what have been discussed before, body language is culturally bound, gestures can be different across cultures. Here is a story which should draw full attention of Chinese people who want to live in America around Americans:

Nikita Khrushchev, the irrepressible leader of the U.S.S.R. in the late 1950s and early 1960s. During his visit to the U.S.A., he aroused some controversy by some of his behaviour. One of his controversial gestures was raising his clasped hands in a sort of handshake over his head. He apparently meant to express greeting and show his friendship to people of the U.S.A. However, his gesture was not appreciated by those who saw him in person or over TV; because in the U.S.A. the gesture indicates the sign of victory after a boxer has defeated his opponent. Furthermore, he had made earlier remarks about the burial of American capitalism, and many Americans regarded his gesture as a boastful gesture signifying he had already won. (Deng&Liu,1989:135-136)

The story tells us that ignorance of gestures from the target language culture will lead to misunderstanding and even serious consequences. It's that we should learn more about gestures of American style during the communication between our Chinese and Americans.

### 3.5.6. Eye Contact

Eyes are the windows of the soul. In spite of the facial expression, eye contact is also an important means for communication. In some exiguous emotions, eye contact plays an important role, which cannot be substituted by verbal language and other nonverbal language.

Man's face is more vivid with the eyes blinking. Generally speaking, people do not gaze at other's eyes for a long time in order not to offend other's privilege, which complies with our Chinese eye contact custom; people do not stare at each other in order to show their modesty and respect. Gazing at others will be considered to impolite and provocative.

However, because of the existing of the cultural differences, it is really complicated to use the eyes, especially for Americans. In America, people are required to gaze at others' eyes, for this is a mark of honest. If one dares not to look at others' eyes, he will be considered to be dishonest, timid, indifferent, and so on. What's more, while communicating, Americans usually make eye-to-eye contact with their listeners for about a second, and then glance away for a while. After that, they re-establish their eyes to contact with their listeners to make sure if their listeners are still attentive, and then glance away once more. The listeners, meanwhile, keep their eyes on the face of the speaker, allowing them to glance away for a short time. This kind of eye movement conveys the information that they are equal with each other. That means we should do the same action of eye contact when we communicate with Americans.

### 3.5.7. Touching

Touching is an effective way to communicate with others. Touch or body contact provide rich and powerful tools for communication. Touch can show 12 meanings including affection, announcing a response, appreciation, attention getting, and compliance, departures, greeting inclusion, playful affection, playful aggression, sexual interest or intent. The way we touch and amount we touch are almost totally different in Chinese culture and American culture.

In China, touching a child's head is a way to show care when meeting, and also their parents take it willingly. It can be said that it's our traditional necessary to do that during Spring Festival; while we need to know that physical contact is generally avoided in conversation among ordinary friends or acquaintances. Touching a child, especially a female child, is not allowed. It is considered as obscene if a male adult touches or embraces a female child. It is noticed that Western mothers often complain that Chinese friends fondle their babies and very small children. Such behaviours—whether touching, patting, hugging or kissing can be quite embarrassing and awkward for the mothers. Besides, they know that no harm is meant, and that such behaviours are merely signs of friendliness or affection, therefore they can not openly show their displeasure. In a word, we should bear in mind that such actions in their own culture would be considered intrusive and offensive and could arouse a strong dislike and repugnance.

Generally speaking, the five aspects of American body language are easy to master, which of course will promote communication in Sino-US process.

Research has proved that varies of non-verbal expression may easily cause the misunderstanding and hostility in the communication. Thus, hypothesis regarding to the barriers of not-verbal differences can be illustrated as follows,

(1) Misunderstandings take place when people from Anglo-Saxon and Chinese culture origins encounter at the shop-floor level and corporate management level.

(2) Improper treatment of non-verbal actions and personnel distance between people from different culture background may bring the damages in IR and HR management, vice versa, appropriate operation of non-verbal may promote the harmonious management.

## 3.6. Findings from culture/language Ratinale

### 3.6.1. Awareness of Culture Differences

The study has evidence that Foreign enterprises in China will inevitably encounter other culture or subculture during their transnational operation. As every culture is unique and different, the contradiction, opposition, rejection or even confrontation between other culture and subculture are inevitable when they contact, thus creating cultural conflict. If the objective cultural difference cannot be addressed properly, cultural shock will be highly likely to arise in the enterprise. The normal business and management will then be negatively affected, and even worse, the enterprise may suffer the failure of transnational operation.

Cultural difference is the difference in culture between different countries and nations. Tradition is an important aspect in cultural difference. It can be represented as unwritten custom, taboo and rewards and punishments. With the "mindset" it provides for people and its great influence upon the moral system, tradition expresses a particular culture. Cultural difference is embedded in each aspect of culture, mainly including: language, material culture, aesthetic viewpoint and values, education, religion and customs. Cheung, Rowlinson & Jefferies(2005) pointed out that the more similarity the two parties share, the lower possibility the conflicts will happen, and vice versa. The theory fits with this study, in which the two parties share great possibility of conflicts while decision-making due to the cultural difference within each other.

### 3.6.2. Difference in Language

Language, as the product of human communication and the most basic tool people use to communicate, deliver information and ideas with one another, is culture's dressing. To understand a country's culture and analyze its sociocultural environment, it's necessary to master its language. In the international communication, both problems created by same language symbols with different meaning and the barrier of understanding exist that same language symbols have different meaning and connotation for people in different countries. Different countries use different languages. Even a few countries who share the same language can have difference in meaning due to their different geographical background and cultural origin. For instance, Chinese will say *"nali, nali, guojiangle"* when they want to express modesty. However, if directly translated into English as "where, where, you talk more!", these words would make no sense to English speakers.

### 3.6.3. Difference in Values

Values are people's basic ideas to judge between right and wrong, good and bad and important and unimportant. The Attitude is people's special sense toward some objects and their durable inclination toward way of act. Different cultures have different values and attitudes toward time, change, material wealth, risk, etc., which have an influence upon people's consuming behaviour and consuming pattern. People from different countries, different nations or of different religious beliefs always have visible

66

differences in their values. For instance, a lot of westerners pursue the maximum freedom of personal life, laying emphasis on sensual pleasures in real life and tending to enjoy the pleasures of the moment even with deficit spending. Easterners, however, stress on frugality and simplicity, tending to concern themselves more with the future than the present life.

### 3.6.4. Difference in Religious Belief

Religious belief is an important component of a country's social culture. Most countries in the world have believed in religion throughout their history. The world's major religions are Christianity, Catholicism, Judaism, Islam, Hinduism and Buddhism. The main contents of religion include way of life, belief, value and custom. These can make a great impact on social and personal opinion and on the interacting relationship between personal opinion and social one. With its dominant position in tradition, religious belief plays an essential role in shaping a country's national character. National character is represented as a stable value system, where the values have been shaped through years of accumulation and then penetrate every detail in people's daily life. This strong and lasting influence is hard to convert.

### 3.6.5. Difference in Aesthetic Viewpoint

Difference in aesthetic viewpoint is related to the artistic interest of a culture. For instance, Chinese and American people have different aesthetic values, which are reflected on the interest the two peoples have on art, literature, music, etc. To understand one culture, we need to study how this aesthetic values influences people's behaviour. Different countries and nations have different aesthetic standard, aesthetic consciousness, aesthetic method, aesthetic habit or different aesthetic psychology about nature, art, social life, etc. Aesthetic psychology means the aesthetic standard and aesthetic judgment of a specific group of people. It comes from the art forms like modelling, acting and literature imperceptibly and has prominent impact on internationally intercultural business activities. In addition, when selecting clothes, American people emphasize on their individuality in pursuit of novelty and uniqueness, while, different from American people, Chinese people tend to be refined, implicit and gregarious. Some things have special symbolic meaning under a certain cultural background, while the symbolic meaning can be totally different in different

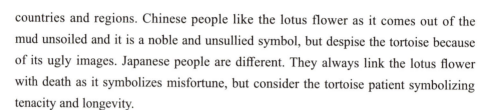

countries and regions. Chinese people like the lotus flower as it comes out of the mud unsoiled and it is a noble and unsullied symbol, but despise the tortoise because of its ugly images. Japanese people are different. They always link the lotus flower with death as it symbolizes misfortune, but consider the tortoise patient symbolizing tenacity and longevity.

### 3.6.6. Difference in Customs

A custom is the rule of people's way of behaving in their culture. Compared with the abstraction of value, a custom is people's concrete daily behaviour and is frequently linked with concrete and specific scenes and situations. A custom shows traditional folk culture where the etiquette culture is the core. For example, people's decisions on major events like birth, funeral, marriage, etc. as well as decisions on small things in daily life like sacrifice, festival, dressing, dietary habit, relationship with others, speech and language and so on have shown folk customs. Other examples can be difference in dietary habit or marriage. As for marriage, Chinese people bow to Heaven and Earth as part of a wedding ceremony whereas westerners are baptized in the light of god in church.

### 3.7. Culture in macro and micro layers

The development of a theoretical model for this research must, therefore, be based on the above considerations, which clearly suggest an interdisciplinary approach. Given that previous research had been scattered in a very diverse and multi-disciplinary way, it is necessary to categorize it and adopt an approach that is practical for IRs and HRM area. In the context of global business and the cultural uniqueness of different nations, cultural information is delivered through individual perceptions and activities, with the information of certain cultural paradigms thus comprising both the macro layers and the micro layers. When we speak of culture's macro layer, we are referring to the mass of hidden information (Schneider, 2003), which is not easily detected: for example, the value system, religions and belief differences; while the micro level of culture refers to those aspects which may be detected immediately in the course of communication, such as language differences, non-verbal actions, artefacts in certain societies, exotic cuisine, etc. (see Figure 3.3).

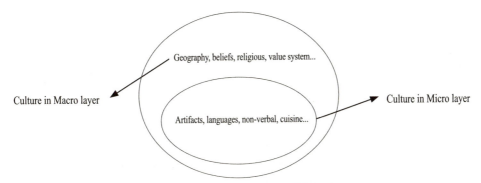

Figure 3.3   Culture in Macro and Micro Layers

Following scrutiny of previous studies in culture (Hall, 1959; Bright, 1976; Smircich, 1983; Hofstede, 1981), it seems that the macro/micro stratification may offer an alternative guidance for cross-culture studies in the context of international industrial relations and the HRM paradigm.

Early in the 1950s, Hall claimed that 'culture is communication', which means that the study of culture is that of communication among different cultures. He is regarded as the founder of the discipline of cross-cultural communication (Rogers, 2002). Generally, it is agreed that Hall's pattern of cross-cultural theories comes from the achievements in four domains, namely cultural anthropology, advances in linguistics in the 1950s, the study of animal behaviours and Freudian psychoanalytic theory. Hall analysed human cultural features, including the formal, informal and technical aspects of human activities.

Later, scholars in different fields presented their research modules in cross-cultural studies in accordance with their unique perspectives (Hofstede, 1980; Trompenaars, 1997; Earley & Ang, 2003; Schwartz, 1994). Rogers et al (2003) presented their Sequential Hierarchy (Figure 3.4.) after a chronological review of the previous findings.

Rogers explained that Schwartze explored the values from different nations, which are the foundation of cross-cultural research, while Hofstede focused on the national level, House explored the impact of national culture on individuals' leadership strategy, Trompenaars and Hampden-Turner were more interested in organizational perspectives and Hall in the interpersonal dimension, while Ealrey and Ang turned their attention to the intrapersonal level.

69

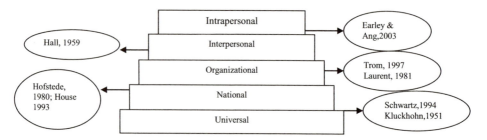

**Figure 3.4. Sequential Hierarchy in cross-culture studies**
*Modified from: Rogers et al, 2008*

## 3.8. Language and communications

The comparative research, with 44% of the studies involving just the UK, the USA, Japan, France and Germany, reflects the analysis within Anglo-Saxon perspectives (Clark et al., 1999). Rapidly industrializing countries such as India, China, Malaysia, and Eastern European countries are attracting more foreign national studies.

Will a MNC be successful in communication and management if it uses a common language, such as English, for its international team? Recent research reveals that it will not (Marschan, 1997). Buckley (2005) argues that "the meaning of words comes not from the objects they designate but from the context in which they are used, so that people with different backgrounds will understand the same word differently" (2005: 48).

By studying translation theories, Janssens et al. (2004) developed three language strategies: a mechanical, a cultural and a political strategy, being applied in MNCs management, which gave explicit explanations for the language function in international business activities. Corporate language strategy has obtained support from some researchers. Welch et al. (2005) argued that it is clear that language is the essence of international business: its impact covers not only cross-cultural communication, negotiation and knowledge transfer, but also the relationship between headquarters (HQ) and subsidiaries, as well as the control, coordination, and integration within MNCs. The development of information technology (IT) communication promotes the integration of HQ and subsidiaries, and even the connection among subsidiaries, but problems emerge in terms of language varieties; thus, the integrity of communication is vital (Kogut and Zander, 1992).

Welch et al. (2005) pointed out that there are different layers of language spoken in the internal structure of MNCs, even if everybody speaks the same language. Problems occur because of the three layers of differences, including the everyday spoken/written language, company speak (the special terms and management process terminology specific to the company), and the technical/professional industry language. Therefore, to understand the functions of language in international business, it seems necessary to illustrate the characteristics of two attributes of language, namely the instrumental attribute and the cultural attribute.

Language is a primary medium of communication, a coding system composed of phonetics, lexical, semantics, syntax and discourse for speaking and reading. When people speak/write, they are encoding the symbols of language and sending the information to the receiver (hearer or reader) who is to decode the symbols and interpret them. Misunderstanding may occur in the process of encoding and decoding, and this incoherent process, along with the other attributes of language (i.e. the social attributes), will eventually complicate the communicating situation and lead to a loss for both encoders and decoders. A number of researchers have shown that an individual's language fluency in both instrumental and cultural attributes exerts a vital function in cross-cultural communication (Hymes, 1971; Scollon and Scollon, 1995; Marschan-Piekkari, 1999; Henderson, 2005).

## 3.9. Cross-cultural Training

Cross-cultural training (CCT) is regarded as an effective way of overcoming these obstacles and reducing failure rates in management (Black and Mendenhall, 1990; Bhagat and Prein, 1996). Some scholars (Earley and Mosakowski, 2004) introduced the term 'cultural intelligence', highlighting that cross-cultural competence is as important as IQ and EQ in the context of globalization. But critics have presented contradictory evidence, saying that CCT may have a negative impact on expatriates, so it is hard to assess its function (Black and Gregersen, 1991; Kealey and Protheroe, 1996). To establish the validity of CCT, Puck et al. (2008) organized a survey involving twenty German MNCs. Even though the research data did not support the positive effectiveness of CCT increasing the expatriates' adjustment, it highlighted the important roles of language in helping the expatriates to improve their cross-cultural competence. Thus, the researchers suggest that expatriate selection should take language skills and language training into consideration in the developing programmes of MNCs, and tailored CCT was proposed on the basis of the expatriates' personal characteristics.

Communication consists of three aspects, i.e., the contents (writing system), the tone as well as the speed(voice), and the body language while communicating. Research shows that in order to achieve the effectiveness of communication, the proportion of the word, voice and the body language should be 7%, 48% and 55% respectively. The effective communication should integrate these three factors together. Effective communication is a dynamic bilateral behaviour, which not only needs the message sender to clearly express the connotation of his/her information, but also requires the feedback. Therefore, the careful listening and feedback are of vital importance (Xie, 2012).

Communication needs skills. Weihrich & Koontz (1993) noted that the effective communication requires the skills as follows: the message given by the sender should be clear, practical and logical; the sender should consider the needs of the receiver and ensure the information could be understood; both of the two parties should pay attention to the factors like the tone, the diction, the context and the emotion; both of the two parties should be responsible for the communication effects. Putti, Weihrich & Koontz(1998) thought that feedback should be the top priority. Only the careful listening can ensure the accuracy of the communication. Additionally, understood language, controlled emotions as well as moderate body language should be applied in the communication. DeCenzo & Robbins (2001) marked that simple and direct language should be arranged. During the communication process, the two parties should attach great importance to the feedback, the bilateral communication, the diversity of communication methods, a trustful and supportive communication atmosphere.

The thesis defines the communication skill as the flexible application of the communication methods. Based on the solid analysis, eight communication skills being selected as the variables to measure the effect of communication. Detailed variable classification are as follows (Table 3.2.):

**Table 3.2.**      **Definition of the variables of the communication skills**

| Variable | Sub-variable | Definition |
|---|---|---|
| X1 Language | Language | Use the language you can understand, convey the information you are familiar with |
| | Speed | Whether you can accept his speaking speed or not |
| X2 Listening | Listening | Whether you can be carefully understood |
| X2 Listening | His thoughts | He discusses in the consideration of your needs, and doesn't talk blindly to his own thoughts |
| X3 Context of Utterance | Chance | Whether you have enough opportunity to express yourself during the communication |
| | Emotion | One's emotion can be controlled and one can communicate in a smooth state |
| | Situation | Voice , tone as well as diction are consistent with the way and the content you talk |
| | Tone | Whether his facial expression and tone can satisfy you or not |
| X4 Nonverbal Communication | Nonverbal communication | Nonverbal communication is well used. |
| | Moderation | Whether you feel that his nonverbal communication is too overcautious or exaggerate. |
| X5 Logic | Aim | Have clear thoughts, aims as well as a strict logic while communicating. |
| | Logic | Whether you think that he is logical or not. |
| X6 Reason | Explanation | Whether he is reasonable or not |
| | View | Offer sufficient proofs to demonstrate one's own views |
| X7 Communication Method | Cooperative ways | Take cooperative ways instead of adversarial ones and use mild language. |
| X8 Standpoint | Standpoint | Whether you know his standpoint clearly or not. |

## 3.10. Conclusion

Culture and language are unique phenomena in human society. Their contents differ between different societies. Differences of culture and language mean that research into effective communications is necessary and valuable, especially in the epoch of internationalization, where capitals, human resources and technologies are transferred on a global scale.

**Table 3.3.      Resaerch Objectives Relating to Culutre/language and IR/HRM**

```
┌─────────────────────────┐                              ┌─────────────────────────┐
│ Culture is shared,      │                              │ Culture shock and Cross-│
│ learned, systematic,    │                              │ cultural Competence     │
│ organized, dynamic,     │                              │                         │
│ and integrated,         │                              └─────────────────────────┘
└─────────────────────────┘
                                                          ┌─────────────────────────┐
┌─────────────────────────┐         ╭─────────╮          │ Cultural theories from  │
│ Culture is way of life, │         │ Culture │          │ Hofstede,Trompenaars,   │
│ collective identity,    │         │Language │          │ Turner, etc.            │
└─────────────────────────┘         ╰─────────╯          └─────────────────────────┘

                                                          ┌─────────────────────────┐
┌─────────────────────────┐                              │ Cooperative principle   │
│ High culture, popular   │                              │ Politeness Principle    │
│ culture, deep culture   │                              └─────────────────────────┘
│ Low and high context    │
│ patterns                │                              ┌─────────────────────────┐
└─────────────────────────┘                              │ Non-verbal Actions      │
                                                          └─────────────────────────┘

┌─────────────────────────┐                              ┌─────────────────────────┐
│ IR and HRM Cultural     │                              │ Language Strategy in    │
│ Features in the context │                              │ MNCs in China           │
│ of China's Transition   │                              └─────────────────────────┘
│ Economy                 │         ╭─────────╮
└─────────────────────────┘         │Industrial│
                                     │Relations │
┌─────────────────────────┐         │ Human    │         ┌─────────────────────────┐
│ Features of ASC and     │         │Resources │         │ Language Barriers at    │
│ Chinese Culture and its │         │Management│         │ semantics, syntax,      │
│ Impact on IR/HRM        │         ╰─────────╯         │ pragmatics, and discourse│
│ Operation               │                              │ level                   │
└─────────────────────────┘                              └─────────────────────────┘

                                                          ┌─────────────────────────┐
┌─────────────────────────┐                              │ Cross-cultural Competence│
│ Non-verbal Actions in   │                              │ Improvement in ASC MNCs │
│ IR/HRM Practice         │                              │ in China                │
└─────────────────────────┘                              └─────────────────────────┘
```

Language and cultural barriers in industrial relations have attracted comparatively little research, especially in developing countries such as China. This research intends to consider culture and language barriers in China's IRs situation, which will offer a new perspective for researchers.

This study, after a search from ratinale findings, is trying to set up a linkage between cultures, language resaerch and IR/HRM practice in the context of China's transition economy. Research objectives were the driving force to the connections. Hypothesis and research modules will be presented in the next chapter.

# Chapter Four
# Literature Review: IR and HRM Studies

This chapter continues literature findings from industrial relations and human resources area. Conceptual modules illustrated in this chapter are the essential base for further empirical research.

## 4.1. Industrial Relations

### 4.1.1. Definition and its development

The understanding of industrial relations has been updated alongside changes in society. British scholars have found early records of academic research in IR in the 19th century (Morrison, 1857). The actual institutionalised IR study began in the US in the period between 1919 and 1929 (Kaufman, 2004).

Traditionally, industrial relations is the "study of the process of control over work relations, and among these processes, those involving collective worker organizations and action are of particular concern" (Hyman, 1975): therefore, it encompasses all aspects of the employment relationship, giving special attention to the relations between labour and management (Katz, 1988).

Industrial Relations not only incorporate structure, organization, and developments within enterprises (across the sector) but also systematically use the influence of the channel of product markets, which tend to be highly significant, and the role of government regulations and public policies. It also provides an explicit role for the influence of shared ideas or ideology.

Scholars with interests in different areas may give different definitions of IR. Kaufman (2008) argued that there were two distinct paradigms of IRs: the so-called Original Paradigm (OIR), focusing on the employment relationship, and the

Modern Paradigm (MIR), centred on unions and labour management relations. This categorization reflects the distinct trajectory for IRs arguments that has been evident for many years. One group insists that IRs studies should restrict its research to the union sector and associated topics, such as collective bargaining, labour management, and the national labour policy (Flanders, 1965; Clegg, 1954; Hyman, 1975; Katz, 1988; Dunlop, 1958; Godard and Delaney, 2000; Kochan, 2000), while other scholars contend that IR kept downward pressure in nearly all countries in the 1980s and 1990s, and that an equal emphasis on other solutions to labour problems, such as human resources management, is a welcome and an overdue development (Blyton and Turnball,1994; Edwards, 1995; Hills,1995; Edwards, 2003; Guest,1990; Strauss, 2001).

### 4.1.2. Three Perspectives of Industrial Relations

The theories and research on the industrial relations have been developing into a deeper level with the development and evolution of the western industrial relations. There are principally three perspectives on modern industrial relations research. The first is the Marxism perspective, which regards the industrial relations as the class opposition and conflicts, which are irreconcilable contradictions, between the labour and the capital owner. The second is the pluralism, which believes that the conflicts are inevitable in the industrial relations. There are simultaneously conflicts as well as cooperation between the labour and the capital. However, the conflicts from this perspective are resolvable. The third is unitarism, which argues that even though sometimes there is partial conflict on profit between the labour and the capital, there is not inherent contradiction between two parties.

### 4.1.2.1. Industrial relations from the Marxism perspective

It is said that the employment relation is an unequal relationship between the exploiting and the exploited based on the private ownership of the means of production, is also the class conflict between the labour and the capital, which is irreconcilable. Karl Marx argues the labour conflicts in the employment organization are essentially class contradictions in the capitalism society because, as Karl Marx said (1867) 'if money, according to Augier, comes into the world with a congenital blood-stain on one cheek, capital comes dripping from head to foot, from every pore, with blood and dirt'. The development of the capitalism will inevitably strengthen the above mentioned conflicts. Therefore, if the proletariat determines to alternate the current circumstance, the only way is to destroy the governance by the bourgeoisie, eliminate the employment and the private ownership and thoroughly resolve the contradictions and conflicts between two parties through the class revolution.

It is believed that the inevitable occurrence of the trade union is the reaction by the labour toward the capitalism system. The employee is impossible to compete with the employer individually. Another problem is that unnecessary competition among individual employees will occur. In order to protect different individuals' benefit and avoid competition, the only solution is to organize as a unity. However, Marxists argue that the trade union and its action, which are only temporary reactions toward the productive mode and inherent contradiction in the social relationships of the capitalism society, will not completely resolve the labour and the capital conflicts of the capitalism society.

From the industrial revolution to the latter half of the 19th, the western society was in the phase of laissez-faire capitalism development. In order to squeeze the surplus value as much as possible, the bourgeois applies the exploiting style to make the workers into accessories to machinery, which leads to the intense conflict between the labour and the capital. The exploitation from the bourgeois induces the workers to realize the necessity to be united, consequently the preliminary workers' organization—early trade union came into being. The tasks are strikes and demonstrations asking for basic wages and working conditions for workers. The bourgeois resist severely against the trade union. The government representing the bourgeoisie's benefits restricts the trade union's actions and activities by means of law. For instance, every country's constitution forbids workers' strikes or demonstrations. The government became the protective umbrella for the bourgeois to exploit the workers and squeeze the value.

Under this historical background, Marx establishes his industrial relations theories from the historical materialistic perspective. In the Manuscript of Economics and Philosophic in 1844, Marx proposes and analyzes the concept of alienation of labour, which reveals the opposition between the working class and the bourgeoisie in the capitalist society. Furthermore, Marx makes a dynamic analysis on the capitalist industrial relations in Das Kapital. He states that the labour is accessory to the capital and sets up the theory of surplus value, which is the core theory of Marxist political economy. The essence of theory of surplus value is actually theory of industrial relations.

There has been a remarkable decline in IR over the last two decades in nearly all western countries. Among the various reasons for this phenomenon, one key factor is reductions of capital-labour conflicts, abandoning of bad-luck and poor-timing working situations: thus, the union movements are declining.

However, in the eastern countries that are undergoing a booming economic revival, such as China, IR retains its traditional significance. Mass labour distributing industries have proved that the capital-labour conflicts that occur in the western countries have been taking place on different scales. A more specific description of IR in China will be given in the next chapter.

As one word, the focus of IRs today tends to be on broader employment relations with more options: not just the traditional pluralist and unitarian employment relationship, but also union and non-union sectors, HRM and collective bargaining, providing a much broader array of solutions to labour problems. Given the changing profile in China's foreign corporations, this research has created a micro and a macro paradigm, trying to include as many factors as possible in the analysis of IRs in China.

### 4.1.2.2. Industrial relations from the unitarism perspective

Since Fox (1966) sorts out the two concepts in 1960s, the unitarism and pluralism perspectives have been dominant in the research of industrial relations for more than 40 years till now.

The unitarism emphasizes the profit congruence among the organization members. It believes that the organization members share the same target and goal. The occurrence of conflicts, because of the trouble makers, misunderstanding and mismanagement, is abnormal. Fox (1966) believes that the organization members share the same benefits and conflicts are accidental and abnormal. The essence of the unitarism is that each specific organization is a harmonious entity share the common object. It is a harmonious and cooperative relation among the members. Cooperation is the logic premise of an enterprise, the performance and efficiency will be improved because of the collaboration between labour and capital. However, the common desire to build harmonious industrial relations should not prevent the conflicts between two parties.

In the framework of this theoretical hypothesis, the unitarism believe that the mismanagement cause workplace conflicts and the improvement in management will reduce workplace conflicts. Lewin argues that if the enterprise applies advanced or high identity management strategy in the pattern of high performance, the conflicts are preventable, and the bilateral relations will be stable. Rose (1988) believes that the enterprise may manage through common goal with right methodology. To solve common problem will help with the cooperation and profit integration between the labor and the capital. Therefore, the conflicts will be alleviated. The unitarism emphasizes that it is not opposition between two parties of the labor relations, the existence of conflicts is the result of mismanagement and inadequate communication, which will encourage the administrator to review the management problems in the organization. That is the reason why many administrators have believed in these theories.

The unitarism prefers to resolve the conflicts from the perspective of the organization. It is much emphasized to adjust and control the conflicts through management strategies. The trade union and the collective bargaining are rejected from this point of view. The trade union is believed to be the third party to interfere. It is said the trade union shall be replaced by means of HR development, management improvement and better HR system. Moreover, the trade union movements will be prevented and replaced by a new type of labor relations. Most of the HR scholars are researching the employment relations from the unitarism perspective, which, to some extent, replaced the traditional research framework.

Since the 1980s', with the development of social production and the workers movements, especially the impact from globalization and the knowledge economy, the economy operation mechanism, economy structure, property relations, enterprise regulations, etc. of the western developed countries have been deeply transformed, the influence of which on the structure of industrial relations is unprecedented. The labor and the capital are supposed to transform the traditional approach and means to adjust conflicts, to mitigate the opposition of industrial relations, furthermore, to create the trend of cooperation between the labor and the capital.

Beaumont (1991) believes that the development of unitarism is related to the integration of the world economy and the impact of products' market competition. Because of the intensified international competition caused by the progress of integration of the global economy, the organization is facing increasing pressure to reduce the employ condition and labor cost. The pressure squeezes the room of compromise from the side of employer and the administrator as well as reduces the room of development of the trade union and collective bargaining. In the circumstance of the international competition stress and the industrial organization's transformation, the trade unions in every country have been weakened in difference levels since the late 1980's. Clarke (1993) argues that the increase of the enterprise competition demand, and the cooperation between the administrator and the employees to maximize the efficiency of the labor and the capital and to make sure the continuous working, shall be the reason of the unitarism occurrence. There are scholars believe that the popularity of unitarism is closely related to the HR management, as well as the thoroughly quality management and the customer-centered, changing organizational structure, organizational culture and values.

### 4.1.2.3. Industrial relations from the pluralism perspective

Pluralism emphasizes the difference of the organization members' profit. Each organization is a multivariate entity; different person wins different benefit and focuses on different points. There are conflicts and cooperation, cooperation in conflicts and conflicts in cooperation between the labour and the capital, neither of which is dominant. The mechanism of pluralism is consistent process of compromise, which will lead to a balance in some point of all aspects of benefits.

Pluralism believes that the conflicts, which can be resolved, are inevitable in the employment relations. In any context of the labour and the capital conflicts, compromise and resolution can be reached if possible techniques and approaches are applied. The principal purpose of industrial relation structure is to resolve conflicts between different industrial profits and groups. The conflicts can be resolved through collective bargaining and labour legislation. Clegg argues that collective bargaining is the right approach to deal with industrial relations in the perspective of pluralism. If the contradiction cannot be solved through negotiation, it can be solved by involvement of the third party such as the government and the like.

Pluralism regards the trade union as the legal representative of the employee's benefit. The trade union organized and consistent reporting the employee's benefit will not lead to conflict, furthermore, it will balance the power comparison between the labour and the capital. Pluralism also believes that the collective bargaining involving trade union will regulate the internal contradiction of the organization. The employer and the employee reach agreement by means of collective bargaining, which will set up rules accepted and followed by both parties in the organization. The goal of stipulating the contradiction will be fulfilled.

From the latter half of the 19th century to the 1980's, free competition is transformed into monopoly in all capitalist countries. The employees' struggle for their rights has never been ceased because of the capitalists suppress. The huge pressure from the workers movement forced the capitalist governments abolished the law banning association. The trade unions have been developed into a new era, and the power comparison between industrial relations has also been transformed. At the same time, the severe opposition between the industrial relations is alleviated with the development of society and economy and the progress of political democracy. The two parties begin to negotiate when problem occurs. Under this circumstance, the governments in each country alter gradually the industrial relations policy in early capitalism which connived and encouraged the capital into the constructive interfere policy. There are many acts and regulations such as Act of Labor Protection, Act on Labor Dispute Resolution, Act on Trade Union, etc. have been introduced. Furthermore, the relevant organs for labor management and administration are established.

During this period, the huge conflicts and severe opposition between the labor and the capital are comparatively reduced through the approaches such as collective bargaining system, labor and capital agreement system and three-party negotiation mechanism. The three-party structure plays a positive role in stabilizing the industrial relations. The resolution of labor conflicts is more and more institutionalized, legalized, and stipulated.

Different perspectives to review industrial relations are developing with different characteristics of different eras, which formed the different phases of research on industrial relations (refer to Table 4.1).

Many scholars argue that these perspectives are exclusive and incomparable. From the historical point of view, the unitarism and the pluralism are opposite. The unitarism recognizes only one legal source of authority, while the pluralism believes there are different interests groups. The unitarism and the Marxists declare opposite

**Table 4.1.    Transformation of Research Perspectives on Industrial Relations**

| Research perspectives on industrial relations | Marxism perspective | Pluralism perspective | Unitarism perspective |
|---|---|---|---|
| Historical background | Free competition period of capitalism; the government is representing the capitalists benefit | Capitalism is transforming from free competition to monopoly; severe pressure from workers' movement; the government applies constructive interfere policy | Global economy integration; promoted by knowledge economy; socialized mass production; deep level of workers' movements |
| Basic hypotheses on industrial relations | It is essentially opposite and confronting conflicts between classes, which is irreconcilable | The labor and the capital are cooperating in conflicts and conflicting in cooperation. | The labor and the capital share the common fundamental interests, but there are conflicts in parts of the interests |
| Reasons for conflicts occurrence | Unequal relations of the exploiting and the exploited between classes | The organization is a pluralist entity, different person concerns different benefits. | The conflicts are caused by mismanagement and inadequate communication |
| Strategies | To eliminate the employed labor and the private ownership through class revolution | Collective bargaining, three-party negotiation, policy interference | Improvement in management will reduce conflicts |

views on labour conflicts. There pluralism and the Marxism believe in different points as well as share some common ideas. Both perspectives state that the interest conflicts between the labour and the capital are inevitable and basic. However, the pluralism believes the labour conflicts are resolvable, while the Marxists insist the labour conflicts are irreconcilable. Clegg proves that the theory of pluralism includes many of the radical Marxists' viewpoints and suggestions. However, the Marxists criticize that the pluralism emphasis on establishing regulation on conflicts. Therefore, each perspective does not exist in only one period; they are developing successively and also co-existing and functioning simultaneously. However, each of the perspectives is comparatively dominant in different developing phases.

To summarize, each perspective shows its own advantage. The Marxism becomes the theory base of labour process cybernetics. The pluralism shows to be the theory foundation of the industrial relations systematic theory. The unitarism becomes the theory cornerstone of the HR management.

## 4.2. HRM: History and its Relations with IR Evolution

HRM as an academic project is to study how to manage the human resources and to maximize employee performance in service of an emplyer's objective. Unlike IR study, HRM focuese more on organizations, its polices and system. Traditionally, HRM designed to surpevise emplyee benifits design, recruitment, employee training and development, and performance assessment (Collings et Wood, 2009). HRM also involves into organizational change and industrial relations in dealing with demands arising from collective bargaining and government regulations (Klerck, 2009).

Generally speaking, there were three developing stages for HRM. The first stage was antecedent personnel management ideas. The industrial revolution initiated some simple ideas in managing workers. The experiences made earlier entrepreneur realized that the well being of workers led to perfect and effective work. Robert Owen and Charles Babbage were the representatives of Managing from Experiences at that time.

In the early 20th century, HRM influenced by Frederick Winslow Taylor who invented "scientific management", also called "Taylorism" focusing on the economic efficiency in manufacturing jobs. Later after Taylor, from 20s to 50s in the 20th century, more and more researchers and scholars developed a series of theories in human relations movement, such as Hawthorne studies (1924-1932), theories from Abraham Maslow (1908-1970), Max Webber (1864-1920), Frederick Herzberg (1923 -2000) and David McClelland (1917 -1998), etc. During this time, personnel management turned to be more systematic, and regulated, and its administrative area expanded as much as entrepreneurs changed their recognition in managing the employees. Full time HR managers and departments came into being.

From the 60s to 70s in the 20th century, modern HRM gradually replaced the traditional personnel administration. In1954, Peter Drucker (2006), in first time, use the term of "human resources" in the enterprises management, and argued that human resource as a special capital earned qualities that the other resources cannot compete, such as competence for compromise, unification, judgment and imagination. The main differences for modern human resources comparing the features from personnel administration (PA) are that HR has the features of long-term orientation, prediction, conformability and strategy. Traditionally PA concerns on external control, while HR advocates employees' self-management, and induvidual committement. Unlike the mechanical and unified attitude to employees, HR takes more flexible ways, high credibility. PA emphasises on minized cost wile HR persudes maximum effeciency.

Since the 1980s, with the development of world economy and influence of globalization, HRM has gradually evoluted to an advanced stage, remarkably in the developed countries, and newly developing countries. HRM turned to be a strategic way for MNCs improving its competitiveness (see Table 4.2.).

Table 4.2.          Origin of human resources management

| Decade | Business Realities | HR Name Changes | Issues |
|---|---|---|---|
| Pre-1900 | Small Business & Guilds | Did not yet even Exist | Owners Owned the HR issues |
| 1900 | Industrial Pevolution | Labor Relations | People as interrchangeable parts |
| 1920 | Civil Service & WW1 | Industrial Relations | Worker rights and more formalized Processes |
| 1940 | Scientific Management & WW2 | Personnel Administration | Efficiency experts and more highly evolved HR processes |
| 1960 | Givil Rights & Compliance | Personnel | Legal Compliance and Reporting; "Policy Police" |
| 1980 | Human Rclations, the Knowledge/Service Economy, and Mergers & Acquisitions | Human Resources People | Relevance in a fast-changing world; Motivation and "Human Relations" theories abound |
| 2000 | Modern Organizations | Organization Effectiveness?Human Capital Organization Capability? | No new official names, but lots of "Morphing" as the transactional parts get outsourced and the transformational parts get defined |

*Source: Developing HR as an internal consulting organization, Richard M. Vosburgh, Mirage Resorts, MGM MIRAGE*

In this study, MNCs in China are mainly involving into labour intensive industry, and less in technology intensive industries, therefore, the traditional IR theories took more influence to the reseasrch, focusing on the tripatite relationship among trade union, management and government. Few technology intensive MNCs have been defined and analyised with HR perceptions.

## 4.3. Comparative Studies in IR and HRM Framework

Statistics show (Clark et al., 1999) that comparative studies in Industrial Relations (IRs) and Human Resource Management (HRM) have been conducted frequently in the past two decades. The main interests for these comparative studies cover six areas:

- Exploration of similarities and differences in IRs/HRM systems in respective nations.
- What are the causes and impacts of these similarities and differences?
- Is there a trend for divergence or convergence in HRM systems?
- How should a multinational organization be managed?
- How can an organization of one culture adapt to another culture in a different situation?
- What are the benefits for both cultures?

It seems, from a number of studies (Robert 1970; Neghandi, 1974; Child, 1981; Bhagat and McQuai, 1982; Adler, 1983; Sekaran, 1983; Roberts and Boyacigiller, 1984; Adler et al., 1986; Redding, 1994), that the research has highlighted major methodological, epistemological and theoretical deficiencies, which can be summarised as follows:

- Lack of integration of studies of individuals, groups and organizations (Robert, 1970; Bass, 1965; Neghandi, 1974; Lachman et al., 1994; Earley and Singh, 1995)
- Ambiguous definition of culture and distinction of culture and nation (Child, 1981; Smith, 1992; Tayeb, 1994; Chapman ,1996)
- An ethnocentric bias impact on the studies (Clark, 1999)
- Most of the reviews present methodological inadequacies, such as no equivalent functions for the comparative sectors, samples of organizations, while individuals and nations are loosely matched.

The core resources for this research consist of four components: culture, language, industrial relations and human resources management. As shown in Figure 4.1., this research attempts to establish the links between these four components and apply them in practice in China's developing economic situation. Modules and findings generated from this study are expected to offer some helps.

Apart from the previous findings of comparative studies, this study is trying to find out cultural features for China's IRs in the transition economic period. How is its tripartite relationship in relating to the ASC and China cultural envrionment? Right after the open policy in the early 1980s, China's government advocated "harmony industrial relations", a typical traditional culture concept applied into the IRs practice

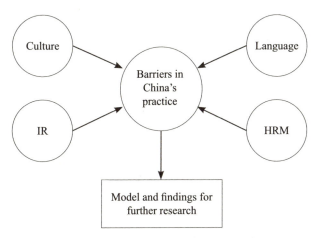

**Figure 4.1.  Research Components and its Achievements**

which is somehow controdictory with the ASC traditions.

## 4.4. Conclusion

Employment relations are the relations of different cultural and language encounters. People with various cultural and language backgrounds will use their respective policies and strategies to meet the needs of industrial relations in the specific context. Language and cultural barriers in industrial relations have attracted comparatively little research, especially in developing countries such as China. This research intends to consider culture and language barriers in China's IRs situation, which will offer a new perspective for researchers.The three main IRs theories rooted from unique historical background and have once play important roles in guiding the IRs movement. Human recources management as newly develped subject focuses more on individual achievement and assessment. Therefore, labour intensive concentrated MNCs in China are more adoptive to apply with IRs studies.

# Chapter Five
# Literature Review of Empirical Study

Some of the prior empirical studies conducted by scholars and practitioners of IR/HRM are collected and analyzed in this chapter, focusing on cases in both developed and developing countries. This chapter sets out to explore the similarities and differences of culture/language impacts on MNCs in different nations, which may be applied in the context of China.

## 5.1. Empirical studies of language and culture barriers in MNCs from developed countries

Scholars have noticed, in the course of internationalization, the impacts of culture and language on the management of multinational corporations. Given the varieties of culture and language factors in the respective countries and regions, researchers in conflict studies have directed their attention to different paradigms.

MNCs from the developed countries refer to those whose subsidiaries are located in a developed country, which is a sovereign state that has a highly developed economy and advanced technological infrastructure relative to other less industrialized nations. Most commonly, the criteria for evaluating the degree of economic development are gross domestic product (GDP), the per capita income, the level of industrialization, the amount of widespread infrastructure and the general standard of living (Wikipedia,2014)

Black (2005) suggested that, with reference to Hofstede's cultural dimensions, IRs may present the obvious different features in complying with respective cultural trends. He realized the primary determinant of national culture, after his empirical test by linking Hofstede's dimensions with industrial relations variables, this becoming a force for ongoing diversity in labour market systems in different nations. In his critique of previous theories' frameworks in Industrial Relations, such as the system theory, Marxist theory, strategic choice theory and neo-institutionalism, the author found that they all "largely ignore the role of national culture", except for Meltze's (1993) amended system model and Pool's (1986, 1993) strategic choice model. Furthermore, Black proposed a series of hypotheses that a cultural perspective may explain the differences in IRs in different nations, such as trade union density, collective bargaining coverage, bargaining centralization and decentralization, high or low collective bargaining coordination, federal and government involvement in bargaining, and levels of earning dispersion.

Black's research had an important implication for IRs research in different national contexts. It was the first time that it was suggested that national culture "is the main predictor of the characteristics of the industrial relations systems investigated" (1995: 1152). But some obvious flaws in his research should be mentioned. First, the data resources for IRs were collected mainly before 1995. In the past decade, there have been gigantic changes in the world economic structure, just as with the industrial relations in different countries. Second, the three groups of IRs are mainly from European countries, plus the USA and Japan, which obviously do not cover all of the world's thriving economic areas. Third, the awareness of the impact of national cultural on IRs is undoubtedly a revolutionary step for both research and practical guidance, but it does not explain how those differences have a positive or negative impact on IRs, and obviously needs more exploration.

Lincoln et al. (1995) noted the importance of cross-cultural management in MNCs. The study of Japanese companies in Germany was trying to find the answers to three questions: What are the cultural differences in terms of language issues, interpersonal styles (personality and politeness) and norms for responsibility? How should the impact of national cultural differences be managed at the corporate level? What are the industrial relations for Japanese companies in North Rhine, Germany?

Smircich (1983) earlier identified two ways to analyse the corporate culture. The first is culture as a 'variable' – tangible artefacts (e.g. stories, myths, legends, jargons, logos, décor etc.) brought into or imposed on the organization from outside, devices, mechanisms that can be controlled and manipulated. The second regards culture as a 'root metaphor': a process of enactment, not 'external' to the individual, but an ongoing process, created, recreated and shaped by human interactions and by how we understand things, make sense of them and give meaning to them. Lincoln's comparative study gave explicit support to culture as a variable, but it seems that the researchers did not continue the exploration of culture as a root metaphor, but attempted to take into consideration hierarchies such as German specialism vs. Japanese generalism. Thus, readers can find answers at the corporate level, but cannot find out what factors are underpinning the 'tangible artefacts'.

The collapse of communism in Eastern Europe brought a new round of economic revival and cooperation with Western European enterprises. Cyr (1996) selected three typical joint-ventures located in Poland, Hungary and the Czech Republic and explored the human resource management at corporate level. The three joint-ventures, cooperating with different foreign partners, have similar backgrounds and were founded in the same year, all in the manufacturing sector and at the time when foreign investment was beginning to flourish.

Cyr's case study demonstrated that culture barriers are core considerations for improving joint-venture HRM strategy. Furthermore, thirty-seven items in the questionnaire offered valuable references to other comparative culture studies. But it seems that there is a lack of evidence, as the researcher puts it in the conclusion, to say that the old corporate culture was derived from a communist paradigm. According to Schein's (2004) six cultural dimensions, philosophy and ideology are just part of culture divisions. Cyr offered an instructive research method and methodology for further research in this field.

In the case study of analyzing corporation discourse in the Italian multinational corporation FIAT, Manzella (2012) investigated some examples of the complex relationship between languages and concepts in the field of labour law and industrial relations. The study argued that a new strand of research, the Linguistics of Labour Law and Industrial Relations (LLLIRs), should be addressed in an in-depth manner in the course of cross-cultural or cross-border analysis. Due to the absence of corresponding practice, processes or concepts in the target culture, plus mistakes during translation, comparative study of industrial relations and labour law is becoming 'impracticable'.

## 5.2. Empirical studies of Language and Culture Barriers in MNCs from the developing countries

In considering China's management, researchers are trying to depict core parts of Chinese managerial characteristics from multiple perspectives, such as the cultural impact in the context of MNCs' HRM issues. Gamble (2000) found, from his survey of Japanese, Korean, Hong Kong and European ventures in China, that localizing management in China was inhibited due to 'practical, cultural and strategic factors': thus, his research suggests that culturally literate expatriates or qualified local managers are vital to MNCs. When discussing the cultural impacts, Gamble argued that there were five factors intervening in management: firstly, the cultural stereotypes from headquarters (for example, Japanese MNCs were reluctant to localize the management role in consideration of local managers' loyalty to the company, organizational skills, and attention to quality); secondly, insider/outsider dichotomies, borders in variable fixity and porosity of boundaries in Chinese definitions of their relationship with people; thirdly, the *guanxi* factor, a much-debated topic in the structure of Chinese personnel networks; fourthly, modernity and prestige, a special issue reflecting the complexity of the Chinese attitude towards foreign culture, in which expatriates can usually wield more leverage in doing business with their Chinese counterparts due to government and domestic prejudice regarding western achievements; fifthly, the expatriate as 'mother's brother', with a special Chinese personnel relationship being granted to expatriates in which outsiders are treated as insiders of the group.

Another empirical study, conducted by Verburg et al. (1999), argued, after a comparative survey of 70 Chinese industry sections (40 state-owned enterprises and 57 joint-ventures) and 47 Dutch industrial enterprises, that there exist distinctive features in cognitional structure, cultural values and labour regulations. The research adopted Globe (Den Hartog,1997) culture scores from the Netherlands and China and defined key points in HRM practices, mainly in respect of personnel selection and placement, pay and rewards, performance appraisal and personnel training. The research found, by comparing HRM practices in two countries, that the distinction is big. The traditional Chinese culture and value perception has experienced a transition in the process of recent socio-economic changes and new labour laws.

=Choi's (2008) findings relating to East Asian-owned firms (EAIEs) in China categorise three forms of managerial style: regulative, authoritarian and paternalistic. In search of the reasons contributing to labour disputes, it suggests that various factors, mainly the organizational characteristics, the institutional arrangements, the working conditions, and the composition of the labour force and managerial style, lead to different forms of labour dispute. The research revealed that "labour disputes are significantly and differentially influenced by various crucial variables according to the national origin of the firms" (2008: 1953), and, except for the institutional and economic factors, the "cultural factors still exert a persistent effect on the labour disputes, concurrent with the salient variations in managerial styles among EAIEs" (2008: 1956). Unfortunately, the author did not scrutinize the cultural influence in this research.

As China is becoming one of the most dynamic and significant economies in the world, policies of HRM such as the hiring of local managers are being adopted by many MNCs. Li and Nesbit (2013) noted this phenomenon of cultural contradictions at the managerial level. When local managers are working in MNCs, how do Chinese traditional cultural values encounter the Western-based cultural values? Li and Nesbit selected some key points, first, to define the research area: the HRM cultural values of Chinese staff working in MNCs; second, to identify the significant differences of HRM values from both sides; third, an effective research method to approach the objective.

The Western-based HRM values, as the researcher has pointed out, were 'Anglo-Saxonized', as all the MNCs were sampled from the US and Europe, which can be categorized into three dimensions: fundamental orientation towards human resources, the hard approach and the soft approach. By searching the literature on Chinese culture and history, the author has been able to identify Chinese values associated with people management, which follow the three abovementioned dimensions (Li and Nesbit, 2013). The methodology adopted in this research is from George Kelly's Repertory Grid Interview (RGT) approach (1955), which involves 455 bi-polar constructs obtained from seven elements, and 23 master constructs with definitions were finally concluded by interviewing 37 Chinese managers. The authors compared value differences under the same dimension, and found that there was a strong influence and assimilation of western values among Chinese managers, while, of course, some traditional Chinese values such as personal relationships *(guanxi)* and group orientation were deeply imbedded into the managers' minds, although others had disappeared, including the 'harmony' and 'virtue' concepts which were once the key values held in the Chinese tradition. Furthermore, 14 of 36 participants emphasized that coaching, mentoring and career planning are the key concerns in human resource management, which are closely connected with the personal networks of traditional Chinese values.

This research has some limitations, as the authors admitted that sample chosen was narrow, focusing only on 36 interviewees from just American and European MNCs, and not taking consideration of MNCs from other nationalities, which probably bring different values of perceptions for the managers. Nonetheless, it provides useful guidance for further research, as well as some hints that some Chinese management values may become integrated into a hybrid international HRM. The research method presented in this study offered an effective and validated method for research relating to HRM and industrial relations.

A research of automobile industry IR situation in China (Jurgens & Krzywdzinski, 2014) found that there was extensive use of fixed-term contract for up to 10 years as a transitional phase before blue-collar workers get an unlimited contract. Temporary contract was a main contract-based employment, plus another type of temporary pattern was from labour agency which was as high as 28% of total work force (See Figure 5.1. ).

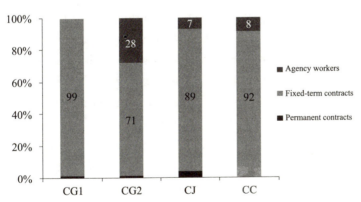

**Figure 5.1.  Structure of blue-collar workforce by form of contract (in %) in automobile manufacturing plants**

*Source: Jurgens & Krzywdzinski,2014:7*

The research found that there were stable sources for blue-collar work force supply, unlike the lower levels of the value chain, mainly from the contract based vocational high school or vocational college. Few of migrant workers have been enrolled into the automobile industry. Even though, automobile industry took much more concern on the competence improvement of employees on the shop floor level. The competence required from auto firm comprised the factors not only in operational skills, such as multi-skilling for several workplaces with the team, preventive routine maintenance for tools and machine, knowledge of quality control, but also the skills relating to communicating with the team, supervisors and engineers. The later demands were actually the competence of cross-cultural communications.

A qualitative empirical research in looking for host country language proficiency of MNCs expatriates has presented evidence on the importance of corporate language strategy (Zhang & Peltokorpi, 2016). There was a large number of expatriates working in China's MNCs or FDI which was estimated to be 220,000 in 2012 (Global Economics, 2012), and researchers interviewed 70 expatriates and their host country national (HCN) guided by the social identity theory. The study was trying to find out the impact of host country language proficiency on work and non-work-related adjustment.

The 70 interviewees come from 13 Nordic subsidiaries in the Beijing and Shanghai areas in 2006-2007 and 2012-2013. It has been argued that language proficiency took a positive influence on interaction adjustment in a study of expatriates in several host countries (Shaffer et al.,1999), which may cover various issues like coordination, communication, control, knowledge transfer, social identity and power and career advancement, this study has found out that expatriates host country language proficiency has multi-faceted effects on expatriates' performance with local employees, social support, and network related and non-work adjustment.

The industrial transition reforms after 2008 economic recession has also led to some changes of trade union election. According to the contents of Constitution of Labour Law, trade union must be built in the workplace, plus, there was an increasing workers' protests after 2006 (Chan,2010), the All China Federation of Trade Union (ACFTU) has strengthened the trade union building in private and trans-national corporate. Apart from the old "top-down" state-driven, a trade union election manipulated by government and high level trade union, and TNCs-induced patterns, an echo of strong consumer movement in Western countries requiring for the corporate social responsibility, for the election of trade union at enterprises level, a new type of strike-driven union election has caused much attention by scholars and government (Hui & Chan, 2015). Although critics saying it is hardly to be believed a new democratic trade unionism by this strike-driven election, just a kind of internal affairs, strong filtering mechanisms excluding rank-and-file workers from the higher levels of the union structure, it is, from the cultural perspective, compatible with China hierarchical and authoritarian social structure.

Researchers and practitioners recently are thinking of more HRM and IR into environmental management issues, which being called green competences (GCs). It is because that HRM is taken as an entity in supporting and promoting the adaptation of environment protection practices (Jabbour,2013;Renwick, Redman, & Maguire,2013). China was regarded as the world's most seriously polluted country (Tan & Lau,2010), thus, improving the individuals GCs from the employees working in the MNCs and FDI looks necessary and mandatory. A study of GCs in China (Subramanian, et al., 2016) industries in automotive manufacturing, raw material extraction, IT and other sectors proved that acquired GCs were driving force in shaping their effective GCs, even though there may exist different interpretations of harmonious development.

## 5.3. Cross-cultural conflicts

Scholars, on the early stage, regarded conflict as an interaction form among different sides' interest, perception and preferences(Brown, 1979). Some scholars define conflict as perceived incompatibility or opinion differences perceived by participants or interpersonal incompatibility, and regard conflict as the significant decision making mechanism of senior management team(Jehn, 1994). There is irreconcilability in interest-related conflict and objective. Generally speaking, two sides in conflict usually have different objectives, or one side, in pursuit of objective or expected interest, unavoidably becomes a hindrance to the other side. Compared with conflicts caused by the same culture, cross-cultural conflicts are usually caused by different interpretations of a single event. People from the same culture can share with one another and they will have similar interpretations of a single event; however people from different cultures will have different interpretations and can hardly share with one another. Thus cross-cultural conflicts exist in conflicts of different sharing systems.

Cross-cultural management became known around the late 70s of 20th century. With the further economic development of USA after the second world war, an increasing number of multinational corporations came into being; however, their management and experience which proved to be successful within USA could hardly and unexpectedly work out i n their overseas subsidiary corporations. While Japanese corporations, by combining experience of their American counterparts and their own national management mode, have surprisingly achieved success. Thus, research on the management phenomena above has been continuously conducted by theoretical circle, and finds out it is the differences of national cultures and values that result in cross-cultural management conflicts. Those conflicts exert direct influence on multinational management and finally cause business failure. Since then, research, from the perspective of cultural differences, on cross-cultural management conflicts have been the emerging fields for theoretical research. Scholars have not only given the definition and classification of cross-cultural conflicts, but also researched the relationship between cultural conflicts and management performance.

### 5.3.1. Classification of cross-cultural conflicts

Rahim(1992) and Druckman(1993) classified conflicts into conflict of interest, conflict of values and conflict of opinions. Conflict of interest is caused by sides' different possession orientation on interest allocation; conflict of values means different value orientation on the same thing or the same event which lead to different values and opinions; conflict of opinions stands for different opinions, plans and methods when facing the same event. Jehn (1994) classified conflicts into conflict of task and conflict of relationship. Conflict of task means interpersonal incompatibility, namely

Table 5.1.                    Classification of Cross-cultural Conflicts

| Representative Figures | Classification of Conflicts |
| --- | --- |
| Rahim(1992); Druckman(1993) | conflict of interest, conflict of values, conflict of opinions |
| Jehn(1994) | conflict of task, conflict of relationship |
| Robbins(2001) | conflict of task, conflict of relationship, conflict of process |
| Amason(1996) | conflict of perception, conflict of emotion |
| Deutsch(1990) | self-conflict, interpersonal conflict, intergroup conflict, inter-organizational conflict, conflict between country and nation |
| Pondy(1989) | potential conflict, perceptual conflict, intentional conflict, behavioural conflict, outcome conflict |
| Coser(1956) | constructive conflict, dysfunctional conflict |
| Coser(1956) | zero-sum conflict, win-win conflict |

*Data Source: made by author according to relevant materials*

inharmonic within a team, or people holding prejudice or hatred against other team members. Similarly, Amason (1996) classified conflicts into conflict of cognition and conflict of emotion; Robbins (2001) classified conflicts into conflict of task, conflict of relationship and conflict of process. Conflict of process, during the allocation of job responsibility and organizational resources, stands for the conflict among members when completing a task. In fact, conflict of process is one form of conflict of task. Furthermore, conflict of task can be subdivided into conflict of task content and conflict of task process. In addition, according to different conflict subjects and interaction objects, conflicts can be classified into self-conflict, interpersonal conflict, intergroup conflict, inter-organizational conflict, and conflict between country and nation(Deutsch, 1990); according to the effect that conflicts have on organizations, conflicts can be classified into constructive conflict and dysfunctional conflict; according to the natures, conflicts can be classified into zero-sum conflict and win-win conflict(Coser, 1956); according to the forming process and existing form, conflicts can be classified into potential conflict, perceptual conflict, intentional conflict, behavioural conflict and outcome conflict(Pondy, 1989).

### 5.3.2. Conflict and Performance

Conflict is closely related to performance (Yao, 2006; Jiang, 2008; Liu, 2008; Bao, et al, 2007). According to the research of Thomas & Schmidt (1976), in order to boost organizational performance, enterprise managers will usually spend over 20% of their time preventing and handling conflicts. However, theoretical circle hold different opinions on the relationship between conflict and performance. Generally speaking, scholars believe that there is a positive correlation between conflict of task and organizational performance; a negative correlation between conflict of relationship and organizational performance. For instance, Amason & Schweiger (1994) hold that conflict of task can contribute to the improvement of organizational performance, during which the conflict helps to enhance team members' information processing of nonconventional task with high uncertainty, and to improve members' understanding of problem through conflict and discussion to further boost organizational performance. According to the research of Simons (2000), he believes the relationship between conflict of task and organizational performance depends on how soon the decision can be made. Within a senior management team who can make quick decisions, conflict of task contributes to the improvement of team performance; within a senior management team who can hardly speed up decision making, conflict of task goes against the improvement of team performance. According to the research of Amason (1996), conflict of task, within a senior management team, contributes to team members' understanding of decision to further make them emotionally easier to accept the decision and to finally improve the team's decision quality. In contrast, conflict of relationship will compromise the decision quality and make team members emotionally harder to accept the decision. Janssen et al (1999) and Lin (2008) believes that there is a negative correlation between conflict of relationship and organizational performance, which means team members in relationship conflict have to spend plenty of time handling personal problems and relationships - their information processing ability being compromised and the team performance being undermined. Dedreu & Weingart(2003), based on 35 papers regarding the relationship between conflict and organizational performance, concluded that there is a medium negative correlation between conflict of task/relationship and organizational performance; conflict of task, conflict relationship and organizational performance interact with one another, during which conflict of relationship affects the correlation between conflict of task and organizational performance. Wang et al (2007) hold that the negative factor, within conflict of relationship, such as conflict of emotion will compromise the decision quality; the positive factor, within conflict of relationship, such as group cohesion will benefit the team performance. Lewicki et al (1992) believe d that there is an inverted U-type correlation between conflict and performance, which means neither conflict too intense nor conflict too weak can benefit organizational performance and only conflict of a moderate intensity can stimulate self-criticism, learning and innovation inside the organization to achieve ideal organizational performance.

In addition, Wu (2010) found out that the differences of team members' values have a negative effect on team conflict and team performance; while team conflict has a positive effect on team performance.

Contribution and Shortcomings: as to cross-cultural management conflict, scholars from all over the world have conducted detailed research on aspects like definition and classification of cross-cultural conflict, relationship between conflict and performance, resolution of cross-cultural conflict. Mature research on definition and classification of cross-cultural conflict has been recognized in theoretical and practical fields and widely utilized; although positive or negative correlation between conflict and performance still remains controversial within theoretical circle, it is an unquestioned fact that there is a strong correlation between conflict and performance, which means more research should be conducted on management of cross-cultural conflict. In this essay, Amason's (1996) conclusion will be adopted that conflict of cross-cultural management classified into conflict of perception and conflict of emotion, and lay emphasis on conflict of perception to research how cultural differences make Chinese and German subjects differ from one another in decision making and cognition of everyday management decision. Everyday management decision involves cross-cultural enterprise decision on production, personnel, innovation, finance, etc.

### 5.3.3. Communication Strategy Resolving Cross-cultural Conflicts

Modern and contemporary scholars have conducted systematic and detailed research on communication strategy that can resolve cross-cultural conflict, among which there are two-strategy theory of Deutsch(1949, 1990) and Tjosvold (1988), communication conflict mode of Putnam & Wilson(1982), four-strategy mode of Pruitt(1981), conflict management grid theory of Blake & Mouton(1964), etc.

Two type theories, proposed by Deutsch (1949, 1990) and Tjosvold (1988), resolve cultural conflict by cooperation and competition. Lovelace & Shapiro & Weingart (2001) found out that how understanding inconsistency affects team performance depends on cooperation or competition of members' communication. Tjosvold and Law & Sun(2006) proved that cooperative communication can mitigate both conflict of task and conflict of relationship while competitive communication would intensify conflict.

According to communication conflict mode - three type theories - of Putnam & Wilson (1982), they believe that conflicted should be resolved by avoiding, solution orientation and controlling.

Pruitt(1981) held that, under different circumstances, resolution of conflict includes problem solving, contending, accommodating and inaction. Problem solving means facing conflict directly and evaluating problem objectively and fairly to find out effective solution. Contending means convincing the other side in conflict to accept one side's opinion or proposal by contending and demonstrating. Accommodating means, according to circumstances, accepting opinion or proposal of the other side in conflict by compromising. Inaction means coping with conflict by inaction, wasting time and delay.

Singh & Vlates (1991) concluded five strategies that communication resolves conflict: avoiding/withdrawal, accommodating/smoothing, compromising, forcing and integrating/problem solving.

Buller & Kohls & Anderson(2000), American scholars on cross-cultural management, proposed decision tree model. They believe communication strategy, continuous as a whole, comprises six strategies like avoiding, educating, forcing, compromising, cooperating and accommodating. One strategy is optimal in one situation. Under certain circumstances, suitable strategy should be adopted to achieve best results.

In addition, Wang Jing(2008) pointed out that cultural difference costs and cross-cultural transaction fees exert influence on organizational performance, and further proposed a cross-cultural management mode suitable to Chinese enterprises, namely "cultural integration and integrated mode".

Weihrich & Koontz(1993) believe that effective communication are often supported by communication skills including: information conveyed by people should be clear, realistic and logic; attention should be paid to communication needs of

Table 5.2.            Conflict Strategy Theory

| Name of Theory | Representative Figures | Conflict Strategy |
|---|---|---|
| Two-strategy Theory | Deutsch(1949, 1990) Tjosvold(1990) | cooperation, competition cooperation, competition |
| Three-strategy Theory | Putnam & Wilson(1982) | avoiding, resolution orientation and controlling |
| Four-strategy Theory | Pruitt(1981) | problem solving, contending, accommodating, inaction |
| Five-strategy Theory | Blake & Mouton(1964) Singh & Vlates(1991) Thomas(1976) | withdrawal, consoling, intimidating, compromising, problem solving withdrawal, smoothing, forcing, compromising, problem solving avoiding, accommodating, compromising, contending, integrating |
| Six-strategy Theory | Buller, Kohls, Anderson(2000) | avoiding, forcing, educating, negotiating, accommodating, cooperating |

*Data Source: made by author according to relevant materials*

information recipients and make sure they understand; both sides in communication should emphasize intonation, wording, context and emotional factor; both sides in communication should be responsible for results. Putti, Weihrich & Koontz(1998) believe that, during communication, feedback information and listening play an important role in getting accurate information; understandable language should be used in communication; emotional controlling is important in communication, so is non-verbal communication, which means proper use of body language. De Cenzo & Robbins(2001) hold that organization members should use simple and direct language in communication; in communication, both sides' feedback information should be valued and so is two-way communication; the diversity of communication methods should be paid attention and so is the supportive and reliable communication atmosphere.

### 5.3.4. Cross-cultural Management in China's MNCs

The problem facing transnational corporations in China is how to build up the new-type modern enterprise culture and avoid cultural conflict. Accompanying foreign funds and technology when they were introduced in, various values, management thought and pattern, mindset, ethics and code of conduct also brought in communication and clash. On one hand, foreign-funded enterprises operating within China should comply with Chinese laws and regulations and their organization management system should also adapt to Chinese culture; on the other hand, since the cross-cultural management of foreign-funded enterprises is bidirectional, Chinese employees who account for a majority have to adjust themselves to the management pattern of transnational corporations. The communication between Chinese and foreigners could be multi-sided and multi-layered, and integration between different management patterns could also last for long. However, the infiltration and integration of oriental and occidental cultures are surely to be a catalyst for globaliztaion, high-efficiency and diversity of transnational corporations.

In order to make a great achievement in transnational operation, Western countries currently pay much attention to cross-cultural management, which proves to be effective in practice. According to the opinion of Nancy J. Adler, a famous Canadian expert on cross-cultural organization and management, there are three approaches to resolve cross-cultural conflicts: first is dominance, which means one kind of culture's dominance over other kinds of cultures. One kind of culture dominates the entire decision-making and behaviour within the organization while other kinds of culture were oppressed. Advantage is obvious that "uniform" organizational culture could be constructed in a short time but it makes it impossible to draw on others' strong points, and staff's aversion to cultural oppression would worsen the conflict. Second is compromise, which means compromise and concession among different kinds of culture. Harmony and stability inside the organization are achieved through seeking common grounds while keeping minor differences. Dangers, however, still lurk behind harmony and stability. Only when the cultural difference is minor can we turn to this approach. Third is integration, which means a brand new kind of organizational culture integration built on mutual respect, complement and coordination and based on acknowledgment of and emphasis on cultural diversity. This kind of uniform culture not only boasts high stability but also benefits from its "hybrid", which proves to be the most effective means to facilitate the cross-cultural management in transnational operation.

There are two aspects, based on an experiment research (Xie, 2012), to analyzes the cross-cultural management decision in the relation between the communication frequency and the conflict resolution (See Figure 5.2.). On the one hand, the author

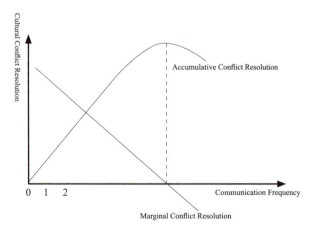

**Figure 5.2. Diagram of the Relation between the Communication Frequency and the Conflict Resolution of Cross-cultural Management**
*Source: Xie, D.M. 2012. Behavioural Experiment on Cross-cultural Decision-making Conflict Management by Communication between Chinese and Germen.*

compares the consensus degree of the subjects from Sino-German Testing System of the different communication frequency; and on the other hand, the author also compares the degree of subjects' changing their views from Sino-German Testing System.

The experiment results as follows:

A negative correlation between communication frequency and the marginal conflict resolution of cross culture is found. That's to say, with the increase of communication frequency, the marginal conflict resolution will decrease.

When marginal communication utility>0, there is a positive correlation between communication frequency and accumulative resolution of cross-cultural conflicts. That's to say, the higher the communication frequency is, the less the accumulative resolution of cross-cultural conflict will be.

When marginal communication utility<0, there is a negative correlation between communication frequency and cross-cultural conflict resolution. the higher the communication frequency is, the more the accumulative resolution of cross-cultural conflict will be.

The accumulative resolution turns out to be an inverted U shape curve with the increase of communication frequency. When the marginal conflict resolution equals zero, the accumulative resolution reach its maximum, during which the communication frequency is regarded to achieve to its best threshold.

## 5.4. Industrial relations in China's MNCs

### 5.4.1. Labour Contract

With more and more employees are recruited into foreign-funded enterprises, a problem sticking out is the lack of contract signing standardization. It is common that employees are bounded by quite a few clauses in the contract but employers are usually bounded by less clauses or none. Especially low-level employees suffer more. As the most important legal basis of labour-capital employment relationship, the devoid and perversion of labour contract prove to be the major cause that result in employers unscrupulously infringing on employees' rights, employees bearing no sense of belonging to the companies, and frequent job hopping. For instance, there are cases that female employees are more likely to be laid off once their pregnancy become known; there are cases that employers find an excuse to dismiss their employees before the end of the year to avoid the 12th and 13th month pay. It is noticeable that labour relationship remains more confused in labour intensive industries of garment, shoemaking and toy, especially in small-scale enterprises of short-term joint venture.

### 5.4.2. Trade Union and Workers' Congress

At present, the actual status and function of labour union of foreign-funded enterprises are extremely far from what has been stipulated in Trade Union Law and Labour Law of PRC. For example, in 2007, among 480,000 foreign-funded enterprises established in China, 160,000-only one third-of them have trade unions (Yao, 2007). In some enterprises, it is often seen that employees' benefit and claim cannot be well expressed by labour union, chairman of the trade union can be easily fired at employer's will, or trade union is reduced to act as employer's spokesman. Even in some large-scale American or European joint ventures with high standardization, power and function of labour union also remain restricted.

Soon after the economic recession in 2008, the Chiense government proclaimed a campaign which called Industrial Upgrading to change the old economic modules of labour intensive export production with low technological capabilities. An empirical study (Butolllo,2013:166) for the gament and IT sector research which located in Guangdong's Pearl River Delta from 2010 to 2011 has proved that moch of those enterprises still lie on the low-skilled and badly paid migrant workers (Butollo,2013:166). To prevent the unrest from migrant workers, collective bargaining on wage and some other bread-to-butter issues was advocated by local government for the purpose of creating harmonious industrial relations.

## 5.5. Questions from empirical studies

The empirical studies of MNCs in the world reflect some changes of HRM and IRs. A distinctive feature is that, considering the gaps in culture and language, MNCs' stakeholders and managers focus their interest in people's management in different areas.

### 5.5.1. HRM and IRs

Since HRM "comprises a set of polices designated to maximize organizational integration, employee commitment, flexibility and quality of work" (Guest, 1987), MNCs with Anglo-Saxon cultural backgrounds establishing subsidiaries in the developed countries tend to adopt a range of HRM strategies. It has been argued that, at an individual level, there is so much variation in people's age, tenure, educational background, gender and motivation that a unitarist and individualistic approach to management brings more benefits for the companies and for employees. Changes in the economic and political climate have resulted in a decline in trade union pressures on management in the developed world. However, the developing countries, including the remarkably newly thriving economic giants such as China and India, have trade unions whose power remains underestimated, and which play important roles in many dimensions of MNCs' daily management. Mass labour-orientated industry distribution as well as cultural difference have led to the prosperity of the trade unions, providing a quite unique profile of industrial relations compared to the situation in the developed countries.

### 5.5.2. Culture and Language Barriers

Research has demonstrated that interference from culture and language is a key factor manipulating the HRM and IRs policies in the respective subsidiaries, with corresponding culture and language strategies leading to better and more effective management, no matter whether HRM or IRs strategies have been applied.

For subsidiaries located in developing countries, at the individual level, cultural interference has been demonstrated in personal career planning, personal networking, and working performance assessment. Language, as a carrier of information, is a carrier of culture as well, so that communication problems occur because of language misunderstandings. Research has identified that language barriers for MNCs are not a matter of whether one can speak a foreign language, but whether one can *think* in that language. It has been demonstrated that the consequences of communication could be worse if one could not grasp a foreign language well enough (Liu, 2010). Questions may arise in terms of the HRM and IRs in the context of a multi-language situation, as follows:

- What language strategy should MNCs take in HRM and IRs management?
- Do mono-language strategies work in a MNC?
- How can cross-cultural competence be obtained in HRM or IRs practice?

• What are the criteria to prove that the employees working in the MNCs are qualified in foreign language communications?

Along with the questions from previous chapters of literature review, this research expects to find answers from coming in-depth studies in the context of MNCs in China.

## 5.6. Conclusion

The empirical cases discussed in this chapter demonstrate the importance of culture and language interference in the management of MNCs' subsidiaries in both developed and developing countries. Although the IRs paradigm in the Anglo-Saxon countries is losing the interest of entrepreneurs and scholars, who favour a more unitarist and individualistic management style, it still has an impact on many enterprises in mass labour intensive industries in developing countries like China.

Empirical findings from previous scholars offer a valuable theoretical framework underpinning the studies in newly thriving economic regions. Questions and hypotheses come under their research trajectories. The issue of how culture and language strategies impact a country's HRM and IRs operations is a relatively neglected question. That is exactly what this study is intending to answer.

# Chapter Six
# Industrial Relations in Contemporary China

This chapter presents a profile of Chinese industrial relations from the beginning of China's industrialization early in the 1910s to the giant changes today. The Chinese economic reform, starting in 1978, was a key turning point that involved changing from a planned economic system to a socialist market-oriented economy. One consequence of this economic reform was that it created the diverse and complex industrial relations that can be seen in China today, which originated from three branches: the traditional cultural heritage, the communist ideology and the impacts of the marketing economy.

## 6.1. Industrial relations: lost in translation

When talking about the translations of industrial relations, researchers found that it is a quite complicated thing. Early report from the literature review proved that the correspondent term with industrial relations was translated as "产业关系(*chan ye guan xi)*", but Chinese word *chan ye* traditionally refers to the manufacturing industries. Later when Marxism perspective IRs theories spread in China, people used to analyze the industrial relations from social conflicts way. Actually, for being quite a long time, scholars in China took the term of **Labour Relations** instead of industrial relations to generalize the relations between empolyers and employees (Cheng, 2002:3). In China, one who got paid to work for an organization or for another person else can be called employee. But the term of employee is always confused or misused by other terms such as labourers, workers, staff members etc.

When using the term labour relations, it refers mainly to the relations between capital and labourers, emphasising the contradictory features from two sides. The term industrial relations "劳工关系" (*lao gong guan xi*) in Chinese is a employee-centred concept, and took more concerns on employees' organization, the trade union, and the process for collective barghaining with employers (Cheng, 2002).

Another Chinese term in employee relations is "劳雇关系" (*lao gu guan xi*) which took more cares on the legitimate relations between employees and employers in their responsibilities and accountabilites. Later on, Chinese scholars adopted a new term of employee relations "劳使关系"(*lao shi guan xi*) from Japanese empirical studies (Cheng, 2002) which took more emphasis on the technical issues of management, but less care about value judgement, took more measures on creating mild and intimate relationship, but less confrontational structure.

Moer or less, the study of relations between trade union, management and goverment in China has included every layer under the principles of socialism system with Chinese charateristics. Connotation of industrial relations or employment relations in China is not same as that of in ASC cultural context, and mistakes always occured because of wrong interpreation.

In this study, the term of industrial relation is translated as "劳动关系" (*lao dong guan xi*), which used to be translated as Labor Relations(LRs) "产业关系" (*chan ye guan xi)* by some Chinese scholars (Cheng, 2002; Chang, 2005) because LRs has been featured to much of idealogical charateristics.

Another reason for the necessity of using one independent chapter describing industrial relations in China is, as explained in the previous chapter, that this study focuses mainly on mass labour intensive MNCs in China which is one of typical features in China's emploement system, thus, study of tripatite relationship between trade union, management and goverment takes more significance than human resources management.

## 6.2. Research methods for analyzing industrial relations in China

Industrial Relations exist in an industrial society where there is a "separation of the owners of production and workers who engage in some forms of productive activity in exchange for wages" (Taylor et al., 2003). A better understanding of industrial relations in China comes from a flexible and dynamic approach. Within ninety years of Chinese history of industrialization, there have been dramatic changes to social contexts relating to political mechanisms and the economic situation, and more importantly, global changes with more emphasis and attention to labour rights. It is thus necessary to set up a module to analyze the actors, government, trade union and management in order to make sense of the features of industrial relations in the respective historical period.

Salamon (2000) argued, following the findings by Dunlop (1958) and Wood (1970), that an industrial relations system could be integrated through a broadly accepted common ideology. However, they had different opinions in terms of the objective of such systems. Dunlop took the system primarily as a means to achieve stability and its own ultimate survival, while Wood (1975) insisted that the system is to satisfy the functional need for order within the production system, thus placing the need for social control above the social welfare needs of employees (See the simplified I.R.S., Figure 6.1).

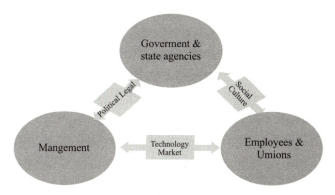

**Figure 6.1.  The System of Industrial Relations**

*Source: Modified from Salamon, M. 2000. Industrial Relations: Theory and Practice, 4th Ed. Prentice Hall.*

## 6.2.1. Dunlop's System Model of Industrial relations

The American scholar Dunlop constructs a relatively complete system analysis frame of industrial relations in his classic *Industrial Relations System*, which means employment relations comprise, on every stage of development, specific actors and environment, ideology of employment relations system, and rules that regulate the workplace. Actors of industrial relations system stand for operators, organizers and workers, and governments that makes and executes the strategies of industrial relations. The factor of environment comprises economic, political and social environment. Ideology, as a complete set of concept and faith that actors hold to link the system as a whole, is the common thought and concept that decide the role and status of every actor. Effective functioning of the system is based on the common ideology. Dunlop believes that, under the influence of environment, the interaction among different actors of industrial relations would produce a series of complex rules that regulate the factory and workers. He points out that rules are like a network that comprises substantive and procedural rules. Substantive rules comprise the results caused by actors action and interaction in industrial relations system, such as wages and welfare, labour condition, working hours, etc. Procedural rules decide the code of conduct in actors interaction, such as solutions to labour disputes, procedures of collective bargaining, etc. Rules in turn exert a direct restriction on the functioning of industrial relations (See Diagram 6.1).

Dunlop's theory lays a foundation for system analysis of industrial relations, but

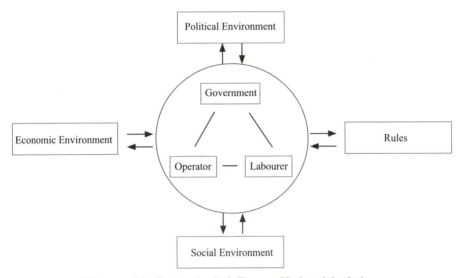

**Diagram 6.1.  System Analysis Frame of Industrial relations**

*Date Source: John T. Dunlop. 1958*

what needs to be improved is its lack of dynamism and consideration for the factor of environment, its failure to clarify the relationship among four constituents, and its ignoring the reaction of industrial relations system on environment.

### 6.2.2. Sandver Model

The American scholar Sandver (1987), under the influence of Dunlop's system model of industrial relations, proposed a theory model regarding industrial relations analysis in his book *Industrial relations: Process and Results*.

Sandver believes that, during the functioning of industrial relations, factors of external environment and workplace and personal factor act as the basic causes leading to labour disputes. Resolving labour disputes hinges on management, individual withdrawal and labour movement organized by trade union. Labour movement resolves labour disputes mainly by collective bargaining with employers on wages, labour condition, working hours and the like to work out labour contract and relevant agreements. The influence that labour contract and relevant agreements exert on workplace improves the workplace and further influences the external environment. The improvement and development of external environment in turn influences the functioning of industrial relations (See Diagram 6.2).

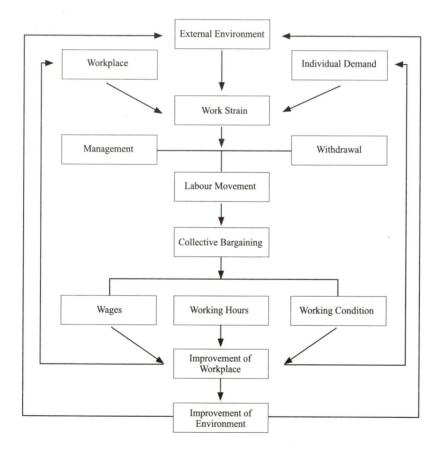

**Diagram 6.2.  Improvement and development of external environment**
*Data Source: M.H. Sandver. 1987:26-34*

### 6.2.3. Gunderson Model

Gunderson model (1995) is made of four consecutive parts of "Input, Actor, Transformation, Output", among which the natures of input and actor are under the direct and indirect influence of transformation and output. Thus in the industrial relations system, interaction among different parts within the system should be taken into fully consideration when analyzing the output (See Diagram 6.3).

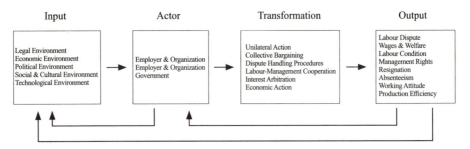

**Diagram 6.3. Gunderson Model**

*Source: Gunderson, Morley, 1995*

### 6.2.4. KKM Model

*The Transformation of American Industrial Relations*, a book coauthored by Kochan, Katz and Mchersie in the year of 1986, made an amendment to Dunlop's classic theory of industrial relations. They lay more emphasis on the change of external environment and industrial relations actors' response to environmental change. A dynamic factor of "Strategic Choice" has been added into the system model of industrial relations and it has also been pointed out that the change of industrial relations is the outcome of environmental pressure and organizational strategy. Selection and judgment of industrial relations actors like workers, operators and governments exert huge influence on the direction and structure of industrial relations system. KKM believes that external environment influences institutional structure and further influences performance output. The change of external environment urges employers to adjust business strategy, during which operators' decisions are restricted by their ingrained values (See Diagram 6.4.)

KKM's theory of "Strategic Choice" divides the action of industrial relations actors into three layers: the uppermost layer that decides strategic choice, the middle layer that decides collective bargaining and personnel policy, and

**Diagram 6.4. Gunderson Model**
*Source: Kochan, Katz, & McKersie, 1986*

the lowermost layer or the workplace layer that directly influences staff and managers. As is shown in Table 6.1, operators, trade unions and governments perform different action on different layers.

Table 6.1.        Operators, trade unions and governments perform
different action on different layers

| Layer | Employer | Trade Union | Government |
|---|---|---|---|
| Long-term strategy and strategy making | Business strategy Investment strategy Human resources strategy | Political strategy Representative strategy Organization strategy | Macroeconomic and social strategy |
| Collective bargaining and personnel policy | Personnel strategy Bargaining strategy | Collective bargaining policy | Labour laws and supervision |
| Relationship between workplace and individual/organization | Management style Workers' involvement | Contract management Workers' involvement Job design and organization of work | Labour criteria Worker's involvement Individual rights |

However, KKM has laid the values and strategy of operators in the core location of analysis frame of industrial relations, over stressing the leading role of managers within industrial relations system while ignoring the independence and status of trade union and employees.

## 6.2.5. PDR System of Hyo-Soo Lee

In different system models of employment relations, attention are usually paid to summarize "input" and "output" but not to illuminate or conclude the transformation mechanism that links both of them. In order to overcome the shortcoming above, Lee (1996), in the perspective of integration and interaction of three parts - production, distribution and rule making, conducts research on employment relations and proposes the PDR system of industrial relations. The system comprises four parts that decide industrial relations: environment, actor, content and interaction of PDR system, and performance. The factor of environment exerts huge influence on the actors' values, power and status and further on the actors' strategic choices within the PDR system; the content and interaction of PDR system decide performance. Hyo-Soo Lee divides environment into competitive environment and total environment, in which the former includes technology, capital, product market, labour market, corporate governance, and enterprise scale; the latter stands for social and cultural atmosphere, economic and political conditions. Environment's influence on actors' values, power and status would be exerted indirectly on PDR system (See Diagram 6.5.).

One key point of PDR theory is the comprehensive and balanced system running mechanism. In the systems, production system greatly influences distribution system and rule making system through creative thinking in human resources management. The imbalance within P, D, R could result in disputes among people involved and low efficiency.

PDR system, rejecting the thoughts of classical economics, is likely to resolve the interest disputes. Thus, PDR theory is philosophically constructed on Commons' stable and human-based capitalist theory, which, as a kind of neoclassical economics, regards labour force as a commodity. PDR, from the human-based perspective, holds that workers have thoughts and potential which are different from merely production factors like capital, land, etc.

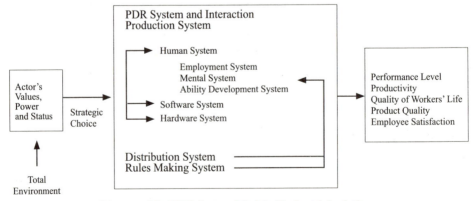

**Diagram 6.5.  PDR System Model of Industrial relations**

*Source: Lee, 1996, Theory construction in industrial relations: A synthesis of PDR systems*

## 6.2.6. IR Research theories from China

In mainland China, there have been various expressions to delivery the meaning of industrial relations, such as the industrial relations, industrial relations, labour-capital relations as well as the employment relations.

Qin Liuqin (1995) noted that industrial relations referred to the relations generated in the labouring process between the labour and the employees, like enterprises and other units. It is an important content in the productive relations, which has a direct impact on the productivity. Judging from the main body, this is a narrow conception of the industrial relations, however, the contents of which belong to a relatively broad concept.

Hei Qiming (2004) marked the industrial relations as a combined relation derived from the group social work, including the labourers like the trade union, as well as the users of the labour force, like the Enterprise Manager Association and the Employer Association. These two parts form the main body of the social industrial relations. Obviously, it is a broad definition of the industrial relations.

Chen (2002) believed that industrial relations come from the employment organizations to study the relevant issues about the employment management, showing the total sum of the cooperation, conflicts, strength and power. This defines the labour relation from the aspect of the management of the industrial relations in companies.

Chang (2005) thought that labour relation refers to the direct part of the labour in the productive relations. Specifically speaking, it is a social economic relation combined by the labourer and the user of the labour force in the working, which are a relative comprehensive concept as well as the concrete manifestation of the combination between the production materials and the labourers in the process of social production.

This study of IR in China will look at three actors and their performances in the respective periods of Chinese history. China's industrialization started in the 1910s, soon after the collapse of China's Qing Dynasty, which is why Dunlop's actors' framework is used to illustrate that the roles of actors may be played differently due to the changes in China's social and cultural environments.

China has a tradition of authoritarian regimes since long before the Zhou Dynasty, a feudal political structure that was established 3000 years ago. This political cultural heritage has had a deep impact even from the beginning of China's capitalist revival in the late 19th century. China's industrialization, driven by both government intention and capital from overseas Chinese, started at the beginning of the 20th century because of the then-government's defeat by the British Empire. A famous statement from Mr. Wei Yuan, a famous translator and senior official in the Qing dynasty, said that China must take the national strategy of "learning merits from the foreign to conquer the foreign". Industrialization was undoubtedly one solution for 'learning merits' at the time. Early factors of industrial relations in China actually had two components: the management itself was the representative of government or state agencies, while for the private industry, China has strong family business characteristics.

In the 1920s, in light of the success of China's Revolution of 1911, the foundation of a new government and the Republic of China, China's industrialization developed into a new epoch, a more thriving stage, with private capitals taking large proportion in some special industrial areas, such as agriculture, textiles etc. The tripartite conflicts between government, management and employees were the driving forces leading to industrial actions and some social revolutions.

In the 1950s, after the liberation of new China, the communist party dominated government, private capitals were demolished almost totally in the process of socialization and corporate employees became 'the masters of the country'. The Trade Union organization changed its character, functioning as a government body. The tripartite relationship between government, management and employees became merged as one body.

After 1978, the Opening-up Policy in economics swept across China. Private economy was encouraged and special economic zones where entrepreneurs could enjoy special tax-free privileges were set up in the Pearl River Delta in South China. The tripartite relationship returned to three independent factors in the private economy. According to China's Xinhua news agency, the private economy accounted for more than 60% of national GDP, and more than 90% of new employment positions were offered by the private economy until 2012 (Xinhua News, 2012), while in state-owned corporations, factors of industrial relations still retained the characteristics of the socialist structure. The metaphor of the 'iron bowl' and the 'gold bowl', was used to describe work opportunities in the state-owned enterprises and the public sector respectively, the latter still being the dream job for the young generation.

## 6.3. Chinese industrial relations: a historical review

From a Marxist point of view, China was a country of feudalism for more than 2000 years, where peasantry was the dominant relationship between landlords and peasants. This legacy is deeply embedded in Chinese society. In 1840, the Opium War between China and Britain took place. China lost this war and signed the Nanjing Contract with the British government, under which British businessmen were allowed to set up factories in five chartered trade cities, namely Canton, Fu Zhou, Xia Men, Ning Bo, and Shanghai. By 1894, there were 34 thousand labourers working in 191 foreign-owned enterprises, and 40 thousand in 48 state-owned enterprises, with another 27 to 30 thousand workers in 135 private enterprises (Liu, 1985)

### Formation of Chinese IR from its early industrialization

In 1911, the Xinhai Revolution broke out, and China's Qing Emperor was overthrown by the Republic of China. With regard to the organization of labour, from 1840 and the Opium War to the collapse of the Qing Dynasty in 1911, there was no formal trade union organization, but labourers were organized into so-called "Townsmen's Associations", referring to people from the same regions. The Qing Emperor strictly prohibited any type of industrial action. In the time of the Xihai Revolution, with the appealing slogan of *Three Principles for the People*: the people's democracy, the people's rights, and the people's wellbeing, the new government advocated the establishment of labour organizations. In addition, a series of labour laws and regulations were released (Wagner: 1938), covering labour organizations, labour disputes, security, and working environment.

However, this situation changed quickly with the influence of the Russian revolution in 1917, as the expansion of Marxism drew the attention of the Chinese intelligence. Marxist learning teams were founded in the big cities of Beijing, Shanghai and Canton. On the 4th of May, 1919, the news that China had lost its own land in Shan Dong Province, which used to be a German concession, came to Beijing.[1]

---

[1] When World War I came to an end, the Chinese people, having long suffered from imperialist aggression and full of hopes for national independence, had hailed "the victory of truth over might" and the "14 Articles of Peace" put forward by U.S. President Wilson. But the method of dealing with the Shandong issue at the Paris Peace Conference rid the Chinese people of their illusion and made them realize that they themselves needed to "take direct action." The May 4th Movement thus broke out. Source: *China Daily*

Students from Peking Universities rushed into the streets and demonstrated for the refusal to sign the Treaty of Versailles. This May Fourth demonstration developed as an unprecedented movement in support of Chinese democracy, freedom, and science. Historians, since then, have talked about the "May Fourth Spirits". College students, along with labour workers, played an important role in this movement. Two years later, Marxism learning teams scattered throughout the main cities of China organized their first representative session in July of 1921 in Shanghai, in which the Communist Party of China (CPC) was officially founded. In its first session, the CPC clearly stated that the Party's essential mission was to conduct research, to lead labour movements with different forms and to strengthen its control of the trade unions. Both the CPC and *Kuomindang*, then the ruling government party, realized the importance of the thriving labour power in China. Since then, the control of China's IR has been a powder keg between the two parties and the trade unions.

Trade unions were split into two groups: one group was led by the CPC, the other by the *Kuomintang*. Early in December 1920, the first "modernized trade union", compared with the old labours' Townsmen's Associations, which was named the Shanghai Trade Union of Machinery, was founded under the guidance of Chinese communist activists. After the foundation of the CPC in 1921, a new branch, the General Secretary Department of All China Trade Union (GSDACTU), was formed, directed by Zhang Guotao. Later in May 1925, GSDACTU was replaced by a new All China Federation of Trade Unions (ACFTU), which continues today (Gao, *et al*: 2008:85).

As for the *Kuomintang*, after holding power, notably after the impact of the May Fourth Movement, the *Kuomintang*-controlled government issued a series of regulations to earn support from the working class. In February 1922, the first Chinese Law of Trade Union Regulations was released, and soon after that, in 1938, the Sino-Japan War broke out. The *Kuomintang* government had ameliorated a series of laws relating to industrial relations. They are: the Trade Union Law, amended in 1929, 1931, 1932 and 1934; the Enterprises Regulations, released in 1929 and amended in 1932; the Regulations

---

http://www.chinadaily.com.cn/china/2012cpc/2011-07/27/content_15842136.htm
direct action." The May 4th Movement thus broke out. Source: China Daily
http://www.chinadaily.com.cn/china/2012cpc/2011-07/27/content_15842136.htm

of Labour Dispute Process, released in 1930, amended in 1932 and 1933; the Law of Collective Contract, released in 1930; the Labour Contract Law, released in 1936; the Minimum Wage Law, released in 1936; and the Law of Mineral Enterprises, released in 1936 (Gao et al., 2008: 58). But there were critics – for example:

> *"The accomplishment of labours' law is a great leap forward for our government and our country. It is unprecedented progress in the Far East countries, but it is almost hopeless in practice. So far, our government has not been ready to make it happen: those regulations are just waste papers..." (Translated by author)* (Gao, et al: 2008:58)

Nevertheless, the legitimated labour construction had a positive influence on social stability and created a government-for-the-people reputation in international society. China was one of the founding members of the International Labour Organization (ILO) (Gao et al., 2008: 59). From 1919 to 1928, China appointed overseas diplomatic staff as representatives to attend the ILO conference. Starting in 1929, the *Kuomintang* government sent a delegation, including members respectively standing for government, employers and labourers, to attend the ILO conference. In 1944, China became a permanent member of the ILO.

Born from the "half feudalism and half colonialism environment", China's trade unions were growing, with a strong influence on ideology. They had close relations with local customs, political regimes and investment orientation.

## 6.4. Industrial relations during the planned economy (from 1949 to 1978)

The period between 1949 and 1978 was a time when the CPC adopted a pattern, partly learnt from the Soviet Union, and partly from localized Marxist interpretations, to guide its industrial relations under the planned economy environment. An analysis of the industrial relations came from its economic-rational roots, with macro and micro aspects (Taylor et al., 2003). In detail, Taylor et al. say:

> *Micro-analysis examines work-based employment relations, examining a range of workplace-based employment issues, and the operation of the labour process ... while, the macro-analysis focuses on social-level institutions, such as the state, trade*

*union organs and employers' organizations, and maps the overall industrial relations framework within society. (Taylor et al., 2003:3)*

After the liberation in 1949, the CPC-controlled government paid much attention to dealing with industrial relations. A cradle-to-grave welfare system was set up and private enterprises almost disappeared from the country. The working class was the leading class and the masters of the country. The wages, employment, and welfare provisions were all taken by the government, which was called the 'iron rice-bowl' (*tie fan wan*). An employment unit, namely *danwei*, functioned as a small country, offering not just working facilities, but also the necessary catering services, such as hospitals, schools, grocery shops, cinemas, and even clubs.

From a macro perspective, workers' employer was the Party (government), which had a special name, *Zhi Gong* (worker and staff). The term '*Zhi Gong*' includes workers in workshops, administrators in the office, engineers, technicians, and all the people working inside the *Dan Wei* (working unit). During the period of the planned economy, all the enterprises were just workshops of the state-factory. Following this socialist ideology, the interests of labour (workers), enterprises, and country (government) became the same, while trade unions lost their function from the previous period of civil and anti-colonial wars, but became an assistant and subsidiary department of government organs. Wang (1992) concluded that the objective of trade unions in the planned economy was to "organize labour contests, technical innovations, and increased production drives and propagandizing worker's management of such activities as organizing sports and entertainment events for workers, supervising the implementation of occupational health and safety and providing sanatoriums, rest homes and public welfare services for workers". In other words, the trade union, ACFTU, was acting as a 'transmission belt' between the Party (government) and workers and staff in the planned economy, with a strong unitarist ideology.

## 6.5. Current industrial relations in China: a dynamic change
### 6.5.1. Role of the Party (government) and legalization
The unitarist ideology faced challenges beginning in 1978. On December 18, 1978, the CPC held its third Plenary Session of the 11th Party Central Committee in Beijing. This historical plenary session had two themes: one was to criticize the "Two Whatevers"

guidance (whatever Chairman Mao says is right; whatever Chairman Mao demands, we shall follow), saying 'practice is the only way to evaluate the truth'; the second was to stop the wrong-doing in the Cultural Revolution, change the Party's job from "taking the fight between classes" to "taking economic construction as the key job of the people and the country". The Party was trying to adopt a market economy as an effective way to reimburse its losses during the Cultural Revolution period.

The Party subsequently promoted a series of economic reforms, and released new policies encouraging private business and township collective business. With the development of China's economic reform, foreign capital as well as investments from Hong Kong and Taiwan rushed into mainland China because of its cheap labour and its convenient and well-constructed infrastructure. Within 30 years, China's GDP was growing by two digits per year, which is quite rare in the history of the world economy. In 2001, China entered the WTO and enhanced its cooperation with world developed economies. China became the wonderland for global enterprises. The workers were no more than masters of the enterprises, and there were divergent industrial relations. Statistics showed that the number of employees working in the State Owned Enterprises (SOEs) industries shrank from 112.61 million in 1995 to 76.40 million in 2001: a loss of almost one-third (NBSC: 2002).

It was a hard time for those people who were laid off (*xia gang*): statistics showed (Luo, 2011) that each year between 1988 and 2011, seven to nine million people were laid off, until there were about 40 million laid-off workers in China. Most of those laid-off workers, of whom females tended to be aged 40 and over and males were 50 and over, came from China's old industrial bases and undeveloped economic territories: for example, 25% of them were from the North-East part of China, an old industrial belt in the 1950s.

The increasing complexity of industrial relations forced the Party to bring its policy up to date. In terms of social public management, the aims of the Party (government) were as follows:

### 6.5.1.1. Maintaining a planned economic system

The actions and policies for the market economy were very cautious, because traditionally the Party believed that the free market economy violated the spirit of socialism and was typical of capitalism. From 1978 to 1992, the economic policy was "giving first place to the planned economy and second place to market regulation" (*jihuajingjiweizhu, shichangtiaojieweifu*) (Fan, 1994). Unemployment was another challenge for the government. During the Cultural Revolution, nearly 17 million urban youth were assigned to the countryside to accept "re-education" according to Chairman Mao's allegation. To ease the crises, the State Bureau of Labour (1981) instituted a policy to perfect the employment situation in urban areas: in contrast to the previous system of job allocations by the government, people were allowed to find employment through recommendations from any of the state-run labour service departments, the provision of jobs by voluntary organizations, or by finding jobs for themselves.

To attempt a new style of employment relations, the government introduced the 'economic zone' policy. In 1980, four coastal cities were defined as special economic zones. They are Shen Zhen near Hong Kong, Zhu Hai near Macao, Shan Tou and Xia Men near Taiwan. A principle of "special treatment inside the special economic zone, and a new policy for new things" (*teshiteban, xinshixinban*) was applied in the economic zones (Ke, 1988). Generally speaking, there was co-existence of different wage systems, overall application of labour contracts in all enterprises, wage levels were generally higher than in inland cities, and the labour social security system was widely applied. Government in economic zones set up special departments for labour service and labour insurance (Ke, 1988). The experience in economic zones later expanded and is being applied widely in China.

### 6.5.1.2. Filling in the 'gap' between the two systems

For quite a long time, two systems of employment existed: the state-controlled enterprises and those workers working for Township and Village Owned Enterprises (TOEs, VOEs), or Joint-venture Enterprises (JVEs). Social provisions varied and a gap emerged. Plus, large surplus labour resources from the countryside were rushing into cities. Those peasant workers (migrant workers) offered cheap labour for the enterprises, but competition with the urban workers caused social conflicts in some areas. Migrant workers were required to apply for work permits from local governments before they could legally move into cities. Dealing with the conflicts because of the gap at the micro level was a key job for the government, as the former minister of labour once said:

*Labour administrative departments ... must make efforts to establish and perfect a macro-control mechanism over labour and wages which can be compatible with the operation of the market. On one hand, resorting to the market as a means to allocate the labour force; on the other hand, employing the plan, by taking its advantages of overall balance and emphasis on the long-term, to compensate for the absence in the former. (Ruan, 1996: 50-66)*

### 6.5.1.3. Function of establishing market mechanism

The initiative and driving forces for economic reform were to 'bring order out of chaos' (*bo luan fan zhen*). China's new round leaders realized that the old extreme 'left' way was pushing China into chaos. Deng Xiaoping once said, "It is a death road if we do not follow the socialism principle, do not take the opening policy, do not develop economics, and do not change people's life for the better" (Li, 2012). The government realized that low economic efficiency was the key problem of China's State Owned Enterprises. The 'iron bowl' must be broken. In 1993, the Third Plenum of the 14th CC-CPC released a decision on "Some Issues of Establishing a Socialist Market Economy". Following this principle, the Chinese labour market is a 'labour force employment market' (*lao dong li jiu ye shi chang*), as explained by the Ministry of Labour and Social Security (MoLSS), in which all parties can come to buy or sell labour with no need for a trade union, collective bargaining, etc. (Taylor et al, 2003)

At the beginning of the economic reform, the government believed that the old employment system was a barrier hindering enterprises' rights to employability. After 1993, the government announced that it would give enterprises entitled autonomies in a variety of aspects of personnel management. A new system of social security was built to meet the demands of SOEs changes: for example, the housing welfare system (Tang & Xi, 1994). Early in 1987, the government called for an individual contract between workers and enterprises, and proclaimed it as a means to establish new employment relations. Since then, the government has gradually withdrawn its management at the micro level of internal industrial relations, instead taking care of industrial relations at the macro level. In 2007, the new Labour Contract law enforced the necessity for collective contracts, and has attempted to establish a harmonious and self-adjusting mechanism for industrial relations.

Apart from the above functions, the government has been attempting other roles. The government is a regulator, inspector and arbitrator.

As a regulator, the government issued a number of regulations and laws, such as the new Labour Law (2007), the Regulation for Collective Bargaining (2004), the Law of Trade Union (Reversion) (2001), the Labour Tribunal (2007), the Employment Promotion Law (2007), etc. Obviously, the government is trying to put China's labour regulation into a legislative trajectory. As an arbitrator, the government has given more autonomy to the enterprises and focused on social stability, social status and collective bargaining with workers, and on maintaining a harmonious tripartite relationship among trade unions, enterprises and management. As an inspector, the government holds the power to stop any acts against the labour laws, and to order rectification where appropriate. But the government's intention to act as a third party has failed due to Chinese tradition and cultural heritage, as workers are ultimately much more reliant on direct appeals to the government when there are unresolved labour disputes.

As a country with thousands of years of authoritarian tradition, China's government officials take unlimited responsibility towards the people. For example, if one official is nominated as a prefect, people may call him/her Parent-like Official (*fu mu guan*), and people living in the prefecture area are just like his/her children. From the other side, the prefect will take endless responsibility to take good care of his citizens. This family concept of administrative patterns has created a stable and long-lasting social structure in China: even today, the CPC warns its officials to be a good *fu mu guan* (parent-like officials) for the people.

By and large, any successful reform taken in China should involve combined power from top-to-bottom, from the government, and bottom-to-top, from the ordinary citizens. In China, effective solutions for social disputes can be achieved only if both government and people approach consensus: otherwise, setbacks can easily destroy people's efforts.

### 6.5.2. Trade Unions

The preface to the CPC Constitution (2007 version) states that the CPC is "the vanguard both of the Chinese working class and of the Chinese people and the Chinese nation." Thus, it is clear that Marxist ideology has been the dominant theory since its foundation in the 1920s. Earlier in the 19th century, trade union organizations in China originated, in most periods, from 'townsmen's associations', which are still active today in some underground trade unions in South China, with some trade unions being manipulated by the capitalists. Since its foundation, the ACFTU has been assigned the function of 'transmission belt' and the responsibly to transmit the government's policies (Taylor. et al., 2003). For example, in the latter half of the 1980s, the ACFTU tried to free itself from the control of the CPC and to be independent, but failed (Jiang, 1996). The new Trade Union Law (2001) stated that the trade union shall abide by the leadership of the CPC. The highest body of the ACFTU is the National Congress of Trade Union and the Executive Committee elected by the national congress, while the chairperson of the ACFTU is usually among the most powerful political leaders: that is, a member of the China politburo.

In the time of the planned economy, the trade union was acting as an assistant or subsidiary department of government organs. Its main function was to assist government or enterprises' management in order to urge workers or staff to accomplish the production targets set by the central government. In the time of absolute planned economy, combining the experience of the Soviet Union and practices in China, there was a 'three-in-one' guideline for trade unions, which meant "taking production as the central task, and paying attention to workers' living and education" (Taylor et al., 2003). Thus, it is no surprise that trade unions at the enterprise level were busy organizing labour contests,[①] technical innovations and increased production drives and propagandizing workers' political and ideological thinking.

Since the market economy, the ACFTU has faced a contradictory situation. On the one hand, it is the representative of the workers, but since 1978, with the expansion of the private economy and the loosening policy for citizen mobility, the situation has become more complex. Statistics showed that in 2009, there were 200 million migrant workers who were the core parts of China's manufacturing industry. It is becoming a challenge for the ACFTU to attract more workers and stabilize the workforce in the process of reform. On the other hand, ordinary workers and staff require the ACFTU to represent their interests and protect their rights. Recent cases of industrial actions such as strikes and demonstrations, and even rival/illegal unions, have stimulated changes in the official trade unions. The ACFTU is attempting democracy-oriented reform in some cities. A pattern

---

① From 1975 to 1978, trade unions in Dawei, state owned industries and the public sector organized some sporting events and competitive performances as a means of stimulating labour motivation and maintaining political control.

of direct election of trade union leadership has been applied in some FDI enterprises and SOEs, such as the Japanese direct invested 'Ricoh Shenzhen Subsidiary',[①] 'Panasonic Shenzhen Subsidiary',[②] and the state-owned 'Yantian International Container Terminals (YICT)' (China Newsweek: 2012). It could be predicted that such reform might lead to uncertainty for official trade union career paths and disrupt bureaucratic stability, but the ACFTU is making the experiment work with democracy-oriented working arrangements.

### 6.5.3. Workers and staff
### 6.5.3.1. Definition

There have been debates over the definition of the term 'workers', because it carries both a descriptive and an ideological significance. Following the traditional Marxists definition, the working class is a definite social group, whose common identity is their lack of means of production and thus independent survival, selling their labour power for wages and holding the status of employees (Braverman, 1974). However, at the time of China's revolutionary history, there was a successful revolt against feudalism, and many more jobs relied on peasant mobilization. Thus, in the first official version of the Chinese Constitution, both the working class and the peasant class were defined as the key parts of the state socialist system (Chapter 1, Article 1). Thus, some scholars argued that the main body of the working class was industrial workers, but it also included commercial and agricultural workers who were registered as permanent

---

[①] In October 2010, workers in the Japanese Ricoh Shenzeng Subsidiary went on strike. Workers asked for re-election of their own trade union representative, and furthermore, considering the background of the two Ricoh subsidiaries undergoing amalgamation, workers demanded compensation for those who lost their jobs and higher salaries for those who remained working in the new amalgamated enterprise.

[②] On 24th May 2012, in the Japanese Panasonic subsidiary in China, Oumu Electronics Ltd. Com., a new trade union chairman was elected by the workers, not appointed by the enterprise, which was the model being used by most Chinese enterprises. The newly elected chainman of the trade union was one of the achievements of three months' demonstration and strike by workers. After this action, the Oumu Electronics executive expressed to the media that the enterprise would emphasise four issues in the future: first, to provide a budget of 100 thousand Yuan each year to support the trade union management; second, to set up a system for collective negotiation between the enterprise management and trade union, including acceptance of employees' complaints, and to release the enterprise's annual report twice a year; third, to address the employees' salary standard though a collective bargaining system directed by the trade union; fourth, to pay attention to the training of trade union leaders from the ordinary workers. Source: China South Daily, http://www.lgzgh.org/detail.aspx?cid=8797

residents in urban localities (*chengshihukou*). More than that, some researchers insisted that the working class may also have included other staff and intellectuals engaged in educational, scientific and health work units (Chang, 1988; Kuang, 1984). Therefore, the new concept of 'working class' was composed of four social strata: 'blue-collar' workers who provide their physical labour (*tililaodong*), 'white-collar' workers who provide their mental labour (*naolilaodong*), intellectuals engaging in educational or scientific work, and civil servants/managerial cadres working in the public sector (Liu, 2001). Since the CPC has been a political party of the Chinese working class since its foundation, the challenge that it faces in the new era is to maintain a social ideology in the context of a market economy.

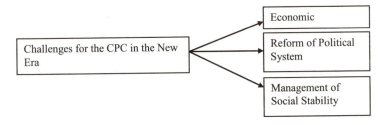

**Figure 6.2 Challenges for the government in the new era**

On 15 November 2012, Xi Jinping was elected to the posts of general secretary of the Communist Party and chairman of the CPC Central Military Commission by the 18th Central Committee of the Communist Party of China. the Communiqué released in the plenary answered questions on how the CPC shall take a series of policies ensuring social development; further, the new government published a set of Explanatory Notes for the "Decision of the Central CPC of China on Some Major Issues Concerning Comprehensively Deepening the Reform", from which more specific measures and policies being taken by the government were explained.

To understand the policies that central government is taking, three aspects should be take into consideration. The first is the function of free marketing principles: for a long time, the CPC did not admit the function of market-oriented economy – instead, a socialist planned market system dominated China's economy for more than thirty years until Mr. Deng undertook economic reform from 1978. The direct consequence of the planned market system led to extremely low efficiency of output, to more than 40 million laid-off workers, and to severe damage to the Chinese nation's competitiveness in the world. Economic construction is still the essential strategy for the CPCP government, which was clearly expressed in the Communiqué of the 3$^{rd}$ Plenum of the 18$^{th}$ CPC, which stated that, "in the coming 10 years, we should respect the function of the market-oriented economy, let the market play a decisive role in allocating resources", and that the government should leave the free market alone, with less interference.

Secondly, in the coming ten years, the CPC should take great care with political system reforms: its targets are to achieve a less authoritarian but more democratic government, and one that is more effective and less corrupt. In 2014, the Xi government cracked down on a group of corrupt senior officials: according to China's Xinhua news agency, nearly fifty government senior officials above the provincial governor level have been arrested and given jail sentences since Xi's new government was founded in 2013. This anti-corruption storm has set up a much more positive image of the CPC to Chinese people and the international community, and also strengthened the power and administrative capability of the new government.

Thirdly, maintenance of social stability is another challenge for Xi's government: that is, in the coming ten years, the government should "explore social equality and justice, further promote social harmony and stability, and further improve the Party's leadership and governance" (*adopted from the Decision, translated by author*). Given the constant social riots, demonstrations and industrial strikes taking place in recent years, people appeal for their benefits by any possible channel, legal or illegal. The question for the new government is how to create a more "just, transparent, harmonious, and ecological society" in the course of China's industrialization and urbanization. Today, if one walks into a village in the countryside, no matter which province it is in, one remarkable thing is that there are only old people and teenagers living in it: most of the young people have left their home towns and gone to the cities as migrant workers (*nong min gong*)[①]. New types of industrial relations, different from

---

[①]  The term "migrant worker" has different official meanings and connotations in different parts of the world. The United Nations' definition is broad, including any people working outside of their home country. Some of these are called expatriates. Several countries have millions of foreign workers. Some have millions of illegal immigrants, most of them being workers also. The term can also be used to describe someone who migrates within a country, possibly their own, in order to pursue work such as seasonal work. Overall, the

that of the traditional state-owned enterprises, are formed and challenge the tripartite relations.

### 6.5.3.2. Workers and staff in the planned economy period

During the planned economy period, the premises where workers and staff worked, known as *Danwei*,[1] were strengthened with the birth of SOEs in 1950s. There are different opinions on the origins of *Danwei* (Lu, 1997; Yeh, 1997; Sil, 1997), but they supplied almost all the social needs of their workers and staff, such as housing, schools, medical care and recreation. They thus became the basic administrative unit of urban society during the planned economy. Workers and staff earned their privileges through different types of *Danwei*, and stood as an elite group in the working class of China.

However, this "cradle-to-grave" welfare system has encountered unprecedented challenges since China's second generation of leadership held power in 1978. Extremely low efficiency of productivity, nepotism, and political favouritism forced the government to undertake a 'socialist style economic reform'. All the SOEs were required to follow the principle of economic reform: that is, 'increasing efficiency by downsizing staff'. The government subsequently released a series of policies encouraging workers and staff who had earned a certain skill or competence to develop private businesses, termed *Xiahai* (go swimming in the sea), while those who lacked skills or were disadvantaged by their age or financial supports were required to *Xiagang* (be laid off), and step down from their working position.

---

Chinese government has tacitly supported migration as a means of providing labour for factories and construction sites and for the long-term goals of transforming China from a rural-based economy to an urban-based one. Some inland cities have started providing migrants with social security, including pensions and other insurance. In 2012, there were a reported 167 million migrant workers, but with trends of working closer to home (within their own or a neighbouring province, a wage drop of 21%. Migrant workers in China are notoriously marginalized, especially by the hukou system of residency permits, which tie one stated residence to all social welfare benefits (source: http://en.wikipedia.org/wiki/Migrant_worker)

[1] *Danwei* in China has been described as a "small city" (O'Leary, 1998: 54) which was able to meet all the basic social and welfare requirements of urban living and in which "individuals are born, live, work, and die" *(Naughton, 1997: 170)*

### 6.5.4. Changing patterns in the transitional economic period

In the three decades since 1978, the government has undertaken new economic reforms, aiming to increase efficiency. One remarkable change is the decreasing number of SOEs, with an increasing number of private enterprises and a new legal structure for firms. These changed employment patterns have caused considerable variation in labour standards and employment conditions. For example, in terms of standard wages, who will make the decision on the price of labour? It is not simply determined by the state as usual, but by the employer and employees. An open labour market may let the employees leave their *Danwei* to find new jobs. Statistics show that in private and FDI enterprises, labour disputes, collective bargaining, and industrial action are increasing due to the improvement of workers' awareness of their social identities and their right to a better life, and more importantly to the formation of grass-root trade unions. For most people, being a skilled or white-collar worker in a foreign invested enterprise, or securing any job in an SOE, is still the ultimate pursuit.

### 6.5.5. Cultural characteristics of mainland Chinese Eemployees in foreign enterprises

Scheneider (1988) once noted that human resources policies are related not only to organizational culture but also to the national culture of where the subsidiary company is located. Therefore, practices of human resources management(HRM) such as planning and employment, performance evaluation and rewards, selection, socialization should not only match with the enterprise strategy but also adapt to the culture of subsidiary company.

Holton (1990), by conducting multiple depth interviews with employees from Sino-foreign joint ventures, found that there are several following cultural characteristics of Mainland Chinese employees:

- Employees attach importance to interpersonal harmony and fear losing face. Therefore, managers who are accustomed to Western enterprises should make alterations to their management pattern. In terms of staff training and performance evaluation, they are suggested to keep a reserved and low-key profile.
- Long surrounded by Chinese state-run enterprises, employees expect job security and crave "iron bowl".

- Employees tend to be obedient and unwilling to shoulder responsibility; meantime, they are averse to "initiative" or "innovative" way of doing things for fear that the internal harmony of organization could be broken. Mainland Chinese managers are less courageous to shoulder responsibility but more willing to obey orders.
- Mainland Chinese managers are reluctant to conduct horizontal communication inside the organization and they perform poorly in cross-functional coordination.
- They tend to economic egalitarianism and believe that there should not be a large gap between the salary of a high-level employee and that of a low-level one.
- In Chinese social culture, the senior are widely venerable for their rich experience and wisdom and often regarded as "sages".
- A lack of technical employees, engineers and managers, and they are not easy to be transferred.
- Abundant grass-roots employees who are willing to be trained, but supervision is needed to sustain their performance.

### 6.5.6. Some observations on China IR development

In the time of industrial upgrading initiated from 2010, China industrial relations are facing a new round of challenge in many aspects. As for the structure of labour law, it has not got too much differences from that in other countries, but is has been substantially influenced by international labour standards.

The traditional hierarchical culture legacy has had impact on China work law legislation, and it can be predicted that this hierarchy may reflect the economic and ideological assumption for a long time. In China, different categories of workers enjoy different payment and welfare. Foe example, Cooney, et al. (2013) sorted out six entitlement of workers in China sequencing from higher to lower degrees of protection. The six position of workers are: (1) permanent workers;(2)workers engaged directly by employers under fixed contracts;(3)workers engaged on fixed contracts on labour hire arrangements;(4)casual workers;(5)so-called employees who are not engaged in labour;(6)independent contractors. In shop floor operation inside the enterprises, the Labour Contract Law does much to protect the conditions of the first three workers, and largely neglects the other three (Cooney, et al., 2013:146).

Any changes, following the authoritarian tradition in China, in law and regulations of work situation, must be stat-centric. The involvement of civil society participation will be marginalized due to the need of social stability. Unlike the social structure in Western countries, non-governmental organizations are vulnerable and conflicted in China industrial relations. But government may take extra-legal methods of implementation to promote innovative legal norms and process.

### 6.5.7. Legitimacy Awareness

Traditionally, China has been taken as an authoritarian country for many years, but the situation is changing thanks to 35 years of Open Reform policies taken since Deng's government. This reform movement was taken from the top to the bottom social classes by advocating the belief of "ruling the country by law". On one hand, China has the world's most complete legitimated rules regulating industrial relations, such as the Trade Union Law, which requires a trade union organization in every company when the number of employees reaches a certain point, and the Regulations of Collective Bargaining, which call for legal procedures in trade unions' negotiation with employers, but on the other hand, trouble might arise if one company does everything following the laws and regulations without taking cultural factors into consideration. Thus, it is suggested that IRs and HRM of MNCs in China need complete consideration of cultural factors as well as references to laws and regulations.

### 6.5.8. Interference of Traditional Value Systems

The value of culture in guiding us as to what is good and what is not worthy of doing plays an important role in reconciling the conflicts of IRs and HRM. The collectivism featured in Chinese culture plays a special role in IRs and HRM. Theories that are well-developed and verified in the West may not work in the East: for instance, Fan and Ingmar (2003) investigated 62 MNCs in China to examine the relationship between HRM and firm performance, and found that the cultural environment can function as leverage to amend the connections of HRM and firm performance. Expatriates in MNCs may find that the work is easy to accomplish if a previous understanding is established or a short training programme relating to Chinese traditional value systems is taken before coming to China.

It is noted that value systems may advance with the times in contemporary Chinese society. The big changes to the economic and political structure have overturned a number of China's traditional values. For example, old Chinese philosophies taught that a man developing his career in society should follow the principles of 'cultivating one's moral character and governing one's family, and, last, managing the state', which was the creed for life, but today, the concepts of family and state may not be prioritised by young men looking for a job and a decent and comfortable life with a better treatment at work, which is the new Chinese dream for ordinary people.

Nevertheless, traditional values control people invisibly, so insight into local culture and customs is important for expatriate managers when dealing with employees.

### 6.5.9. Role of the Trade Union: a Double-edged Sword

MNCs shall take the trade union as a serious organization when doing business in China, unlike the situation in the West; for example, there are no trade unions or similar organizations in the American MNCs such as Wal-Mart, KFC, McDonalds or some hi-tech companies, nor in the IT giants such as Microsoft, Apple Inc. But when the above companies set up subsidiaries in China, trade unions became a reliable partner in many cases.

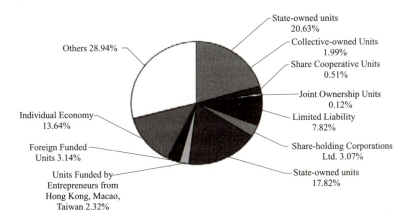

**Figure 6.3.  Urban Employment Distribution in Different Ownership Structure**
*Source: People's Daily:2009*

There are always two edges to a sword: if trade unions, as research has found in some MNCs in the south of China, work together with the managers, this may greatly improve the output of products. Misunderstandings about the role of trade unions might arise for the MNCs' managers because of the cultural and ideological differences and interference from their home country. The following reasons might be relevant:

- Taking a trade union organization as a political construction, which will have a negative impact and hinder the company's business;
- Concern that the trade union and management will have two opposite parts, which will threaten the company's development.

Another situation deterring the development of trade unions could be concluded as follows:

- Employees tend to be poorly motivated with regard to joining a trade union because most companies are labour-intensive and young women with comparatively lower education make up the majority of workers. There might also be negative attitudes and lack of support from the companies' management towards the trade union organization;
- Even if the trade union is set up by the requirements of law, it might not work effectively because of employees' strong mobility, rapid turnover, and internal management system;
- The confusing attitude from the grass-roots trade union organization, which takes MNCs as a special zone, is hard to communicate, and helping MNCs to set up a trade union is often a thankless job.

## 6.6. Conclusion

The same actors and institutions can be identified in Chinese industrial relations, but there are marked differences. Their interests and nature of function are similar to their counterparts in the Anglo-Saxon world. But, due to the historical, economical and cultural differences, the actors in China's industrial relations hold unique characteristics in this system. A typical example is that the ACFTU is not just a union, but a quasi-government organ in which there are different opinions in its internal system on how to achieve the aim of maintaining social peace. More than that, "differences between public and private, between orientations to managerial authority and the application of government legislation are all different from liberal capitalist institutional arrangements" (Taylor et al., 2003). Across the market economy period, the government tried to change its emphases from the traditional control of everything to a focus on more general macro-level management: for example, to regulate the private sector and its industrial relations via the adaptation of union organisation, collective bargaining and labour provisions. The government is still playing an important role in industrial relations and the positions of workers are steadily declining, while overt conflicts of interest are becoming more pronounced.

After more than three decades of economic development, there has been a two-digit increase in annual GDP. China's economy is still performing strongly, and has been called the locomotive of the world's economy. The various forms of employment relations, along with the complex international economic situation, mean that China's industrial relations represent a more provocative issue, not just relating to China's political and economic life, but also to that of the world.

# Chapter Seven
# Research Design and Methodology

In light of the variety of cross-culture, language, and IRs/HRM themes discussed in previous chapters, both quantitative and qualitative research methods are adopted in this empirical study. Preparations for the case studies are necessary in order to give a clear description, develop the hypothesis to be tested and define the research subjects and areas as well as the theoretical model for the present research.

## 7.1. Qualitative and quantitative approaches

The study intends to use both qualitative and quantitative methods. Both research methods have their advantages and disadvantages: for instance, quantitative research is "well suited to providing certain types of factual, descriptive information—the hard evidence", while qualitative methods are regarded as "providing rich data about real people and life situations and being better able to make sense of behaviour and to understand behaviour within its wider context." On the other hand, the two methods invite criticism, the quantitative being accused of being "sterile and unimaginative" and the qualitative for "lack of generalisability, (being) too reliant on the subjective interpretation of researchers and incapable of replication by subsequent researchers" (De Vaus, 2002: 5).

Regarding to qualitative methods, case study could be an ideal strategy to explore "how" and "why" questions (Yin, 2003) because the "essence of case study" is that it "tries to illuminate a decision or set of decisions: why they were taken, how they were implemented, and with what result" (Schramm, 1971). A qualitative research method including case study, different types of interview, observation have been applied with this research which will be described in more details.

## 7.2. Questions and research framework relating to the research

As discussed in previous empirical studies, a wide range of culture and language barriers exist in the course of MNCs' management. Given the economic shift in China, particularly its entry into the WTO since 2000, and MNCs' prosperity in China's special economic developing zones, it can be assumed that there must be some uniqueness of cultural management in HRM and IRs areas. Thus, the following questions arise:

What are factors of Chinese traditional cultural that is impacting the corporate HRM and IRs? Are those influences positive or negative for corporate management? What language strategies are used by MNCs in China? Do non-verbal actions play an important role in the workplace? If yes, how? Is cross-cultural awareness training necessary and helpful for employees? What are the criteria and strategies within the MNCs that both foreign and local employee expect?

Different research methods are used in this study, of which a questionnaire is one of the most effective ways to ensure validity and credibility in quantitative data collection. Questionnaires designed for this comparative study have taken into consideration the following factors:

- Translations and item equivalence
- Trade unions or work council review
- Length of time to administers
- Varying privacy guidelines/attitudes
- Methods for administration
- Difficulties in working with multinational teams
- Varying acceptance of such data gathering in different countries

Having examined previous academic research, it is possible to classify culture into macro and micro layers. Languages and non-verbal actions at the micro level transfer values and other factors to the macro level when people communicate. Research in the process of communication channels argues that languages, as carriers of cultural material, are important for all cultural-related activities, including international IRs and HRM. Thus, questions and hypotheses may be submitted by following new categories from the micro to the macro paradigm (see figure 7.1.).

There has been debate about the definitions and inter-relations of the terms 'IRs'

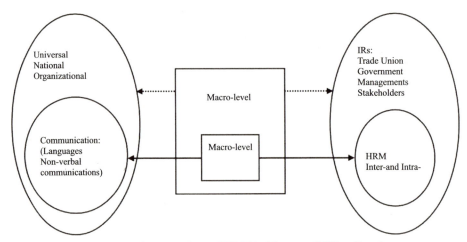

**Figure 7.1. Culture, IRs and HRM in Macro and Micro Levels**

and 'HRM' (Salamon, 2000). Some scholars (Kaufman, 2008) argue that there are just two different paradigms of IRs, one centred on the employment relationship and the other centred on unions and labour-management relations. Therefore, it could be concluded, by developing Kaufman's illustrations, that IRs and HRM are two different dimensions in the research on human relationships in the context of industrial society. In complying with the previous cultural categories, IRs aims to analyse employment relations from the macro level, i.e. the relationship between different actors: the government, managers, and unions, while HRM explores more specifically the aspects of inter- and intra- groups of people in the companies, as illustrated in Figure 7.1. Research into cultural and language barriers in the context of IRs/HRM should take into consideration both the macro and micro levels; only then may it provide a panoramic view of cultural management. The model will allow the hypothesis generated from these premises to be tested.

## 7.3. Hypotheses derived from literature reviews

A number of hypotheses have been constructed from the assertions of the theoretical patterns derived from the previous literature review in terms of cultural, language barriers in IRs/HR management in MNCs in China. Certain type of MCNs from ASC background in China have been identified and selected by this research where most of them were located in Beijing-Tianjing Economic Zone in north China, the Shanghai

Yangtze Economic Delta in east China and the Canton Pearl River Economic Delta in South China. Dieeferent research methods have been taken in collecting the data. For eample, oberservation without interfrence, Semi-interview with the office staff or workers at the workshop level, designed questionnarie distributed to the relevent workers.

This study took care about a certain type of people involving the trageted enterprises relating with research objectives, for example, the senior managers who are usually the expatriates from the headquaters, the medium officials, and ordinary staff or workers.

From the previous cultural studies, it can be seen that value is key concept which makes culture diffetrent and lead to barriers initiation. Althought scholars like Schwartz (1994) and Kluckhohn (1951) etc. have systemic descriptions on the values conflicts, it can be suggested, if putting it into the shoes of industrial relations in China, the following:

Hypothesis 1: Differences of value systems in different cultures contribute to the characteristics of different systems of industrial relations. Value differences lead to heterogeneous strategies for trade unions in terms of a build-up of characteristics, interpersonal coordination, and societal demands for group welfare and survival.

With the in-depth interview and questionaires distribution, evidence and facts shall come to prove if an affetive method can be defined by taking the cultural and languages differences into considerations. From the previous rationale findings (Hofstede 1987, 2015; Trompennaars, 2004; Laurent, 1983; Triandis, 1990, 1995, etc.), we can also suggest:

Hypothesis 2: Theories from the scholars' findings present an effective and applicable method to distinguish the Chinese IRs systems in terms of collective bargaining, industrial actions, labour disputes and organizational structures.

As for the theories in analyzing organizational charatistics and national cultural features, we expect the following:

Hypothesis 2a: Organizational categorizations present effective methods for organizational systems, decision making, and labour tribunals.

Hypothesis 2b: Organizational patterns expose the differences of western and eastern managerial features because of national cultural uniqueness.

It is believed that it is necessary for peole working in the MNCs graping certain skills of awareness in cultural intelligence (Hall,1956; Earley & Ang,2003), when dealing with issues in industiral relation, we can suggest:

Hypothesis 3: Cultural intelligence is essential as a compulsory skill for upper and middle level managers and trade union leaders in MNCs in terms of making effective decisions.

Further to the resaerch of language strategies and communication skills (Grice, 1989; Leech, 1983; Hall,1976, Harzing, 2008,2013; etc), when aiming to the communicative skills and barriers (language and non-verbal actions) in the context of HRM practices from the inter- and intra-personal perspective, assumptions can be conducted:

Hypothesis 4: Language communication in the context of MNCs requires HRM to pay attention to the cooperative principle. Differences in understandings of etiquette/behaviour cause conflicts in communication, and misinterpretation of non-verbal actions can lead to disastrous consequences during inter- and intra-personal communication.

On the other hand, previous resaerch proved the importance for language structures which may interfere people's behaviours, thus, it can suggest:

Hypothesis 5: Differences of language structures and expressions create obstacles in HRM management, such as recruitment, performance assessment, awards and labour disputes.

It could be predicted that discoveries of language and culture impact in hindering the communications in IR and HR management shall present a contribution to the knowledge and practice of MNCs in China. So far, little evidence can be collected from this area.

## 7.4. Challenges of Comparative Research

Translation is one of the most problematic issues for comparative studies in terms of language and cultural barriers. The questionnaire designed should be in bilingual format, with one version for the Chinese native speakers and one for the international staff. It should also be ensured that the two version forms are the same. One solution is to use the Back Translation method, having translators convert the translated forms back into the original language, to verify whether the back-translated version is the same as the original. This back translation method has been used in the present study, notablely in the time of interview and case studies.

The case study approach is a positive one, but choosing good cases for extremely small samples is a challenging endeavour (Gerring, 2007). Thus, finding a typical case as the subject of research is crucial for the qualitative method. A typical case, also known as a representative case, focuses on a case that exemplifies a stable, cross-case relationship (Seawright and Gerring, 2008), from which some causal mechanism at work could be explored.

This research intends to select two typical corporations as exploratory samples to detect the influence of culture and language strategies due to the industrial distribution profile in China. One is a joint-venture corporation in which the partner side is from the Anglo-Saxon cultural region and the other is an Anglo-Saxon FDI corporation. Both are middle-sized industries: that is, they have between 300 and 2000 employees and their annual product output value is more than 4 million US dollars (NBSC, 2003). They are located either in Shanghai, the centre of the Yangtze River Delta, Tianjing, the Tianjing Special Economic Zone, or in Canton, the centre of the Pearl River Delta. These economic deltas are responsible for one-third of China's industrial output, and the largest numbers of MNCs are found in these regions.

A number of proposals derived from the hypothesis have been used and developed into case designs. The evidence comes mainly from six sources: documentation, archival records, interviews, direct observations, participant observation and physical artefacts.

A pilot pre-test is designed to verify the reliability and validity of the research. A reliable measure is one with which people obtain the same result on repeated occasions (De Vaus, 2002). The following factors will be taken into consideration:

- Selection of research objective (what corporations are regarded as typical models, and in which industry to conduct the research).
- Selection of interviewees (people at different levels of management and origin).
- Distribution relating to gender, age and education background.

Regarding research validity, a valid measure "measures what it is intended to measure" (De Vaus, 2002: 53), and three types of validity must be taken into consideration: criterion validity, content validity and construct validity. Literature contributions from scholars have established valuable criteria for this comparative research, while models of correlations of culture/language and IRs/HRM illustrate the measures that the research aims to use.

Samples for the quantitative phase of the research will be collected on a large scale from FDI and JVCs in the main industrial cities of China, such as Tianjing in the north-east, Shanghai in the east and Canton in the south. A questionnaire survey is the ideal way to collect quantitative data. The study will focus mainly on the MNCs' origins to ensure their cultural correlations between China and countries of Anglo-Saxon cultural origin. Indicators of origins for this research shall come from two resources: Chinese employees as the majority group, and foreign expatriates at management level as the policymakers.

Previous studies (e.g. Hall, 1959; Hosfeted, 1998; GLOBE 1996; Trompenaars, 2004; etc.) have demonstrated that most of time, the patterns of polarized research dimensions can be applied in cross-cultural studies, but the real situation is always more complicated and not easy to illustrate in full. For instance, it may not be surprising to see a culture with strong collectivist characteristics (for example, in China's collectivist cultural tradition) sometimes presenting individualistic trends, and vice versa.

A survey questionnaire was designed for distribution both through the internet and by post throughout the national economic zones located in the north, east and south of China. To make the survey more convenient and easier for collection, a website *(http://www.ctgunews.com/)* was designed in 2014 by the author and his research team. Soon after the online publication, it has been proved an effective method for data collection, approximately nearly half of the data was coming from this website resources. While the other half of questionnaire data were collected by the distribution of printing paper.

## 7.5. Data Collection

### 7.5.1. Questionnaires

The questionnaire is made up of two parts (see the appendix 4-7). The first part is for collecting participants' demographic information, such as their language proficiency, experience of living abroad, frequency of interaction with foreign counterparts, position in the corporation and years of employment.

The questionnaires were disseminated both in hard copy form and online on the official website of an international university network. Online investigation presents a more convenient and effective way for researchers to communicate with others and to collect survey data.

Nearly 2000 printing paper were distributed to the MNCs, JVCs and FDI scattered in three different regions in China, that is, the Beijing-Tianjing Economic Zone in the North of China, Shanghai Yangtze Economic Delta in the Eastern part of China, and the Pear River Delta in the South of China. Unfortunately, adding up the collection from cyber collection, there were, in total, 218 responses were received, only two of which were invalid. Thus, 216 participants' responses were coded for statistical analysis and entered into the computer database. SPSS (Statistical Package for Social Science) for Windows was used for the analysis, and the various statistical procedures adopted are described below (See Table 7.1.). But the survey did not stop completely, thanks to the author's work convenience that the graduates from author's university and foreign visitors encountered with all being invited to continuing the data collecting. The participant involved into this programme came from mainly three resources: the author's students who graduated from the university in which researcher is working, the authors personnel networking, business partnership from researcher' social connection.

**Table7.1.**                     **Distributions of Printing Questionnaires**

| Region | Copies distributed | Copies Received | Time Collected | Categories of Enterprises |
|---|---|---|---|---|
| BTEZ | 500 | 35 | 07,2013 | Automobile, Manufacture, Pharmaceutics, Banking, etc. |
| SYED | 500 | 32 | 09,2013 | Banking, Insurance, Shipbuilding, Automobile, IT, etc. |
| CPRD | 500 | 28 | 07,2013 | Textile, Chemistry, Banking, Garment, IT, etc. |
| HBP | 500 | 15 | 01,2014 | Manufacture, Agriculture, Telecommunication, Electronics. etc. |

*BTEZ = Beijing-Tianjing Economic Zone;*
*SYEZ= Shanghai Yangtze Economic Delta*
*CPRD = Canton Pearl River Delta;*
*HBP = Hubei Province*

The other source of data collecting as mentioned in the previous chapter was to design a website and invited the related people to fill in and submit online which seemed more convenient and easier (see Table 7.2.). But the reality was not as predicted, data received through online submission were not as good as hard copies' distribution, and most of time, the submitted files could not be taken due to various reason, for example, incomplete information, obvious invalid candidate, non-Anglo-Saxon enterprises, etc.

**Table 7.2.**　　　　　　　**Distributions of Online Questionnaires**

| Online Website | Year of Website designed and published | Duration of Data Collecting |
|---|---|---|
| http://pro.ctgusec.com/questionnaire/public/questionnaire/en http://www.ctgunews.com | 2013 | 6 Months |

A five-point Likert was used, with answers ranging from 1 (strongly agree), 2 (agree), 3 (neither agree nor disagree), 4 (disagree), 5 (strongly disagree). A corresponding score is allocated for each item, with 5 for strongly agree, 4 for agree, 3 for neither agree nor disagree, 2 for disagree and 1 for strongly disagree.

Several tests were run in the data analysis part for each research question. Generally speaking, a descriptive analysis was run to give a whole picture of the status quo of employees' cross-cultural understanding. A multiple regression was run to seek correlations among different factors, and independent T-tests and one-way ANOVA were used to find out the connections of demographic variables and cross-cultural barriers.

### 7.5.2. Interviews

Semi-structured interviewees were selected carefully. 30 expatriates and host country national (HCN) employees were recommended from 8 different types of enterprises, namely, MNCs, JVCs and FDI based on the Anglo-Saxon culture umbrella. The enterprises were located respectively in Beijing, Shanghai and Canton regions where most of the above mentions enterprises set its subsidiaries in[1].The positions of the

_____

① Overseas-funded enterprises in China are mainly concentrated in eastern coastal areas. Specifically, the largest concentration area of them are the Pearl River Delta, Yangtze River Delta and the Bohai Bay Rim Area (especially in the area of Tianjin and Dalian), besides, Shandong and Fujian Province also have a lot of foreign companies. In Pearl River Delta region, most of the overseas-funded enterprises are labour-intensive, mainly from Hong Kong and Taiwan; In Shenzhen, there are some manufacturing bases established by Japan and South Korea's big companies; In Yangtze River Delta region, a large majority of business investment is from Japan and South Korea enterprises, besides, a lot of Taiwanese high-tech companies set up the production and processing

144

interviewees ranged from the chief director of corporate to Chinese chief executives, office managers and ordinary employees (See Table 7.3. and Appendix 10).

Table 7.3.         **Number of interviewees in each category of enterprises**

Number of interviewees in each category of enterprises

| No. | Categories of enterprise | Number | Countries | Employees | Job Function/Position |
|---|---|---|---|---|---|
| 1 | FDI in Life Science | 7 | USA | 300 | CEO/General Manager/ Division Manager |
| 2 | JVC in Tourism | 3 | Au | 100 | Department Manager Quality Supervisor |
| 3 | MNC in Garment | 3 | UK | 2500 | Head of Team/Project Manager/Sale Manager |
| 4 | JVC in Automobile | 7 | USA | 1200 | Sales Support/Production Manager/HR Department |
| 5 | JVC in Agriculture | 4 | Au | 1000 | Project manager/Sales Manager |
| 6 | JVC in Shipping | 2 | UK | 700 | Engineer/Quality Control |
| 7 | JVC in Education | 1 | AU | 600 | Quality Control |
| 8 | JVC in pharmaceutics | 3 | UK | 3000 | Project manager/quality manager/ department director |

The industries from which these interviewees were drawn varied from manufacturing to international trade, tourism, life science, agriculture, automobiles, pharmaceutics, consultancy, food and textiles, thus representing most of the JVCs and FDI corporations in China today. It took the researcher a long time to select appropriate candidates. The experience of research proved that finding the right people

---

base in this region; As for Bohai Bay Rim area, Japan, South Korea and European companies are in the majority; Japanese-owned firms are concentrated in Dalian;The Korea-invested enterprises and European companies occupied large proportion in Tianjin; Korean middle and small-sized enterprises, with poor technology, credit and business conditions in common, are gathering in Shandong; There are more Taiwan enterprises in Fujian and the overall situation is still good; Shanghai and Beijing, the largest economic centre and the political centre of China respectively, focused on international business and financial industry, are becoming the first choice for the world's top 500 enterprises to establish their headquarters or representative offices in China; Of course, in Guangzhou, there are some large enterprises which are the first batch of entering China set up headquarters or representative offices in China.

http://zhidao.baidu.com/link?url=KrTGjOdU6Wa3E2k45WcPMNzZ3E4-4CXfnQmv1rNs8j0ny275QExAS_ Pb9lfOF_UBNp4LF_Fuc9r4j0F_MqlbOK to interview was not an easy job. Some of the interviewees were very cautious at first and quite reluctant to agree to be interviewed. They were worried that something private and secret to the business. Some were very cooperative and easy-going. All together, 30 interviewees with 19 expatriate and 11 HCN employees were conducted. Among the 19 expatriates, 5 are female, and for the HCN employees, 3 are female. More details about the interviewees are provided in the Appendix 10.

To make the aftermath work easy to fix up, researcher has asked for the permission of voice recording, even sometime this request was objected by the interviewees. All the interviews were conducted in person by the author in Chinese and English depending on the need of conversation. The premises of interviews varies in accordance with the situation and convenience of the people involved, sometime the venue is at the workplace, sometime in the office, in the coffee shop and in the employees' dormitory. The entire interview started from the introduction of this research purposes and then followed the questions designed by the researcher. Interviews with expatriates were conducted in English except the interviewees is Chinese ethnic or voluntarily speak Chinese Mandarin. Related information, for example, the background of interviews' companies and product achievements were collected by the author from other channels and resources.

Attitude from the interviewees varies as well. The lower the position the employee held in the corporation, the more reluctant they were to be interviewed, and females were even more cautious than males. One episode was impressive: when visiting a food FDI in the city of Dongguan near Canton, the researcher proposed taking a picture with the interviewee, who was the director of a HR department: she agreed, but insisted that any signs or logos relating to the corporation must be kept out of the picture.

However, if the interviewees were introduced via some kind of personal relationship (*guanxi*), the situation was more cooperative. Trust was built between the two sides by the third person, who generally was one whom both sides recognized. This kind of endorsement, for the researcher, was regarded as the typical Chinese traditional pattern for personal networking.

## 7.6. Ethical issues

The research methodology will include written material, some of which might need to be treated confidentially. Questionnaire respondents and interviewees will be subject to the usual confidentiality which is practised by researchers. The research does not envisage any ethical issues to impact on it.

Since it is the first time the researcher will be attempting a cyber questionnaire, some people might be unwilling to give their company names and contact information. Their wishes will be respected.

## 7.7. Conclusion

This chapter has elaborated on the research methods and methodology, such as research questions, respondents, instruments and the data collection process. It is noted that every research method presents advantages and disadvantages, which researchers should bear in mind when looking for valid ways to design a study. Ample data resources were essential for the data analysis: for this reason, a questionnaire and a case study, along with some typical interviews, were necessary for the research.

# Chapter Eight
# Data Analysis of Empirical Research

This chapter gives a complete analysis of data collected from the empirical studies taken from three typical Chinese economic developing zones, the BTEZ, YED, and PRED. As well as the qualitative analysis presented in this chapter, quantitative analysis using SPSS has also been used to test the hypotheses which were given in an earlier chapter.

## 8.1. Data resources

As mentioned in the previous chapter, data for the questionnaire and interviews were collected from different sources.

### Questionnaire

There were two versions of the questionnaire: one written in Chinese, suitable for respondents whose native language is Chinese and one in English for the international staff whose native language is non-Chinese. Five hundred copies were printed in Chinese and five hundred in English. Hard copies of the questionnaires were widely distributed to the Beijing-Tianjing Economic Zone in north China, the Shanghai Yangtze Economic Delta in east China and the Canton Pearl River Economic Delta in South China and some of them were also distributed in the local MNCs. Meanwhile, the researcher designed an e-form version which was published on the official website of the international university network. More than one hundred copies were obtained via this online data collection.

### Interviews

As for the interviews, eight MNCs influenced by ASCs were considered as research subjects for several reasons: firstly, they are from the Anglo-Saxon cultural dominance; secondly, after several unsuccessful attempts to communicate with various MNCs in China, the researcher realized the importance of personal network *(guanxi)*, and finally got the approval from the current corporations from which, for example, one is an international well-known automobile corporation located in East China, one is a well-known international MNC in the garment industry located in the city of Sheng Zhen, Canton province in South China (See Table 8.1.)

**Table 8.1.** **Basic information of interviewees' corporation in China**

| Series No. | Corporate Category | Location | No. of employees | No. of Expatriate |
|---|---|---|---|---|
| A1 | Garment | ShenZhen | 2500 | 10 |
| A2 | Life-Science | Suzhou | 300 | 3 |
| A3 | Tourism | Yichang | 100 | 2 |
| A4 | Education | Wuhan | 600 | 2 |
| A5 | Pharmaceutics | Beijing | 3000 | 20 |
| A6 | Automobile | Shanghai | 1200 | 16 |
| A7 | Agriculture | Shanghai | 1000 | 4 |
| A8 | Shipping | Shanghai | 700 | 15 |

The appendix 8 has presented brief introduction of 8 enterprises which being selected from reliable and practical channels. It took the author nearly one year time to accomplish the interview mission due to some reasons. Hinders for deploying the meeting mainly came from the following aspects: (1) time for setting down the appointment with interviewees; (2) author's personnel time arrangements; (3) explanation and communicating skills, etc.

## 8.2. Quantitative findings

### 8.2.1. Sample description from Chinese version

In the first data table, Chinese candidates in the foreign companies were selected. Thereafter, candidates with >5% missing data were deleted. That is because the author ran this analysis using a statistical program known as SPSS. Concrete and specific data collection is needed to prove the author's hypothesis. Candidates were from various areas all over China, working in foreign-funded enterprises and representing cross-cultural communications in the industry areas.

114 Chinese surveys had been collected from the respondents. Among the respondents, 53.5% are female and 46.5% are male. 28.1% of the respondents are below age 25, while 61.4% are between 26 and 35 and the rest are respondents aging between 36 and 49. Most of the respondents, that is, 50.9% are bachelor degree holder, another 34.2% and 6.1% are master and PhD degree holder respectively, the remaining 7% have obtained associate degree while the last 1.8% are only educated up to high school.71.7% of the respondents do not have overseas experience, while the other 28.1% claim to have been studying or working overseas (See Table 8.2.). Together with the interview materials, these data suggest that most of the respondents realize the importance of language and culture in daily communications, especially in business areas.

**Table 8.2.**                              **Gender**

|  |  | Frequency | Percent | Valid Percent | Cumulative Percent |
|---|---|---|---|---|---|
| Valid | F | 60 | 52.6 | 52.6 | 52.6 |
|  | F | 1 | .9 | .9 | 53.5 |
|  | M | 51 | 44.7 | 44.7 | 98.2 |
|  | M | 2 | 1.8 | 1.8 | 100.0 |
|  | Total | 114 | 100.0 | 100.0 |  |

102 surveys for foreign staff had been sent out and collected from the respondents. Among the respondents, 45.1% are female and 54.9% are male. 4.0% of the respondents are below age 25, while 37.0% are between 26 and 35 and 35.0% are respondents aging between 36 and 49, the rest of the respondents age above 50. Most of the respondents, that is, 60.8% are Master, MPhil or MBA degree holder, another 18.6% and 16.7% are Bachelor and PhD degree holder respectively, the remaining 2.9% have obtained associate degree. Furthermore, 57.8% or the respondents speak little or no Chinese, 10.8% of them speak moderate Chinese and 28.5% of them claim to speak Chinese fluently or professionally. Among the surveyed, 21.6% are chief managers of the company and 53.9% are middle managers, while the other 21.6% ordinary staff.

As for Chinese staff's English language proficiency, most of the respondents at least know moderate amount of English, only 6.1% of them claim to know little about the language.57% of them hold an English language certificate that is equivalent to an IELTS score of 5 to 6; another 13.2% of the respondents have obtained English language certificate that is equal to IELTS score of 6 to 7; 23.7% of the respondents claim that they possess certificate that is equivalent to IETLS score of 7.5 or above.

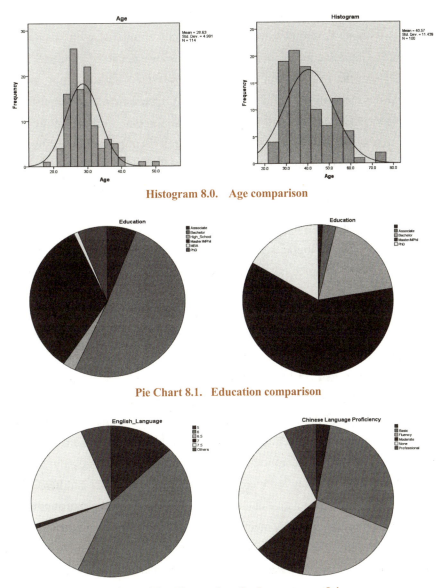

**Histogram 8.0.    Age comparison**

**Pie Chart 8.1.    Education comparison**

**Pie Chart 8.2.    Comparison for Language proficiency**

Among the surveyed, 13.2% are chief managers of the corporation, while 48.2% of them are classified as middle manager and the rest ordinary staff.

### 8.2.2. Chinese staff's level of adaptation to foreign corporate culture

An investigation of Chinese employees' degree of adaptation to the MNCs corporate culture was designed from question 10 to 15. It is found that Question 10 asks the respondents if they think that foreign corporations, compared with state-owned enterprises (SOCs), have more efficient management systems and communication. Question 11 asks the respondents whether Chinese SOCs have a better working environment than foreign-owned companies or not. Question 12 asks them if they think their company has provided employees with a sound working environment and promotion opportunities. Question 13 enquires their feeling of difficulty in adapting foreign-owned companies culture. Question 14 enquires their feeling of the difference between Chinese and foreign enterprise culture. Question 15 investigates the smoothness of communication between the Chinese staff and with their foreign counterparts. The histograms are as followed:

From the foliowing histograms (8.1.-8.6.), it can be concluded that the majority of the Chinese staff do not think or are neutral about the statement that foreign-owned enterprises are more efficient. This finding is somehow not correspondent with tradionally Chinese viewpoint that MNCs have more effective management mechnism. In the following interviews with Chinese managers, some of them even expressed that in some way Chinese companies have more effective managerial structure thanks to its authoritarian system. 35.1% of them are neutral towards the claim that Chinese native companies have better working environment, but an equivalent amount of them vote for or against the argument. Nearly 70% of the respondents do not think that their company has provided them with a sound working environment, and 76.3% of them find adapting MNCs corporate culture difficult. Nevertheless, only 21.5% of the respondents claim that they think corporate culture of the MNCs is different from similar companies in Chinese native enterprises. At last, 63.2% of the staff states or are neutral that in the time of company meeting, communications can be problematic.

Surpringly, it seems that MNCs coporate culture does not have too big "gap" for the local empoyees as imagined. Partly it is because two factors: one is the educational background for local employees, and the other is localization strategy for MNCs

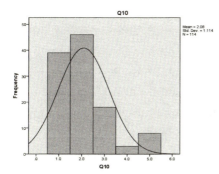

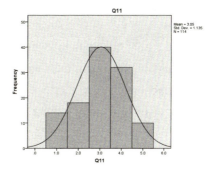

**Histogram 8.1.-8.2.**

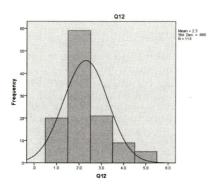

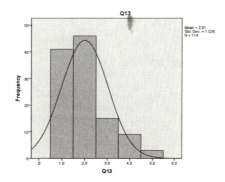

**Histogram 8.3.- 8.4.**

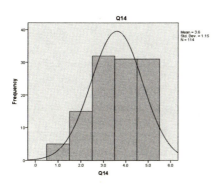

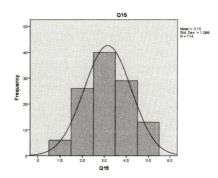

**Histogram 8.5.-8.6.**

adapting more local cultural features. Report from China Ministry of Education showed that more than 540 thousand young people going abroad to accept education mainly in the ASC countries in 2016 (MOE, 2017). This is a persuasive evidence to obtain cultural coherence for local employees working in MNCs, and it is also a quite different demographic change since China became a memener of WTO in 2000.

Running a correlation test among the five questions by calculating the Spearman's correlation coefficient rho using SPSS gives the following results:

From the above table, it can be seen that Q10 and Q13 is moderately positively correlated, indicating that respondents who think that MNCs are more efficient tend to feel comfortable adapting its culture. Q10 and Q11 are moderately negatively

**Table 8.3.**        **Correlations**

| | | | Q10 | Q11 | Q12 | Q13 | Q14 | Q15 |
|---|---|---|---|---|---|---|---|---|
| Spearman's rho | Q10 | Correlation Coefficient | 1.000 | -.422** | .235* | .419** | -.285** | .057 |
| | | Sig. (2-tailed) | . | .000 | .012 | .000 | .002 | .547 |
| | | N | 114 | 114 | 114 | 114 | 114 | 114 |
| | Q11 | Correlation Coefficient | -.422** | 1.000 | -.306** | -.291** | .155 | .115 |
| | | Sig. (2-tailed) | .000 | . | .001 | .002 | .100 | .222 |
| | | N | 114 | 114 | 114 | 114 | 114 | 114 |
| | Q12 | Correlation Coefficient | .235* | -.306** | 1.000 | .276** | -.056 | -.150 |
| | | Sig. (2-tailed) | .012 | .001 | . | .003 | .551 | .112 |
| | | N | 114 | 114 | 114 | 114 | 114 | 114 |
| | Q13 | Correlation Coefficient | .419** | -.291** | .276** | 1.000 | -.010 | -.177 |
| | | Sig. (2-tailed) | .000 | .002 | .003 | . | .920 | .059 |
| | | N | 114 | 114 | 114 | 114 | 114 | 114 |
| | Q14 | Correlation Coefficient | -.285** | .155 | -.056 | -.010 | 1.000 | -.043 |
| | | Sig. (2-tailed) | .002 | .100 | .551 | .920 | . | .649 |
| | | N | 114 | 114 | 114 | 114 | 114 | 114 |
| | Q15 | Correlation Coefficient | .057 | .115 | -.150 | -.177 | -.043 | 1.000 |
| | | Sig. (2-tailed) | .547 | .222 | .112 | .059 | .649 | . |
| | | N | 114 | 114 | 114 | 114 | 114 | 114 |

*\*\*. Correlation is significant at the 0.01 level (2-tailed).*
*\*. Correlation is significant at the 0.05 level (2-tailed).*

correlated, implying that respondents who regard MNCs more efficient tend not to favor the working environment of Chinese native companies. Q11 and Q12 are also moderately negatively correlated, illustrating that Chinese staff who do not favor the working environment of Chinese native companies tend to speak highly of his own company's working environment. As described above, the result demonstrates a certain level of consistency as respondents' adaptation of MNCs' culture is connected to their opinions on native Chinese companies and their own working environment.

To summarize the degree of adaptation for the respondents, a simple model can be established by adding the score of Q10, Q12, Q13, Q14 and minus the score of Q11 and Q15, as the higher the score is for the former 4 questions, the better the adaptation is demonstrated, vice versa for the latter 2 questions. The distributions of the calculated score can be illustrated as followed:

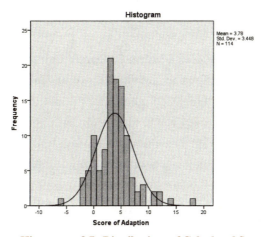

**Historgram 8.7. Distributions of Calculated Score**

Should a respondent give all neutral answers to the question, the score of adaptation should yield a result of 6. Therefore, using 6 as a crucial score, it can be concluded that 86.8% of the Chinese staff do not regard themselves as having adapted the foreign corporate culture.

In addition, Question 16 asks the staff if they think that there has been a significant change in management/employment relations during their employment. The histogram is as followed:

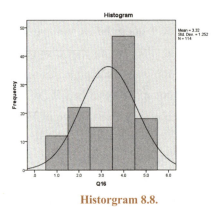

**Historgram 8.8.**

From the graph, it can be seen that 57.0% of the respondents agree with the statement and 29.8% of them disagree. The result indicates that during a Chinese staff's career, significant changes in management relations are not uncommon.

### 8.2.3. Foreign Staff's Impression on Chinese Corporate Culture

Question 10 to 12 are questions regarding the respondents impression on the comparison of Chinese and foreign corporate culture and their own corporation. Question 10 asks the respondents whether they think that Chinese native enterprises have more efficient management systems and communications than foreign-owned enterprises; question 11 investigates whether the respondents think that Chinese native companies have a better working environment than foreign companies or not.; question 12 enquires the surveyed to what scale do they regard their company as one that provides employees with a sound working environment and promotion opportunities. The histograms are as followed:

It can be seen from the histogram that 10.8% of the respondents think that Chinese native enterprises are less efficient, 29.4% are neutral about the statement and 56.0% say that they think Chinese native enterprises are more efficient. Regarding the working environment, 10.8% of the respondents think that Chinese enterprises have worse working environment while the other 41.2% says the contrary. 62.7% of the respondents do not think that their company has provided employees with a sound environment and only 4.9% of them declare the contrary.

To have an overview evaluation on the foreign employees' impression on Chinese

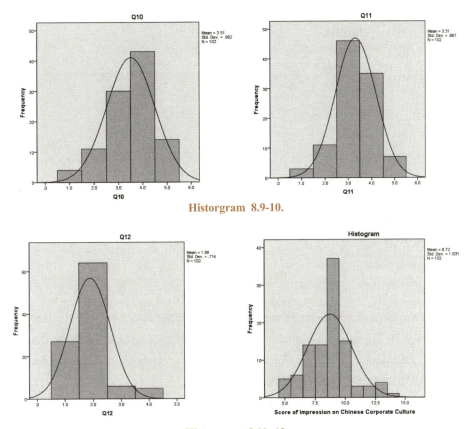

Historgram 8.9-10.

Historgram 8.11.-12.

corporate culture, a score can be calculated by summing the score of the three questions. The e overall score can be found from histogram 6.

The higher the score is, the better is the impression. As a neutral impression should yield an overall score of 9, therefore, it can be concluded that 38.2% of the respondents have a relatively bad impression on Chinese corporate culture 36.3% are neutral and the remained demonstrate different levels of favourability.

### 8.2.4. Foreign Staff's Level of Adaptation to Corporate Culture

Question 13 and 14 are questions regarding the staff's level of adaption to the corporate culture. Question 13 asks if adapting to the working environment in China is difficult, and question 14 investigates if they feel that the enterprise culture of the company is different from similar companies in foreign countries. The histograms of the results are as followed:

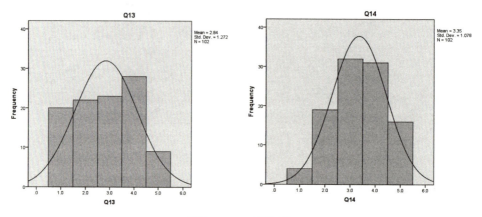

**Historgram 8.13-14.**

From the histograms, it can be seen that 41.2% of the respondents find adaptation while only 36.3% of them claim it easy. 22.5% of the respondents think that the working environment is very different from similar companies in foreign countries, while 46.1% think it is of little difference.

Running a correlation test between the two questions, interestingly, no statistical significant correlation relationship has been found. Indicating that foreign staff's level of adaptation has limited relationship with their opinion on the difference between the Chinese corporations and their foreign counterparts.

**Table 8.4.**                  **Correlations**

|  |  |  | Q13 | Q14 |
|---|---|---|---|---|
| Spearman's rho | Q13 | Correlation Coefficient | 1.000 | -.170 |
|  |  | Sig. (2-tailed) | . | .088 |
|  |  | N | 102 | 102 |
|  | Q14 | Correlation Coefficient | -.170 | 1.000 |
|  |  | Sig. (2-tailed) | .088 | . |
|  |  | N | 102 | 102 |

## 8.2.5. Foreign Staff's Impression on the Corporate Labor Relationship

Question 16 asks if they think that significant changes in management/employments relations during their time in the country have been taken place. 52.9% answered no and 24.5% agreed the statement. The histogram of the answers is as followed, with greater score indicating a greater level of agreement:

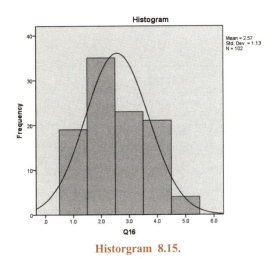

Historgram 8.15.

It can be seen that most of the respondents do not experience major management/ employment relations changes, indicating that the impression on labor relationship in the country is relatively stable.

## 8.2.6. Chinese Staff's Feeling when Communicating with Foreign Peers

Question 15, 17, 19 can be used to investigate Chinese employees' feelings when communicating with the foreign peers. Question 17 enquires whether decision making process in the company are similar to companies outside China, and question 19 asks if they think that foreign employees advocate mutual cooperation and trust between people. A correlation test can be conducted and the result is as followed:

The above table illustrates that answers of Q17 are independent of the answers of the other two questions, indicating that Chinese staff's view on the difference of decision making process between native and foreign enterprises have nearly no relationship with how they view their meetings and their foreign coworkers. Nevertheless, a positive relationship between Q15 and Q19 with significance is detected, implying an association between finding the meeting problematic and regarding foreign staff as people valuing mutual cooperation and trust more. The test therefore suggests a probability that difference of opinions in treating and cooperating with people leading to problematic business meeting.

**Table 8. 5.**                                    **Correlations**

|  |  |  | Q15 | Q17 | Q19 |
|---|---|---|---|---|---|
| Spearman's rho | Q15 | Correlation Coefficient | 1.000 | .036 | .283** |
|  |  | Sig. (2-tailed) | . | .705 | .002 |
|  |  | N | 114 | 113 | 113 |
|  | Q17 | Correlation Coefficient | .036 | 1.000 | .092 |
|  |  | Sig. (2-tailed) | .705 | . | .334 |
|  |  | N | 113 | 113 | 112 |
|  | Q19 | Correlation Coefficient | .283** | .092 | 1.000 |
|  |  | Sig. (2-tailed) | .002 | .334 | . |
|  |  | N | 113 | 112 | 113 |

*\*\*. Correlation is significant at the 0.01 level (2-tailed).*

### 8.2.7. Foreign Staff's Feeling when Communicating with Chinese Colleagues

Question 15, 17, 19 can be used to investigate foreign employees' feelings when communicating with the Chinese peers. Question 15 asks the respondents whether or not communications can be difficult during company meetings; question 17 investigates if the respondents think that decision making process in the company is similar to companies outside China, and question 19 asks if they think that Chinese employees advocate mutual cooperation and trust between people more than themselves. The histograms are as followed:

39.2% of the respondents do not think that communication is problematic during meetings; while the other 16.7% of the surveyed think so. 36.7% of the respondents think that the decision making process is different but a majority of 51.5% think it is similar. At last, 41.2% of the respondents claim that they think China employees does not advocate mutual cooperation and trust more than themselves, with 28.4% of them think the contrary.

Running a correlation test between the answers of the three questions, it can be discovered that no distinct relationship can be concluded. The correlation table is as followed:

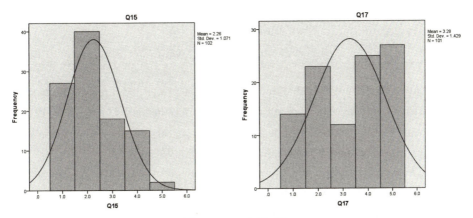

Historgram 8.16.-17.

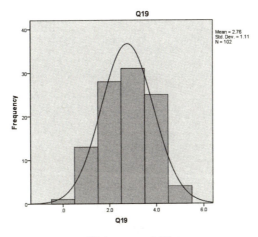

Historgram 8.18.

**Table 8.6.**                **Correlations**

| | | | Q15 | Q17 | Q19 |
|---|---|---|---|---|---|
| Spearman's rho | Q15 | Correlation Coefficient | 1.000 | -.098 | .073 |
| | | Sig. (2-tailed) | . | .331 | .466 |
| | | N | 102 | 101 | 102 |
| | Q17 | Correlation Coefficient | -.098 | 1.000 | .087 |
| | | Sig. (2-tailed) | .331 | . | .385 |
| | | N | 101 | 101 | 101 |
| | Q19 | Correlation Coefficient | .073 | .087 | 1.000 |
| | | Sig. (2-tailed) | .466 | .385 | . |
| | | N | 102 | 101 | 102 |

As can be seen from the table, the correlations between the three questions are of no statistical significance. The result indicates that foreign staff's view on the easiness of business meeting; similarity of decision making process and their impression on the Chinese colleagues' value of trust have very limited correlation.

### 8.2.8. Chinese Staff's View on Individualism and Collectivism

Question 21 asks if the respondents think that collectivism should be advocated more than individualism. The results are as followed:

**Table 8.7.**                **Q21**

| | | Frequency | Percent | Valid Percent | Cumulative Percent |
|---|---|---|---|---|---|
| Valid | 1.0 | 18 | 15.8 | 15.9 | 15.9 |
| | 2.0 | 43 | 37.7 | 38.1 | 54.0 |
| | 3.0 | 37 | 32.5 | 32.7 | 86.7 |
| | 4.0 | 9 | 7.9 | 8.0 | 94.7 |
| | 5.0 | 6 | 5.3 | 5.3 | 100.0 |
| | Total | 113 | 99.1 | 100.0 | |
| Missing | System | 1 | .9 | | |
| Total | | 114 | 100.0 | | |

From the table, it can be seen that only 13.3% of the staff agree on this statement.

This indicates that only a limited amount of Chinese staff think that collectivism is superior, while the rest of the staff does not necessarily think so.

### 8.2.9. Foreign Staff's View on Individualism and Collectivism

Question 21 asks if the respondents think that collectivism should be advocated more than individualism. The results are as followed:

**Table 8.8.**                                                    **Q21**

| | | Frequency | Percent | Valid Percent | Cumulative Percent |
|---|---|---|---|---|---|
| Valid | 1.0 | 18 | 15.8 | 15.9 | 15.9 |
| | 2.0 | 43 | 37.7 | 38.1 | 54.0 |
| | 3.0 | 37 | 32.5 | 32.7 | 86.7 |
| | 4.0 | 9 | 7.9 | 8.0 | 94.7 |
| | 5.0 | 6 | 5.3 | 5.3 | 100.0 |
| | Total | 113 | 99.1 | 100.0 | |
| Missing | System | 1 | .9 | | |
| Total | | 114 | 100.0 | | |

From the table, it can be seen that only 13.3% of the staff agree on this statement. This indicates that only a limited amount of foreign staff think that collectivism is superior, while the rest of the staff does not necessarily think so.

### 8.2.10. Chinese Staff's View on Power Distance

Question 22 asks if the respondents think that Chinese employees favour clear authority and hierarchy within a company. The result is as followed:

**Table 8.9.**                                                    **Q22**

| | | Frequency | Percent | Valid Percent | Cumulative Percent |
|---|---|---|---|---|---|
| Valid | 1.0 | 26 | 22.8 | 23.0 | 23.0 |
| | 2.0 | 36 | 31.6 | 31.9 | 54.9 |
| | 3.0 | 33 | 28.9 | 29.2 | 84.1 |
| | 4.0 | 16 | 14.0 | 14.2 | 98.2 |
| | 5.0 | 2 | 1.8 | 1.8 | 100.0 |
| | Total | 113 | 99.1 | 100.0 | |

**Cont.**

|  |  | Frequency | Percent | Valid Percent | Cumulative Percent |
|---|---|---|---|---|---|
| Missing | System | 1 | .9 |  |  |
| Total |  | 114 | 100.0 |  |  |

54.9% of the surveyed disagree the statement and 16% are for it. Therefore, in general, the Chinese staff does not regard themselves as employees that value long Power Distance.

### 8.2.11. Foreign Staff's View on Power Distance

Question 22 asks if the respondents think that Chinese employees favour clear authority and hierarchy within a company. The result is as followed:

**Table 8.10.**                           **Q22**

|  |  | Frequency | Percent | Valid Percent | Cumulative Percent |
|---|---|---|---|---|---|
| Valid | 1.0 | 36 | 35.3 | 35.3 | 35.3 |
|  | 2.0 | 35 | 34.3 | 34.3 | 69.6 |
|  | 3.0 | 19 | 18.6 | 18.6 | 88.2 |
|  | 4.0 | 9 | 8.8 | 8.8 | 97.1 |
|  | 5.0 | 3 | 2.9 | 2.9 | 100.0 |
|  | Total | 102 | 100.0 | 100.0 |  |

69.6% of the survey disagree the statement and 11.7% are for it. Therefore, in general, the foreign staff does not regard Chinese colleagues as employees that value long Power Distance.

### 8.2.12. Chinese Staff's View on Uncertainty Avoidance

Question 23 asks the staff if they think that foreign employees are more risk-taking. The results are as followed:

**Table 8.11.**                                           **Q23**

|        |        | Frequency | Percent | Valid Percent | Cumulative Percent |
|--------|--------|-----------|---------|---------------|--------------------|
| Valid  | 1.0    | 13        | 11.4    | 11.5          | 11.5               |
|        | 2.0    | 55        | 48.2    | 48.7          | 60.2               |
|        | 3.0    | 29        | 25.4    | 25.7          | 85.8               |
|        | 4.0    | 10        | 8.8     | 8.8           | 94.7               |
|        | 5.0    | 6         | 5.3     | 5.3           | 100.0              |
|        | Total  | 113       | 99.1    | 100.0         |                    |
| Missing| System | 1         | .9      |               |                    |
| Total  |        | 114       | 100.0   |               |                    |

From the results, it can be seen that 60.2% of the respondents are against the statement, indicating that most of the Chinese staff find themselves in the same level of uncertainty avoidance compared with their foreign peers.

### 8.2.13. Foreign Staff's View on Uncertainty Avoidance

Question 23 asks the staff if they think that Chinese employees are more risk-taking. The results are as followed:

**Table 8.12.**                                           **Q23**

|       |       | Frequency | Percent | Valid Percent | Cumulative Percent |
|-------|-------|-----------|---------|---------------|--------------------|
| Valid | 1.0   | 11        | 10.8    | 10.8          | 10.8               |
|       | 2.0   | 7         | 6.9     | 6.9           | 17.6               |
|       | 3.0   | 25        | 24.5    | 24.5          | 42.2               |
|       | 4.0   | 28        | 27.5    | 27.5          | 69.6               |
|       | 5.0   | 31        | 30.4    | 30.4          | 100.0              |
|       | Total | 102       | 100.0   | 100.0         |                    |

From the results, it can be seen that 17.6% of the respondents are against the statement, indicating that most of the foreign staff find Chinese colleagues having a stronger risk-taking tendency than themselves.

### 8.2.14. Chinese staff's cultural masculinity and femininity

Question 24 asks the staff whether or not they think that foreign employees prefer detailed instructions.

**Table 8.13.**                                        **Q24**

| | | Frequency | Percent | Valid Percent | Cumulative Percent |
|---|---|---|---|---|---|
| Valid | 1.0 | 24 | 21.1 | 21.2 | 21.2 |
| | 2.0 | 27 | 23.7 | 23.9 | 45.1 |
| | 3.0 | 38 | 33.3 | 33.6 | 78.8 |
| | 4.0 | 18 | 15.8 | 15.9 | 94.7 |
| | 5.0 | 6 | 5.3 | 5.3 | 100.0 |
| | Total | 113 | 99.1 | 100.0 | |
| Missing | System | 1 | .9 | | |
| Total | | 114 | 100.0 | | |

For this question, 45.1% of the respondents disagree and only 21.2% of them agree. Therefore, Chinese staff does not see themselves possessing more cultural femininity compared with foreign counterparts.

### 8.2.15. Foreign staff's cultural masculinity and femininity

Question 24 asks the staff whether or not they think that Chinese employees prefer detailed instructions.

**Table 8.14.**                                        **Q24**

| | | Frequency | Percent | Valid Percent | Cumulative Percent |
|---|---|---|---|---|---|
| Valid | 1.0 | 33 | 32.4 | 32.4 | 32.4 |
| | 2.0 | 36 | 35.3 | 35.3 | 67.6 |
| | 3.0 | 18 | 17.6 | 17.6 | 85.3 |
| | 4.0 | 14 | 13.7 | 13.7 | 99.0 |
| | 5.0 | 1 | 1.0 | 1.0 | 100.0 |
| | Total | 102 | 100.0 | 100.0 | |

For this question, 67.6% of the respondents disagree and only 14.7% of them agree. Therefore, foreign staff does not think Chinese staff as possessing more cultural femininity compared with foreign counterparts.

But there is one debatable issue for the connotative understanding of masculinity and femininity between foreign and Chinese staff. Due to the historical and cultural differences, it is hard to approach consensus on the uniderstanding of masculinity/ femininity for Chinese who got used to live in with a strong hierarchical society. Statistics from the above analysis partly support the corporate cultural assimilation.

### 8.2.16. Foreign Staff's View on the Chinese Culture

Question 25 asks the respondents about their opinions on the significance of traditional Chinese culture. The results are as followed:

**Table 8.15.**                                              **Q25**

|       |       | Frequency | Percent | Valid Percent | Cumulative Percent |
|-------|-------|-----------|---------|---------------|--------------------|
|       | 1.0   | 27        | 26.5    | 26.5          | 26.5               |
|       | 2.0   | 48        | 47.1    | 47.1          | 73.5               |
| Valid | 3.0   | 22        | 21.6    | 21.6          | 95.1               |
|       | 4.0   | 5         | 4.9     | 4.9           | 100.0              |
|       | Total | 102       | 100.0   | 100.0         |                    |

It can be seen that almost 95.1% of the respondents are either neutral or against the statement. To further investigate, an ordinal regression model can be fit to examine if any relationship exists between the respondents' education level, overseas experience, Chinese fluency and their opinion towards the importance of traditional Chinese culture. The result is as followed:

**Table 8.16.**                         **Goodness-of-Fit**

|          | Chi-Square | df  | Sig.  |
|----------|------------|-----|-------|
| Pearson  | 84.766     | 91  | .664  |
| Deviance | 72.019     | 91  | .929  |

Link function: Logit.

From the above tables, it can be concluded that no distinct relationship can be concluded between the three factors and their opinions on the importance of Chinese traditional culture.

### 8.2.17. Chinese Staff's View on the Importance of Chinese Culture

Question 25 asks the respondents about their opinions on the significance of traditional Chinese culture. The results are as followed:

**Table 8.17.**                                                                 **Q25**

|         |        | Frequency | Percent | Valid Percent | Cumulative Percent |
|---------|--------|-----------|---------|---------------|--------------------|
| Valid   | 1.0    | 33        | 28.9    | 29.2          | 29.2               |
|         | 2.0    | 40        | 35.1    | 35.4          | 64.6               |
|         | 3.0    | 33        | 28.9    | 29.2          | 93.8               |
|         | 4.0    | 4         | 3.5     | 3.5           | 97.3               |
|         | 5.0    | 3         | 2.6     | 2.7           | 100.0              |
|         | Total  | 113       | 99.1    | 100.0         |                    |
| Missing | System | 1         | .9      |               |                    |
| Total   |        | 114       | 100.0   |               |                    |

It can be seen that almost 94% of the respondents are either neutral or against the statement. To further investigate, an ordinal regression model can be fit to examine if any relationship exists between the respondents' age, overseas experience, English fluency and their opinion towards the importance of traditional Chinese culture. The result is as followed:

**Table 8.18.**                                     **Goodness-of-Fit**

|          | Chi-Square | df | Sig. |
|----------|------------|----|------|
| Pearson  | 74.491     | 97 | .957 |
| Deviance | 79.917     | 97 | .896 |

Link function: Logit.

From the above tables, it can be concluded that no distinct relationship can be concluded between the three factors and their opinions on the importance of Chinese traditional culture.

## 8.2.18. Chinese Staff's Experience in Communicating with Foreign Colleagues

Question 26 investigates Chinese staff's opinions towards whether communication with foreign colleagues is more effective with a knowledge of foreign culture and customs, and 27 asks if he would sometimes find it difficult to find the right expression.

**Table 8.19.**                                                       **Q26**

|       |        | Frequency | Percent | Valid Percent | Cumulative Percent |
|-------|--------|-----------|---------|---------------|--------------------|
| Valid | 1.0    | 35        | 30.7    | 31.0          | 31.0               |
|       | 2.0    | 53        | 46.5    | 46.9          | 77.9               |
|       | 3.0    | 16        | 14.0    | 14.2          | 92.0               |
|       | 4.0    | 6         | 5.3     | 5.3           | 97.3               |
|       | 5.0    | 3         | 2.6     | 2.7           | 100.0              |
|       | Total  | 113       | 99.1    | 100.0         |                    |
| Missing | System | 1       | .9      |               |                    |
| Total |        | 114       | 100.0   |               |                    |

**Table 8.20.**                                                       **Q27**

|       |        | Frequency | Percent | Valid Percent | Cumulative Percent |
|-------|--------|-----------|---------|---------------|--------------------|
| Valid | 1.0    | 16        | 14.0    | 14.2          | 14.2               |
|       | 2.0    | 53        | 46.5    | 46.9          | 61.1               |
|       | 3.0    | 22        | 19.3    | 19.5          | 80.5               |
|       | 4.0    | 12        | 10.5    | 10.6          | 91.2               |
|       | 5.0    | 10        | 8.8     | 8.8           | 100.0              |
|       | Total  | 113       | 99.1    | 100.0         |                    |
| Missing | System | 1       | .9      |               |                    |
| Total |        | 114       | 100.0   |               |                    |

The results are illustrated in the tables above. It can be seen that for both questions, most of the respondents disagree with the statement. Indicating that in general, Chinese staff does not find it useful knowing the foreign colleagues' cultural background well, nor does he find it difficult finding the right expression.

### 8.2.19. Foreign Staff's Experience in Communicating with Chinese Colleagues

Question 26 asks if the respondents think that communication with Chinese colleagues is more effective with knowledge of Chinese culture and customs, and question 27 asks if they think that when communicating with Chinese colleagues, sometimes it would be difficult to find the right expression.

**Table 8.21.**                               **Q26**

|       |       | Frequency | Percent | Valid Percent | Cumulative Percent |
|-------|-------|-----------|---------|---------------|--------------------|
| Valid | 1.0   | 45        | 44.1    | 44.1          | 44.1               |
|       | 2.0   | 36        | 35.3    | 35.3          | 79.4               |
|       | 3.0   | 14        | 13.7    | 13.7          | 93.1               |
|       | 4.0   | 6         | 5.9     | 5.9           | 99.0               |
|       | 5.0   | 1         | 1.0     | 1.0           | 100.0              |
|       | Total | 102       | 100.0   | 100.0         |                    |

**Table 8.22.**                               **Q27**

|       |       | Frequency | Percent | Valid Percent | Cumulative Percent |
|-------|-------|-----------|---------|---------------|--------------------|
| Valid | 1.0   | 15        | 14.7    | 14.7          | 14.7               |
|       | 2.0   | 45        | 44.1    | 44.1          | 58.8               |
|       | 3.0   | 26        | 25.5    | 25.5          | 84.3               |
|       | 4.0   | 14        | 13.7    | 13.7          | 98.0               |
|       | 5.0   | 2         | 2.0     | 2.0           | 100.0              |
|       | Total | 102       | 100.0   | 100.0         |                    |

The results are illustrated in the tables above. It can be seen that for both questions, most of the respondents disagree with the statement. Indicating that in general, foreign staff does not find it useful knowing the Chinese colleagues' cultural background well, nor does he find it difficult finding the right expression.

### 8.2.20. Chinese Staff's View on the Importance of Cultural Training

Question 28 asks if the respondents agree that the way to solve communication problems is by languages and culture training, and question 29 enquires if they need to seek help from a third party when misunderstanding happens.

**Table 8.23.** Q28

|  |  | Frequency | Percent | Valid Percent | Cumulative Percent |
|---|---|---|---|---|---|
| Valid | 1.0 | 27 | 23.7 | 23.9 | 23.9 |
|  | 2.0 | 42 | 36.8 | 37.2 | 61.1 |
|  | 3.0 | 25 | 21.9 | 22.1 | 83.2 |
|  | 4.0 | 14 | 12.3 | 12.4 | 95.6 |
|  | 5.0 | 5 | 4.4 | 4.4 | 100.0 |
|  | Total | 113 | 99.1 | 100.0 |  |
| Missing | System | 1 | .9 |  |  |
| Total |  | 114 | 100.0 |  |  |

**Table 8.24.** Q29

|  |  | Frequency | Percent | Valid Percent | Cumulative Percent |
|---|---|---|---|---|---|
| Valid | 1.0 | 25 | 21.9 | 22.1 | 22.1 |
|  | 2.0 | 62 | 54.4 | 54.9 | 77.0 |
|  | 3.0 | 17 | 14.9 | 15.0 | 92.0 |
|  | 4.0 | 9 | 7.9 | 8.0 | 100.0 |
|  | Total | 113 | 99.1 | 100.0 |  |
| Missing | System | 1 | .9 |  |  |
| Total |  | 114 | 100.0 |  |  |

For both the questions, most of the answers are against the statements. The results imply that most Chinese staff do not find cultural training necessary and would usually not seek help from the third party even when misunderstanding occurs.

## 8.2.21. Foreign Staff's View on the Importance of Cultural Training

Question 28 asks if the respondents agree that the way to solve communication problems is by languages and culture training, and question 29 enquires if they need to seek help from a third party when misunderstanding happens.

**Table 8.25.**                                        **Q28**

|  |  | Frequency | Percent | Valid Percent | Cumulative Percent |
|---|---|---|---|---|---|
| Valid | 1.0 | 19 | 18.6 | 18.6 | 18.6 |
|  | 2.0 | 49 | 48.0 | 48.0 | 66.7 |
|  | 3.0 | 20 | 19.6 | 19.6 | 86.3 |
|  | 4.0 | 12 | 11.8 | 11.8 | 98.0 |
|  | 5.0 | 2 | 2.0 | 2.0 | 100.0 |
|  | Total | 102 | 100.0 | 100.0 |  |

**Table 8.26.**                                        **Q29**

|  |  | Frequency | Percent | Valid Percent | Cumulative Percent |
|---|---|---|---|---|---|
| Valid | 1.0 | 16 | 15.7 | 15.8 | 15.8 |
|  | 2.0 | 43 | 42.2 | 42.6 | 58.4 |
|  | 3.0 | 9 | 8.8 | 8.9 | 67.3 |
|  | 4.0 | 18 | 17.6 | 17.8 | 85.1 |
|  | 5.0 | 15 | 14.7 | 14.9 | 100.0 |
|  | Total | 101 | 99.0 | 100.0 |  |
| Missing | System | 1 | 1.0 |  |  |
| Total |  | 102 | 100.0 |  |  |

For both the questions, most of the answers are against the statements. The results imply that most foreign staff do not find cultural training necessary and would usually not seek help from the third party even when misunderstanding occurs.

**8.2.22. Chinese Staff's Recognition of Cultural Identity**

Question 30 asks if the respondent agrees that they work more effectively with colleagues who are culturally near to their own cultural; and question 31 enquires the surveyed whether they frequently contact with foreign colleagues or not.

**Table 8.27.** **Q30**

|  |  | Frequency | Percent | Valid Percent | Cumulative Percent |
|---|---|---|---|---|---|
| Valid | 1.0 | 32 | 28.1 | 28.3 | 28.3 |
|  | 2.0 | 46 | 40.4 | 40.7 | 69.0 |
|  | 3.0 | 25 | 21.9 | 22.1 | 91.2 |
|  | 4.0 | 6 | 5.3 | 5.3 | 96.5 |
|  | 5.0 | 4 | 3.5 | 3.5 | 100.0 |
|  | Total | 113 | 99.1 | 100.0 |  |
| Missing | System | 1 | .9 |  |  |
| Total |  | 114 | 100.0 |  |  |

**Table 8.28.** **Q31**

|  |  | Frequency | Percent | Valid Percent | Cumulative Percent |
|---|---|---|---|---|---|
| Valid | 1.0 | 12 | 10.5 | 10.6 | 10.6 |
|  | 2.0 | 50 | 43.9 | 44.2 | 54.9 |
|  | 3.0 | 32 | 28.1 | 28.3 | 83.2 |
|  | 4.0 | 15 | 13.2 | 13.3 | 96.5 |
|  | 5.0 | 4 | 3.5 | 3.5 | 100.0 |
|  | Total | 113 | 99.1 | 100.0 |  |
| Missing | System | 1 | .9 |  |  |
| Total |  | 114 | 100.0 |  |  |

Most of the answers are against the two statements. Indicating that Chinese staff in foreign enterprises does not particularly favour people from neither similar cultural background, nor are they in general willing to actively contact their foreign peers outside work.

## 8.2.23. Foreign Staff's Recognition of Cultural Identity

Question 30 asks if the respondent agrees that they work more effectively with colleagues who are culturally near to their own cultural; and question 31 enquires the surveyed whether they frequently contact with Chinese colleagues or not.

**Table 8.29.**                                          **Q30**

|  |  | Frequency | Percent | Valid Percent | Cumulative Percent |
|---|---|---|---|---|---|
| Valid | 1.0 | 28 | 27.5 | 27.5 | 27.5 |
|  | 2.0 | 40 | 39.2 | 39.2 | 66.7 |
|  | 3.0 | 23 | 22.5 | 22.5 | 89.2 |
|  | 4.0 | 10 | 9.8 | 9.8 | 99.0 |
|  | 5.0 | 1 | 1.0 | 1.0 | 100.0 |
|  | Total | 102 | 100.0 | 100.0 |  |

**Table 8.30.**                                          **Q31**

|  |  | Frequency | Percent | Valid Percent | Cumulative Percent |
|---|---|---|---|---|---|
| Valid | 1.0 | 21 | 20.6 | 20.6 | 20.6 |
|  | 2.0 | 21 | 20.6 | 20.6 | 41.2 |
|  | 3.0 | 19 | 18.6 | 18.6 | 59.8 |
|  | 4.0 | 30 | 29.4 | 29.4 | 89.2 |
|  | 5.0 | 11 | 10.8 | 10.8 | 100.0 |
|  | Total | 102 | 100.0 | 100.0 |  |

Most of the answers are against the two statements. Indicating that foreign staff do not particularly favor people from similar cultural background, nor are they in general willing to actively contact their Chinese peers outside work.

### 8.2.24. Chinese Staff's Awareness of Rights

Question 32 and 33 respectively inspects if the staff regard trade union as an important role and whether or not there are different understanding of trade union under different cultural background.

**Table 8.31.**                                          **Q32**

|  |  | Frequency | Percent | Valid Percent | Cumulative Percent |
|---|---|---|---|---|---|
| Valid | 1.0 | 25 | 21.9 | 22.1 | 22.1 |
|  | 2.0 | 42 | 36.8 | 37.2 | 59.3 |
|  | 3.0 | 31 | 27.2 | 27.4 | 86.7 |
|  | 4.0 | 11 | 9.6 | 9.7 | 96.5 |
|  | 5.0 | 4 | 3.5 | 3.5 | 100.0 |
|  | Total | 113 | 99.1 | 100.0 |  |

**Cont.**

| | | Frequency | Percent | Valid Percent | Cumulative Percent |
|---|---|---|---|---|---|
| Missing | System | 1 | .9 | | |
| Total | | 114 | 100.0 | | |

**Table 8.32.**        **Q33**

| | | Frequency | Percent | Valid Percent | Cumulative Percent |
|---|---|---|---|---|---|
| Valid | 1.0 | 21 | 18.4 | 18.6 | 18.6 |
| | 2.0 | 45 | 39.5 | 39.8 | 58.4 |
| | 3.0 | 35 | 30.7 | 31.0 | 89.4 |
| | 4.0 | 3 | 2.6 | 2.7 | 92.0 |
| | 5.0 | 9 | 7.9 | 8.0 | 100.0 |
| | Total | 113 | 99.1 | 100.0 | |
| Missing | System | 1 | .9 | | |
| Total | | 114 | 100.0 | | |

Most of the responses are oppose or neutral towards the two statements. Therefore, The Chinese staff do not view trade union as an important role and they do not think the character of trade union is different under different cultural background. In that case, it is probable that they would not advocate their rights through trade union.

### 8.2.25. Foreign Staff's Awareness of Rights

Question 32 and 33 respectively inspects if the staff regard trade union as an important role and whether or not there are different understanding of trade union under different cultural background.

**Table 8.33.**        **Q32**

| | | Frequency | Percent | Valid Percent | Cumulative Percent |
|---|---|---|---|---|---|
| Valid | 1.0 | 10 | 9.8 | 9.8 | 9.8 |
| | 2.0 | 22 | 21.6 | 21.6 | 31.4 |
| | 3.0 | 26 | 25.5 | 25.5 | 56.9 |
| | 4.0 | 18 | 17.6 | 17.6 | 74.5 |
| | 5.0 | 26 | 25.5 | 25.5 | 100.0 |
| | Total | 102 | 100.0 | 100.0 | |

**Table 8.34.** Q33

|  |  | Frequency | Percent | Valid Percent | Cumulative Percent |
|---|---|---|---|---|---|
| Valid | 1.0 | 33 | 32.4 | 32.4 | 32.4 |
|  | 2.0 | 42 | 41.2 | 41.2 | 73.5 |
|  | 3.0 | 19 | 18.6 | 18.6 | 92.2 |
|  | 4.0 | 7 | 6.9 | 6.9 | 99.0 |
|  | 5.0 | 1 | 1.0 | 1.0 | 100.0 |
|  | Total | 102 | 100.0 | 100.0 |  |

Most of the responses are oppose or neutral towards the two statements. Therefore, the foreignstaff do not view labor union as an important role and they do not think the character of labor union is different under different cultural background. In that case, it is probable that they would not advocate their rights through labor union.

**8.2.26. Chinese Staff's Overall View of the Difference between Foreign and Native Values**

Question 18 is the single question that asks directly the respondents whether they think there is a marked difference between their own values and perceptions from the foreign employees or not. The result is as followed:

**Table 8.35.** Q18

|  |  | Frequency | Percent | Valid Percent | Cumulative Percent |
|---|---|---|---|---|---|
| Valid | 1.0 | 19 | 16.7 | 16.7 | 16.7 |
|  | 2.0 | 30 | 26.3 | 26.3 | 43.0 |
|  | 3.0 | 29 | 25.4 | 25.4 | 68.4 |
|  | 4.0 | 25 | 21.9 | 21.9 | 90.4 |
|  | 5.0 | 11 | 9.6 | 9.6 | 100.0 |
|  | Total | 114 | 100.0 | 100.0 |  |

Most of the respondents give out answers from 2 to 4, indicating that they tend to slightly bias their view compared to neutral stand. Nevertheless, in general, the Chinese staff does not view their own values different from their foreign colleagues.

## 8.2.27. Foreign Staff's Overall View of the Difference between Chinese and Native Values

Question 18 is the single question that asks directly the respondents whether they think there is a marked difference between their own values and perceptions from the Chinese employees or not. The result is as followed:

**Table 8.36.**              **Q18**

|       |       | Frequency | Percent | Valid Percent | Cumulative Percent |
|-------|-------|-----------|---------|---------------|--------------------|
|       | 1.0   | 36        | 35.3    | 35.3          | 35.3               |
|       | 2.0   | 44        | 43.1    | 43.1          | 78.4               |
| Valid | 3.0   | 10        | 9.8     | 9.8           | 88.2               |
|       | 4.0   | 11        | 10.8    | 10.8          | 99.0               |
|       | 5.0   | 1         | 1.0     | 1.0           | 100.0              |
|       | Total | 102       | 100.0   | 100.0         |                    |

Most of the respondents give out answers less than 3, indicating that they tend to be neutral or against the statement that their views are different. Therefore, in general, the foreign staff does not view their own values different from their Chinese colleagues.

## 8.2.28. Test of hypotheses

Hypothesis 1: Different value systems in different cultures contribute to the characteristics of different industrial relation systems

Hypothesis 1 indicated that different value systems in different cultures contribute to the characteristics of different industrial relation systems. Table 6.2 illustrates that value systems have an important effect on the industrial systems (0.275, $p \leq 0.001$). Thus, Hypothesis 1 is supported. As the author expected, value systems play an important and positive role in industrial relations.

Hypothesis 2: Theories of cross-cultural management from Hofstede, Trompennarrs and Laurent present an effective and applicable method to distinguish the Chinese IRs and HRM systems in terms of collective bargaining, industrial actions, labour disputes, and organizational structure.

Hypothesis 2 indicated that the theories of cross-cultural management from Hofstede, Trompennaars and Laurent present an effective and applicable method to distinguish the

Chinese IRs/HRM system in terms of collective bargaining, industrial actions, labour disputes, and organizational structures. The analysis presented in Table 6.2 indicates that the influence of cross-cultural ways is 0.521 ($p \leq 0.001$). Thus, Hypothesis 2 is supported. As predicted, cross-cultural ways play an important and positive role.

Hypothesis 3: the term of Culture Intelligence is essential as a skill for high and middle level managers and trade union leaders in MNCs for making effective decisions.

Hypothesis 3 posits that cultural intelligence is essential as a compulsory skill for upper and middle level managers and trade union leaders in MNCs for making effective decisions. The regression weight is large

enough to support this hypothesis ($p=0.004$). Thus, Hypothesis 3 is supported. As predicted, cultural intelligence plays an important and positive role.

Hypothesis 4: Differences of language structure and expressions create obstacles in employee recruitment, performance assessment, awards, and labour dispute.

Hypothesis 4 predicts that differences of language structure and expressions create obstacles to HRM management: for example, recruitment, performance assessment, awards, and labour disputes. The regression weight is large enough to support this hypothesis ($p=0.002$). Thus, Hypothesis 4 is upheld. As predicted, language structure and expression plays an important and positive part.

Hypothesis 5: Different cultural understanding creates the different perceptions and functions of trade union.

Hypothesis 5 predicts that different cultural understanding creates a different understanding of the functions of trade unions. As shown in Table 6.5, analysis reveals that cultural understanding does not have an important effect on the industrial systems ($p \geq 0.001$). Therefore, Hypothesis 5 is not supported. Contrary to expectations, different cultural understanding does not create a different understanding of the functions of trade unions.

## 8.2.29. Survey on Cross-Cultural Conflicts within the Companies

Only 16.6% of the surveyed companies claim that various cross-cultural conflicts frequently take place within the company while the 49.6% of them disagree and 30.2% of the surveyed companies do not provide an opinion. It can be concluded that the surveyed companies, which are foreign companies in Canton, do not in general suffer from problems of cross-cultural conflicts.

## 8.2.30. Survey on Companies' Tendency of Ambiguity in Indicating the Missions and Methods of Work

74.8% of the surveyed companies agree that "the company tends to specifically indicate the work's missions and methods involved" while 8% disagrees. Furthermore, a 12.2% of the companies surveyed expressed no clear tendency. To conclude, foreign companies in Canton tend to provide specific indication about the work's missions and methods involved.

## 8.2.31. Survey on Companies' Visions that Guide the Staff's Actions

63.3% of the surveyed companies agree that the company has explicit and consistent vision that guides the behaviours of the staff while 12.2% denying it. Another 17.3% retained their opinion on this. Therefore, more than half of the foreign companies in Canton have clear and consistent visions that guide their staff's actions.

## 8.2.32. Further Statistical Analysis
## 8.2.32.1. Descriptive Statistics

This study has collected another 16 items as the elements of cultural items for the MNCs and FDI in China. Descriptive statistics of the companies' cultural items are as followed:

Table 8.37.    Descriptive statistics of the companies' cultural items

| Item | Mean | Standard Deviation | Item | Mean | Standard Deviation |
|---|---|---|---|---|---|
| Manager's Decisiveness | 2.85 | 1.22 | Adoption of new Methods | 3.75 | 1.02 |
| Staff Obedience | 3.01 | 1.25 | Rules Following | 2.98 | 1.16 |
| Transparency | 3.15 | 1.22 | Men Privilege | 2.71 | 1.24 |
| Respect of Elderly | 3.36 | 1.32 | Staff Activities | 3.92 | 1.05 |
| Respect of Seniors | 3.70 | 1.18 | Hero Guidance | 3.56 | 1.16 |
| Seniors' Privilege | 2.34 | 1.23 | Cultural Conflicts | 2.40 | 1.03 |
| Line Managers' Instruction | 3.85 | 1.13 | Meaningfulness of Work | 3.94 | 0.95 |
| Collective Interest | 3.68 | 0.94 | Vision Guided | 3.82 | 1.12 |

Basing on the human resource managers' knowledge of the companies' culture, relatively, the most recognized items are the *Meaningfulness of Work, Adoption of New Methods, Respect of Seniors, Collective Interest, Hero Guidance and Respect of Elderly.* The items that are fairly aligned with the culture are: *Transparency and Staff Obedience,* while *Manager's Decisiveness, Men Privilege, Cultural Conflicts and Seniors' Privilege* are less recognized in the companies value.

### 8.2.32.2. Reliability Analysis

Running a reliability analysis on the dataset using SPSS, a Cronbach's alpha of 0.754 is obtained. Specifically, among the 16 items, except that the *Cultural Conflict* and *Seniors' Privilege* respectively received corrected item-total correlation of 0.190 and 0.051, other items have a corrected item-total correlation that is greater than 0.4. Further examining the Cronbach's Alpha, the Cronbach's Alpha would rise when either of the above mentioned items is deleted from the scale. Therefore, taking the above two factors into consideration, the two items would be deleted and the Cronbach's Alpha is consequently risen to 0.772. A detailed reliability analysis is as followed:

Table 8.38.　　　Reliability analysis of the companies' cultural items

| Item | Scale Mean if Item Deleted | Scale Variance if Item Deleted | Corrected Item-Total Correlation | Cronbach's Alpha if Item Deleted |
|---|---|---|---|---|
| Manager's Decisiveness | 50.254 | 59.664 | 0.453 | 0.731 |
| Staff Obedience | 50.077 | 60.087 | 0.413 | 0.735 |
| Transparency | 49.900 | 60.788 | 0.380 | 0.738 |
| Respect of Elderly | 49.715 | 61.430 | 0.311 | 0.746 |
| Respect of Seniors | 49.315 | 58.776 | 0.527 | 0.724 |
| Seniors' Privilege | 50.746 | 64.237 | 0.190 | 0.757 |
| Line Manager's Instruction | 49.123 | 61.241 | 0.418 | 0.735 |
| Collective Interest | 49.346 | 62.244 | 0.441 | 0.735 |
| Adoption of New Method | 49.300 | 61.638 | 0.421 | 0.736 |
| Rules Following | 50.062 | 63.407 | 0.264 | 0.749 |
| Men Privilege | 50.369 | 62.173 | 0.295 | 0.747 |

**Cont.**

| Item | Scale Mean if Item Deleted | Scale Variance if Item Deleted | Corrected Item-Total Correlation | Cronbach's Alpha if Item Deleted |
|---|---|---|---|---|
| Staff Activities | 49.131 | 64.332 | 0.247 | 0.750 |
| Hero Guidance | 49.469 | 62.049 | 0.338 | 0.742 |
| Cultural Conflict | 50.662 | 67.590 | 0.051 | 0.765 |
| Meaningfulness of Work | 49.108 | 61.554 | 0.481 | 0.732 |
| Vision Guided | 49.231 | 61.853 | 0.413 | 0.740 |

## 8.2.32.3. Validity Analysis

This part of the analysis involves factor analysis on the scale of the corporation organizing studying events. First Kaiser-Meyer-Olkin Measure of Sampling Adequacy and Bartlett's Test of Sphericity are conducted, respectively obtaining the result of 0.844 and 515.899, which attains the significance level, indicating that the scale is suitable for conducting factor analysis.

A Principal Component Analysis Method is then conducted on the scale, resulting in obtaining 4 significant factors: *Manager's Instruction, Organization's Instruction, Convention's Instruction and Staff instruction,* respectively explaining the 17.88%, 15.81%, 12.72% and 11.52% of total variance; all together, the four factors explain 57.93% of total variance.

**Table 8.39.** **Validity Analysis**

| Dimension | Item | Factor Loadings |
|---|---|---|
| Manager's Instruction | Manager's Decisiveness | 0.742 |
| | Staff Obedience | 0.819 |
| | Transparency | 0.532 |
| Organization's Instruction | Respect of Elderly | 0.533 |
| | Respect of Senior | 0.560 |
| | Line Manager's Instruction | 0.542 |
| | Collective Interest | 0.658 |
| | Adoption of New Method | 0.739 |

Cont.

| | | |
|---|---|---|
| Convention's Instruction | Rules Following | 0.834 |
| | Men Privilege | 0.749 |
| Staff's Instruction | Staff Activities | 0.657 |
| | Hero Guidance | 0.722 |
| | Meaningfulness of Work | 0.752 |
| | Vision Guidance | 0.732 |

## 8.3. Qualitative findings

### 8.3.1. TU and HRM

The following section will present the findings from interviews with team leaders, quality control managers, sales managers, HR managers, and some employees at work shop level, from a range of MNCs in the automobile, food, manufacturing and higher education, tourism, life-science and pharmaceutics industries.

On the cultural features of IRs and HRM in MNCs: There were two different typical answers from senior management and ordinary Chinese employees working in the MNCs:

*"The trade union policy is compulsory for Chinese government, so there is a trade union in our company. But they are a very cooperative and reliable partner." (D2, Project manager, Translated by the author)*

However, the HR manager (D7) did not regard the trade union as a shareholder in the company: he saw trade union officials as just like other ordinary employees with "a slightly higher position", as the chair of the trade union was elected by following the legitimated procedure. During the conversation with the HR manager, it seemed that the governance body of the MNC took the trade union as a kind of opponent: the potential hostile side of power.

On the other hand, the managers in MNCs placed more emphasis on HRM. Prior research has demonstrated that "individual rewards and performance appraisals have been used successfully by foreign companies to influence the behaviour of their local employees" (BjÖrkmanet and Fan, 2002). This was verified by the HR (A7) practice in a bio-science industry MNC, the manager of which said when talking about the recruitment of new employees:

*"Our company places much more emphasis on employees' personal career development. There are about 300 staff working in this division, and 46% of them have university degrees; some even have a master's degree. The company respects knowledge and intelligence."(A7, HR Manager, translated by the author)*

When talking to foreign employees, different attitudes towards trade unions and HRM were evident. One expatriate manager said:

*"The Trade Union in my company is a cooperative group obtaining support from both central and local governments, but it is good, you know? We do not encourage trade union organizations in my country, but here in China, the leaders of trade unions can help the company to reconcile conflicts relating to salary, welfare, education and health issues, etc." (A1, CEO in Life Science)*

Further observations were given by other foreign employees: one staff member said (C8): *"by my observation, the trade union in China is not as powerful as the one in my country. Most of the time, if any dispute occurs; the Chinese employees prefer to seek help from their Townsmen's Association"*.

One study focused on the higher education industry. In recent years, statistics from the China Ministry of Education reveal that there are more than 400 programmes of China-Foreign Cooperation in Running Schools (CFCRS: MOE, 2014), in which 95% percent of the collaborators are universities from Anglo-Saxonized nations, such as the UK, USA, Australia, and Canada. According to the Regulations of PRC on Chinese-Foreign Cooperation in Running Schools, there are very distinct requirements for trade union organizations in higher education institutes. For example:

*Article 28. The teaching and administrative staff of a Chinese-foreign cooperatively-run school shall establish their trade union and other organizations in accordance with law, and participate in the democratic governance of the Chinese-foreign cooperatively-run school through the staff congress or other means.*

*(Regulations of CFCRS, 2003)*

But in talking with some Chinese staff engaging in the CFCRS programme, their comments on the function of the trade union were as follows:

*"Trade Unions in Chinese universities are a kind of welfare organization. When you are ill in hospital, trade unions send people to see you with gifts; on festival days, trade unions distribute to each member cooking oil, laundry powder and rice. Trade Unions organize annual sporting events and parties for fun, and every participant may easily get gifts for participation. Generally, the chair of the trade union in a university also takes a position as pro-vice chancellor, and if any dispute arises with the university administration, trade union leaders will send people to convince the affected party of the validity of the university policies." (B5, quality control)*

Among foreign staff working for higher education institutes, there are some conflicts between the CFCRS regulations and the Chinese law for trade unions in higher education. To date, foreign employees in Chinese higher education institutes are not accepted as trade union members, and are thus not allowed to attend any activities or events, or enjoy welfare products, from the trade union organization.

### 8.3.2. Culture and languages

Former empirical research has demonstrated that culture and language barriers are key factors that may promote or hinder MNCs' development, depending on what strategies the MNCs shall take, and on how the MNCs manage them in more appropriate ways.

From the study, interviews with managers of MNCs and ordinary employees verified some of the previous research findings. For example, an HR manager (D7) from an MNC in the automobile industry said the following, while talking about culture/language barriers:

*"I must say that culture and language competence are very important for any person working in the MNC. For instance, I have been working in this company for more than 20 years, and because I had majored in English, it gave me so much ease in communicating with my foreign counterparts. Thanks to my knowledge of culture*

*and my fluent English proficiency, I have earned many more advantages compared with those who were very smart and skilful in technology."* (D7,HR manager)

He continued to explain that today, English language proficiency is a requirement when recruiting new staff: "*The CET Band 4 certificate, College English Test Band 4, is the basic requirement for the applicants.*" (D7)

Another expatriate manager working in the agriculture explained that although English is a worldwide language and is the official language of the company, it is not enough. If a foreign manager can speak a little bit of the local language, the situation is very different. You can easily step into local people's life; you can taste much more natural local food, understand their culture, and let them take you as a 'family member'. (B8)

Sometimes, cultural and language barriers can actually promote communications in various ways. A Chinese manager engaging in international trade with British companies explained this as follows:

*"I do not understand English: this is why there are always some mistakes and jokes, and sometimes those funny things are like a lubricant that reduces caution and hostility towards us as strangers. I cannot speak English but I can use body language to express my ideas. It does work, though occasionally, my British friends misunderstand my body language. It's good and normal for those mistakes to happen." (C5, employee, translated by the author)*

As for the language strategies, it seems that different MNCs may take different strategies. For example, a manager in the garment industry explained that there are no formal written documents or regulations as to which languages shall be spoken in the daily running of the business, but added:

*"All the documents, reports, and budgets are written in both English and Chinese. The reason is very simple: you have to make sure that both your foreign boss and your Chinese colleagues can fully understand it."(C4, quality control)*

Ordinary employees can use any language they want, but it is noted that those with multilingual abilities may be more likely to gain promotion.

Language strategy is a major concern for those engaging the CFCRS program. Even the MOE regulations in CFCRS clearly state that "not less than one-third of the textbooks shall be imported from its foreign counterparts." However, the real situation after interviewing representatives from 12 CFCRS programmes is that it is hard to teach 100% in English, in Chinese classrooms, for a number of specific reasons. The first is the students' competence in English: it is quite a challenge for Chinese students to get used to the all-English teaching patterns, and this approach is not accepted by the students' parents. In the Chinese tradition, it is usually not the students but their parents who make decisions on course selection and occupational orientation.

Second, there are variations in understanding of what makes qualified college graduates in professional training. For example, in one program collaborating with an American university on a Nursing course, students were required to learn units such as Sociology, the History of World Civilization and Cultural Anthropology. Those units in the Chinese teaching curriculum are for students majoring in literature, law or other subjects relating to social science, whereas students in Nursing have never learnt these subjects. It took the Chinese counterpart a long time to explain this to the students and their parents.

### 8.3.3. Non-verbal action

While asking about the importance of non-verbal action in work, an employee working in the sale department (D3) admitted,

> "Generally speaking, we do not have too much trouble with our foreign colleagues, except in some special occasion, for example, when people are invited to attend the wedding, birthday party, etc.. You know, they (foreign staff) look like more quiet than us, but good at drinking." (D3, Sales support)

> "I noticed that they are not like us to keep close distance as we had with our good friends and colleagues, and they had more smiles than we gave to the unfamiliar people." (D5, account manager)

Some then gave different opinion towards the same eye contact. A Chinese employee said:

> *"I do not feel comfortable when talking to our foreign staff, you see, they keep looking at your eyes when talking with them for something, it seems like they do not trust on me."* (A3, division manager in life-science)

> *While foreign manager gave the opposite comment when asked about this "they are even not looking at you when you talking with them for something serious. This is very rude, you see!"* (B2, manager in tourism)

### 8.3.4. Training programme for cross-cultural competence

Both sides express their interest and concern on the importance of training programme for improving people's cross-cultural competence. Those who grasped more than one language earned much more opportunities and understandings.

> *"In our company, there are some training programme which are mandatory for those new comers, a programme lasts for three months. We have learnt how to communicate with our foreign staff, and how to understand the cultural differences between us. On the other hand, if you are doing well and get the excellent degree in the annual performance evaluation, you can earn the opportunity being assigned to visit our parent company in the US."* (D6, production manager in Automobile)

> As for the expatriates, the comments are like, *"Almost each expatriate in our company has accepted the CCC training before coming to China, but, even though, there are some problems we have never thought of it until we come here, for example, the crowded public transport and high pollution..."* (C8, department director in Shipping)

## 8.4. Case study: company A

### 8.4.1. Introduction to Company A

The parent company of Company A is one of the Fortune Global 500, which is located in UK. Over the years, the group has always been the largest manufacturer and supplier of industrial sewing thread and zip. In the year of 2004, the group invested

500m yuan in establishing Company A. Up to now Company A has boasted a team of 800 people and 10 foreign staff included. The organization charts of Company A, as shown in Figure 8.1

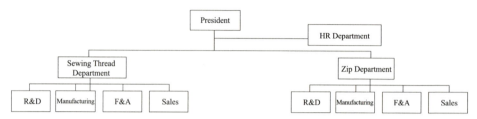

**Figure 8.1.　Organization Charts of Company A**

### 8.4.2. Company's review on macro-environment

Shenzhen City is adjacent to Hong Kong where Company A's China headquarters are located, which bringing cost advantage and that's why Company A was registered as the subsidiary company in Shenzhen.

In terms of talent introduction, ordinary workers are easily accessible in Shenzhen City but Company A has a large demand on textile professionals. The demand cannot be met by local vocational schools due to the quantity and quality of their graduates. Compared with the job markets in inner city of Shenzhen, job markets near Company A are usually on a small scale and scattered, making it extremely difficult for the company to get access to senior technical talents. Furthermore unprofessional employment agencies aggravate the situation by delivering the candidates with a qualified rate of only around 10% and therefore leading to an increase in costs. It is obvious that government has not performed well in providing the companies with necessary vocational training. Thus Company A is eager to see more efforts of government to introduce and develop talents as well as to deliver more efficient training to satisfy the needs of the companies.

Management staff from Company A hopes the government should improve its administrative efficiency especially on handling procedures for foreigners to reduce unnecessary costs of manpower and material resources.

In addition, since fake credentials are rife, government's support for authenticating the credentials and investigating the background of employees will greatly reduce the companies' costs during recruitment and selection and thus boost the operating efficiency.

### 8.4.3. Current situation of HRM in company A

The HR department of Company A is made of ten employees with associate degree or above. Two of them have an educational background of HRM and the rest of them management or related majors (like International Economy). As a service department of Company A, HR department supports other departments in coordinating between employees and the company, department and department. Anyone is free to seek help from HR department on trouble, suggestion or claim.

HR department plays a relatively important role both in parent company and subsidiary one. As one of the board members, HR director is always involved decision making on major issues. HRM system of Company A is based on the compliance with that of company headquarters, reference to the practices of other branches, prediction and planning on demand of human resources in the company's future development, and the condition of local operation.

### 8.4.4. Recruitment, training system and corporate culture construction

In terms of recruitment, Company A benefits from its all-around Internal Vacancy System and flexible external recruiting sources. Any vacancy will be firstly put on the bulletin inside the Company A and two weeks later, if no fit person has been found, open to outside. Under any circumstances, internal candidates will always be given preferential treatment compared with external ones.

As to employee transferring, management and technical staff are generally transferred to different positions inside the company according to post needs and personal willingness. Workers are often introduced from textile vocational technology college or employment agency.

In addition, online recruitment is also one of the major sources of external recruiting. During the recruitment and selection, educational background is not the only factor that decides admission. Applicants are required to take a written test and interview. The written test targets to assess the logical thinking ability by raising mathematics, reasoning questions as well as questions on basic knowledge. The higher the position is, the more weight the interview performance will give.

The yearly turnover of Company A is around 6%-7%, which is the average in the industry. In order to get the real ideas of employee, causes of turnover will be jointly discussed among personnel concerned of HR department and department manager.

The training system consists of new employee training and job skills training, aiming differently on managers and those who are managed. New employee training is conducted inside the company while job skills training will be supported by consulting firms. Every newcomer (regardless of their positions) will be given a one-day orientation which covers the company's culture, history, policy, system, organization charts, safety and health, employee welfare, etc.

The orientation differs from workers to staff members, among which the latter will be given extra training on using telephones and operating computers.

Employees are free to make a training request and its approval by A Company will be upon the actual connection with their jobs; training expenses will be covered by the company if it does enhance the work efficiency, the full-time or part-time training for management staff could be partly subsidized by the company.

On the whole, Company A boasts a relatively all-around training system attended by enthusiastic employees with great willingness on self-directed and collaborative learning.

Every year, the annual celebration of Company A has been hosted by Guangdong TV Station, Shenzhen TV Station, during which the Top Ten Outstanding Employees will be presented the prizes. In addition to this, a monthly collective birthday party as well as a weekly projection and dancing party will be held to enrich the employees' spare time life. The special column of the company will also spare no effort to promote the corporate culture.

The success of Company A's HRM has been guaranteed in following aspects: the importance of HR department has been recognized; HR department's better sense of service has provided employees and other departments with consultancy and necessary assistance; good implementation of incentive system has delivered high employee satisfaction; great attention has been paid on employee skill training, value and enterprise culture education.

However, the current HRM of Company A has still been troubled by various problems, such as the lack of HR personnel and HRM elite; the lack of employees' career management; the less effective HR planning that needs to be improved as well as a relatively high employee turnover of 3% per month, etc.

## 8.5. Conclusion

This chapter has verified the hypotheses and assumptions from the two research methodologies, using a quantitative and a qualitative approach.

The analysis of the questionnaire through SPSS software has demonstrated that IRs and HRM present their own characteristics, deeply rooted in the national and corporate cultural background. From this point of view, it could be concluded that IRs/HRM in MNCs develops toward a much more divergent trend. The theories of cross-cultural management proposed by Hofstede, Trompennaars and Laurent have been proved, once again, to be an effective and applicable method to distinguish the Chinese IRs/HRM system in terms of collective bargaining, industrial actions, labour disputes and organizational structures. Cultural intelligence and cross-cultural training programs provide skills for upper and middle level managers and trade union leaders in MNCs. It must be noted that differences in language structure and expressions create obstacles in HRM management, which present certain challenges for people working in MNCs.

The case studies involving MNCs in the food, automobile, international trade and higher education industries provide a different view. Closer and in-depth interviews have helped the researcher in reviewing the findings acquired from both the questionnaires and the published findings.

The quantitative and qualitative research verified some of the researcher's hypotheses, but not all of them. It needs to be mentioned that research into IRs/HRM in the context of China as a developing economic giant is just on the tip of the iceberg. Plenty of valuable fields as rich mineral resources are waiting to be explored. China's economy as well as its social management system is in a transitional period. No matter how complicated social and economic life appears today in China, one thing is for sure: that China is stepping into the centre of the world economy, and what happens in China is not just a matter of China itself. From this perspective, this study, which applies the theories from Western countries to analyse Chinese businesses, is of special significance. Thus, this research has a contribution to theories of culture and language functions in international management and presents empirical evidence for further research. After a series of investigations into different industries of MNCs in China from the North to the South, this research is able to provide some references for practitioners dealing in international business, especially those who work as expatriates in transition economies. It contributes to both theory and practice in IRs and HRM management for British/European MNCs in China.

# Chapter Nine
# Chinese Culture and its Characteristics

After the analysis and dicussion from the data collection and case stuy in previous chapter, this part is continuing a synthesis of translation/culture/terminology collection for Chinese cultural features and comparison with ASC based on the previous findings and the inferences that can be drawn from them. It is an original dicussion expecting a contribution to knowledge.

## 9.1. Definition of culture from Chinese perspective

It is in the time of data collection and interview the people in MNCs that definition of culture presented its different understandings. The definition of culture from English (Longman,1992) was defined as " the customs, beliefs, art, music, and all the other products of human thought made by a particular group of people at a particular time", while, in China, culture can be interpreted into different images. Culture in Chinese is composed of two words, *wen*（文）and *hua*（化）. *Wen* from Chinese first dictionary of words (Xu, 2013), *Shuo wen jie zhi*, means various type of crossing fine grains, decoration and all type of writings. *Hua* stands for simplification, creating, and nature, that is, to some extension, for changing, and training. In ancient China, culture (*wen and hua*) was the opposite meaning of savage, barbaric, and violence, more often, culture in Chinese was used as a verb, a way to manage the society and of political pursuit.

Current definition of culture from the Contemporary Chinese Dictionary is "a complex of wealth, both in physical and in spiritual, cooumicated in the course of human history, for example, the literature, arts, education and science", which is more similar with the one from Longman's definition. Reseacher (Liang, 2011) argued that the contemprarory word of Wen Hua (culture) was actually not the original meaning of wen hua (culture) in ancient China, but a translation from Japan, an Asian country stepping into Meiji Restoration, a kind of capitalism social renovation, ealier in 1860s.

Thus, it can be said that Chinese culture concepts has close relation with western cultural understandings. But if traced back, the ancient Chinese culture has too much differences, and it's more like a kind of strategy to manage the society and country. To give a complete images of Chinese cultural charactetistics, it is necessary to analiyse it from three dimensions: First, to think of the influence of Chinese tradition; Second, to look at the connection of religious impact; Third, to take the impact of communist ideaology into the account, and fourth, to observe the value changes since the implementation of Open Door policies since 1980s.

## 9.2. Impact of ancient Confucianism

As an independent school, Confucianism was created by Confucius in the late part of the spring and autumn period. The basic intention of Confucianism was to present the thought of "benevolence means to love others" (Confucius, 2008). It advocated "benevolent government" and "rule of governing", emphasized on the value of man's life and the independence of human dignity, and sought for "the doctrine of the mean" and "unity of man and nature", which have laid a profound foundation for Confucianism. Confucianism had grown to be a self-contained and exclusive ideological system after developed by Mencius and Xuncius.

It is said that Confucianism has long been the legitimacy ideology of Chinese nation, which has deep-rooted impact on Chinese culture and influences people's life and ways of thinking even today(Liang,2016). Firstly, Confucianism puts emphasis on education and puts forward a well-known teaching method named "individualized teaching", which means teachers shall focus on students' individual differences and inspire them via relevant teaching ways. Secondly, Confucianism requires people to think highly of morality, ethics, benevolence and righteousness instead of believing in invisible God, the idea of which reflect the idea of humanism and people-oriented. Thirdly, Confucianism put emphasis on agriculture and experience and regarded natural order as the source of human rationality. Dialectical thinking, being one important part of Confucianism, has been highly praised in today's Chinese society. Fourthly, Confucianism advocated ruling country by "Rite".

"Rite" is the laws or regulations and moral rules in Chinese ancient society. As per the law or regulation, "rite" is the reflection of social and political system, and the etiquette in peoples' association. As the moral rules, "rite" is the standard for the behaviour of the leaders of a country and all nobles. Being a key past of ancient law, "rite" can be regarded as the source of Chinese legislation. The ideal order in the past is the highly classification between noble and lowly, superior and inferior, and older and younger. Confucianism requires that people should behave differently according to their social positions, and their lifestyle must in line with their political status. That is what they called "rite". Fifthly, Confucianism have run through a long history of Chinese civilization and have ensured the peace and stabilization for China's history.

Today, Chinese government proclaimed the way of socialism to approach its modernization (Xi, 2014), which requires the construction in both material progress and spiritual progress. In the course of socialist modernization, one vital issue is that the construction of spiritual progress lags behind material progress, which leads to various noxious phenomenons, such as corruption, de-fraudation, money-centric and malfeasance. Therefore, thinking the thoughts of essence in Confucianism have significant impact in China today's spiritual progress.

### 9.3. Impact of religion

#### 9.3.1. Taoism

China is the motherland of Taoism, also known as Daoism which can be traced back to the 4th century BCE. Being a religious or philosophical tradtion, it is deep rooted in Chinese society and it is closely linked with its traditional culture in every aspect. Taoism took much care and studies on living harmony with *Dao*, literally, a right way, which gives principles on the nature, pattern, and substance of everything. Althougth, there are varies of Daoism schools in China after thousands of years evolution, the basic values of the *Dao* (a right way) were followed as: Wu Wei (effortless action), naturalness, somplicity, spontaneity, and the Three Treasures (compassion, frugality, and humility). (Wikipedia: 2017)

Early Taoism were deeply influenced by the book of *Yijng* (book of changes), and the school of *Yinyang* (naturalists), which expounds a philosophical system on how to keep human behavior in accordance with the alternating cycles of nature. Thus, another philosopical book of *Lao Zi*, also named *Dao De Jing*, together with the later writings of *Zhuangzi* (one of famous pholisophers lived in China Spring and War Dtnasty) were taken as milestone works for the Taoism. Taoists, the master of *Dao*, were thought of as hermits or recluses who did not participate in political life. Later on, Taoism evolved into two main groups: *Quanzhen Taoism* and *Zhengyi Taoism*, and was nominated several times as a state religion, but it finally fell from favor after the 17th century (Wikipedia: 2017).

Taoism is closely linked to spirits and fairyland, and it focuses on people's personal desire. Therefore, many Chinese literatures were believed in Taoism since *Tang dynasty*. The fairyland realm and image in Taoism greatly inspired thousands of literati to createmagnificent and charming literature works, which contributed to one distinctive feature in the history of Chinese literature. For example, *Li Bai*, one of the greatest poets in *Dang dynasty*, was deeply fascinated by Taoism. He had traveled to many places to find the wonderland and he even tried to refine magic pills but in vain. However, the fantastic experiences offered him inspirations to create literature works, and many of his poems are related to Taoism.

Almost all the famous novels in Chinese ancient times were affected by Taoism more or less. For instances, *Journey to the West,* one of the four great classical masterpieces in China, tells a story about four Buddhism monks embarked on a pilgrimage to India to obtain Buddhist scriptures. However, many concepts and thoughts that related to Taoism can be found in this book, such as primordial spirit, maid and a Taoism deity featured by the Jade Emperor. Taoism also influenced Chinese medical. The regimen in Taoism is one key part in Chinese medical. Many Taoists contributed a lot to Chinese medical, such as *Ge Hong, Tao Hongjing* and etc. Being part of the four great inventions, gunpowder was invented thanks to alchemy in Taoism.

One can hardly numerate all the influences that Taoism has brought to Chinese culture, further research are needed if more detailed information about this topic.

### 9.3.2. Buddhism

The influence of Buddhism on Chinese culture can be mainly divided into two parts. The first part involves the influence of Buddhism on Chinese ideology. Chinese philosophy thinking was emerged in *Zhou* dynasty (BC1046 - BC256) and flourishing in the Warring States period (BC770 - BC221), during which various thoughts and hundred schools were in competition. Later on, Buddhism was in blooming with the decline of Daoism and one outstanding ideologist *Chuang Tzu* advocated his thought mixed with idea from Buddhism ( Liang, 2011). That is how Buddhism becomes even popular. In *Tang* dynasty (AC618 - AC907), Buddhism became the foundation for the emperor to master Confucianism. Neo-Confucianism was obviously affected by *Hua-yen, Zen* and others Buddhism theories (Feng,1997). In the late *Qing* dynasty (AC1644-AC 1912), Buddhism study was popular among Chinese intellectual circles. The enlightenment of democratic thoughts, such as *Tang Sitong, Kang Youwei* and *Liang Qichao,* were taking some Buddhism theories as their ideological weapon to reform China. Thoughts like equal, kindness, and anicca were of great importance to the Chinese intellectual circles at that time. The second part is the impact of Buddhism on Chinese Literature. *Liang Qichao* once said that Buddhism influenced Chinese culture in 5 aspects. First, the words of Mandarin have been enriched. More than 35,000 words were increased because of the translation of Buddhism classics; second, there were changes in Chinese grammar and stylistic; third, Chinese literature witnessed a great transformation. Many great works were related to Buddhism thoughts in various genres. What's more, Chinese intellectuals were inspired by Buddhism works and they created more unfailing passages, like *Mulan Ballad, Southeast the Peacock Flies* and etc; fourth, musical drama was introduced to China under the influence of Buddhism; fifth, imitation of letters was emerged in China with the spread of Buddhism (Liang,2011). Even today, unlike the situation in India, from where the Buddhism came, 18% of Chinese believe in Buddha (Phoenix News, 2011).

## 9.4. Impacts from the communist ideology

Since 1949, communist doctrines have prevailed in Chinese social life. Ideas from Karl Marx's socialist theories and Leninism from the Soviet Union, as well as Maoist concepts, have become dominant philosophies. Traditional Confucianism was criticized and rejected at the time, but some of its tenets were combined with Marxism and evolved as new patterns of Chinese political ideology: for example, egalitarianism meets traditional collectivism, Confucius's assertions about harmony assertion were accepted by proletarian unions, and the superiority of moral over legalistic obligations was welcomed by socialists' moral expectations.

Egalitarianism, harmony, moral paradigm and paternalism came to be typical characteristics of the nation's state-owned company management.

In 1987, the third plenum of the Eleventh Central Committee conference of the Communist Party of China (CPC) announced its new policy of making the country progress towards the "Four Modernizations", Part of Deng Xiaoping's program for China is the modernization of agriculture, industry, science and technology and the military, following which new epochal economical reforms began. Joint-venture companies were the most successful and beneficial projects that the economic reform ever achieved, from which western management ideas as well as advanced technologies flew in and were accepted by the people after rounds of confrontations and compromises.

### 9.5. Negative impact of China's contemporary social problems

Nevertheless, some social problems occurred along with the 35 years of economic reforms. For example, in September, 2014, the People's Tribune, a magazine of the People's Daily, released a survey conducted by a research group in which researchers collected some negative social problems, which were named the ten social morbidities. In detail, they are: (1) Lack of faith; (2) Bystander attitude or being indifferent; (3) Anxiety over work, life and future; (4) Habitual distrust; (5) Ostentatiousness; (6) Reveling in scandals; (7) Hedonism; (8) Extreme, violent and

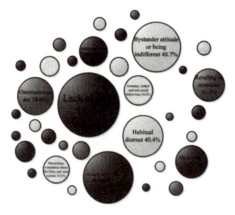

**Figure 9.1.   Social Morbidities in contemporary China**
*Source: modified from the People's Tribune:2014*

anti-social behaviours; (9) Addiction to the internet; (10) Masochism and complaints about the Party and the state system (Figure 9.1.).

Remarkably, more than 55% of interviewees cited Lack of Faith as the main social problem, followed by the Bystander Attitude, cited by more than 48%. The third most frequently cited problem was anxiety over work, life and future. Furthermore, about 24% of respondents cited the credibility deficit of the government as one of main reasons behind the lack of trust in Chinese society.

Although critics argued that the ten social modalities did not fully describe the social illness in contemporary China, they drew the attention of many media and led people in China to examine their own conscience. Research from the People's Tribune offered another profile of contemporary China, which suggested that traditional cultural values are facing challenges due to the development of China's economic structure. Sometime, those negative viewpoints may have a negative impact on IR and HRM practice.

Statistics shows (Economist,2016) that China is also facing the threaten of population decline (see Figure 9.2.). The advantages of China's cheap mass labour resources has been challenged by countries like Viet Nam, Bangladesh, etc. where a number of industries have been resettled down. Those made China government find some ways to upgrade its industry structure.

It is argued that due to this critical transition period in China, values and management structures tend to be complex and diverse. Comparative studies shall follow the specific demands and industries to generate real reflections that will be of use to academia, society and practitioners.

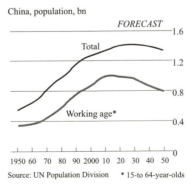

**Figure 9.2. China's Population Decrease**

*Source: the Economist, April, 2016*

## 9.6. China's culture features from Western observation

Hofstede (1987), after proclaimed his four dimensions of cultural analysis, continued the 5th cultural dimension in order to make up the incomplete studies. He designed, by working along with Chinese scholars, 40 fundamental and basic value as the survey contents of his research. (See appendix 2)

With rapid economic and political development of China, Chinese culture has been playing an increasingly important role worldwide. Westerners especially from Anglo-Saxon cultural backgrounds hold various opinions and suggestions on Chinese culture particularly contemporary Chinese culture.

Earl of Cromer from Britain (2006) believes that Chinese culture should pay more attention to humanistic concern and respect among people, promoting Chinese mass culture and enriching people's life. More British scholars suggest Chinese government should not only enlarge hardware investment into cultural construction and facilities, but also make an endeavour to set up a suitable cultural management system, thus promoting enterprise and personal funded cultural programs through tax concessions. Carrillo Gantner, former president of the board of Melbourne Festival, believes that Chinese government should lower the number of general artistic groups but be more supportive of state-level key groups like Peking Opera theatre, in order to preserve the cultural heritage. Andrew Sayers, an expert consultant from New Zealand, holds that Western people now prefer those works of art representing current social development and ideological trend in China, even though Chinese traditional art forms, like Peking Opera and acrobatics, do maintain a huge charm. Mr. Vasari also agrees that Chinese art forms, like *tai chi chuan*, epigram and calligraphy, seem to be less attractive to most Westerners especially young people today while they take more interest in current development of Chinese movie, music and economy, namely Chinese contemporary culture. Sir Simon Rattle, guest conductor of Chicago Symphony Orchestra, suggests that more access to information technology and more exposure to social network platforms would contribute to the promotion of China image and Chinese culture across the world. Furthermore, a healthier cultural market should be developed in China based on cultural institutional reforms to promote income diversification of Chinese artistic groups, supporting cultural development through market, box office and enterprise funds. A search from KPMG (2012) showed that for most MNCs managers who are conducting business in China realized that Chinese culture, as an important component of world civilization, has always been exerting influence on a global scale, because of not only its spectacular historical legacy but also the rising economic power it now supports. Scholars who are studying China generally believe China's huge economic progress would surely lead to people's higher demand in culture and finally result in their pursuit of great rejuvenation.

## 9.7. Chinese cultural characteristics

China's economic importance and its dissociable connections with global society make contemporary China an inevitable theme for researchers. Between 1980 and 2011, China's growth rate (of GDP as a whole and of manufacturing) was the highest in the world, with average annual growth rates of around 10% (China Business Information,2017). Early in 2007, China became the world's fourth largest manufacturing producer, the second largest agricultural producer, the fourth largest exporter of merchandise and the world's third largest importer (Dicken, 2007). But the situation kept changing: in 2011, China became the top manufacturing country in the world, according to the *Financial Times* (2011). In 2012, China leaped from the third to the world's biggest import and export country (Xinhua News, 2013). To understand China's methods of business and management, culture is not the only factor, but *de facto* is also one important reason promoting or hindering managerial activities.

By and large, Chinese contemporary culture is rooted in three constructs: the traditional Chinese cultural legacy, the communist ideology, and impacts from western countries after economic reforms (Figure 9.3).

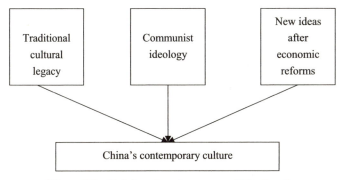

**Figure 9.3. Origins of contemporary China's culture**

## 9.8. China's traditional cultural legacies

Chinese people are proud of their 5000 years of history, arguing that it is the only uninterrupted civilization in human history, as Fairbank (1987) observed:

> "The influence of China's long past is ever-present in the environment, the language, the folklore, and the practices of government, business and interpersonal relations." (1987:367)

However, the term 'traditional culture' is ambiguous, since, in its long dynastic shifts, China has encountered strong ideological confrontations. Confucianism, a philosophical sutra derived from 2000 BC, the Spring & Warring Period, is actually the outcome of compromise of various beliefs. As Shenkar and Ronen (1987) concluded:

> "The culture of traditional China encompasses diverse and competing philosophies, including Taoism, Buddhism, Legalism and a host of local 'little traditions'. Nevertheless, Confucianism is most clearly defined as the foundation of China's great cultural tradition, and Confucian values still provide the basis for the norms of Chinese interpersonal behaviour." (1987: 266)

China's national culture has experienced remarkable changes in the last hundred years. In 1894, Smith Arthur, who wrote a book of *Chinese Characteristics*, in an attempt to classify Chinese cultural features, enumerated 52 characteristics for China at that time, of which nearly two-thirds no longer exist. The values which are still influencing today's Chinese people, as Lockett (1988) suggested, can be illustrated as:
- *Respect for age and strong hierarchy*
- *Collectivism*
- *The preservation of "face"*
- *The importance of relationships, namely "guanxi"*
- *Spiritual pursuit of success*

Evidence from empirical studies (Child, 1995) shows that the above Chinese national cultural features create barriers for business and management and must thus be considered when focusing on international IRs and HRM studies.

## 9.9. When ASC encounters Chinese culture context

The French philosopher Jean-Jacques Rousseau once said: Man is born free yet everywhere he is in chains. Anyone's rights are defined by culture and history.

The development of history has shaped the distinctive characteristics of Anglo-Saxon culture, featuring the pursuit of democracy and science. Democracy and science in the West originated from the medieval theology cantered on religious spirit predominated by Christianity. Generally speaking, Greek rational culture and Jewish Bible constitute Western civilization, which derived from the Reformation and the Renaissance after the Middle Age, while Western religious spirit has undergone significant changes due to the influences of the Reformation, the Renaissance, the Industrial Revolution and World War II. In general, Western culture can be divided into two categories: one is Anglo-Saxon culture represented by British and American culture and with the religious foundation of Protestantism; the other is Latin culture on the basis of Roman Catholic Church and with the representative of France and Italy culture. Huntington once said: The whole Western civilization is a mixture of Christianity, including Catholicism and Protestantism.

Another feature is the establishment of humanism: There are four characteristics of the modernity of Anglo-Saxon culture, namely anthropocentric, individualism, progressivism and new worship. In fact, the first two is humanism, or called person-centered doctrine; this doctrine has two definitions: First, it means human society has its natural legitimacy from the macro perspective; second, it is called individualism from the micro perspective, like democracy, freedom and human rights.

Moreover, mercantilism of Anglo-Saxon culture has a significant impact on economic behaviours. Anglo-Saxon model is based on British and American culture, especially the latter one. Until today, American mainstream society is generally called "WASP", which stands for "White Anglo-Saxon Protestants". Developed business practices give rise to rules respect and limitation of power. Britain has a wise aphorism, "The best training grounds for democracy are football fields in middle schools." because these places are regarded as the cradle of respecting programs (rules of the game) and results. In the eyes of the British and American, justice must not only be done, but must be seen to be done.

By contrast, Chinese culture also has its own unique characteristics, but China today in various aspects, is turning to Anglo-Saxon culture and Protestant culture, in fact, to the culture valuing mercantilism and materialistic. In Chinese tradition, there lack laws, human rights, democracy and freedom which the West boasts. Chinese political culture is characterized by the principles that "people is the most important", "The water supporting a ship can also upset it" and "the emperor serves for his/her people and people are loyal to him/her", which are different from that of the West. Another example is "the controversy of righteousness and benefits". Chinese people put more emphasis on righteousness and do not encourage pursue benefits. The importance of scholars, farmers, artisans and merchants is ranked in hierarchical order, which means that scholars predominates and merchants are less important than farmers and artisans. This point is also different from the West. French scholar Taine (1973) wrote on his book "*The Philosophy of Art*" that there was a time in Italy when it was the ultimate insult that you referred a person to be a scholar.

However, traditional Chinese values are still of enormous significance nowadays. The history origin of collectivism leads Chinese people to especially emphasize personal reputation, or so-called "face perception"; besides, Chinese people are generally interested in building "interpersonal relationships network" under its benign influences and for the pursuit of it, which can be reflected by the mutual-aid organization, such as "fellow-townsman association" and "hometown associations". Furthermore, the Confucian principle that "the emperor performs his duties, the official fulfils his/her obligation, the father meets his duties and the son commits his filial responsibility" ingrains the sense of hierarchy.

Generally speaking, Chinese see the conflict between Anglo-Saxon culture and Chinese culture as the clash of Eastern and Western cultures. Although Anglo-Saxon culture cannot represent Western culture any more than Chinese culture stands for Eastern culture, such an idea has been generally and readily accepted by most people. Therefore, Western culture is referred in particular to Anglo-Saxon culture and Eastern culture does also to Chinese culture in this study.

## 9.10. Conclusion

China had different understanding of culture from its beginning of primitive society, even it came to get consensus with that of western viewpoint. Traditional view of cultural gaps had attracted Chinese philosophers' attention who once noticed that "at first, mankind is kind at heart with natures alike, but habits apart" (Mencius,2016). Here habits refer to culture. Chinese cultural habits firstly originated from its long history of authoritarian mechanism from which Confucianism came to be the main ruling philosophy. Although Taoism had a certain period of flourish among those who lost interest in politics and social management, its philosophic ideas has inspired many intellectuals. When the Buddhism idea spread into China, its value viewpoints like equal, kindness, and anicca, have embraced traditional Confucius ideas. Neo-Confucianism initiated in Song Dynasty was a combination of many ideas from Taoism, Buddhism and other Chinese traditional philosophical viewpoints (Feng, 1997), and became a dominant cultural features.

Communist ideology, in some way, may be regarded as a kind of extension for neo-Confucianism. Many traditional values such as kindness, dialectics, hierarchy can easily meet the demands and are correspondent with the communist revolution. Even after the new round of economic reform since 1980 in China, traditional values facing the challenges from the free economic market defiance, for example, respect for privacy, personal freedom, fair competition, democratic social administration etc., strengths from top to bottom classes of society have created a new type of contemporary Chinese cultural characteristics (as illustrated in figure 9.3.).

Evidence provided from this study has also proved the cultural complex in the transition period that China is no more carrying on the traditional cultural characteristics; some of its features vary in adopting with the changing economic and political demands.

# Chapter Ten
# Findings and Conclusion

One module is designed and come into being in analysing the differences of cultures, languages and its relations with industries and human resources management. This model, as one innovative and original creation from the author, is a tool on exerting the comparative studies in between culture, language and IRs/HRM. Being a contribution to the knowledge in culture studies, this chapter illustrates author's opinions and measures in conducting harmonious industrial relations, and HR management. Furthermore, the empirical research focusing on the MNCs in China has tested several hypotheses proposed by the author and verified some assumptions, which may leave more questions for further research. Some research programmes inspired from this study have been proposed as well at the end of this part.

## 10.1. Constructed conceptual models and contribution to knowledge

In the course of empirical research, the case studies in MNCs in China, the author concluded a model in the aid of relevant work. This model (see Figure 10.1.) will allow the research to use IRs and HRM as a tool to analyse the issues of culture/language barriers. Roger's (2008) classification of culture in five dimensions offers a clear outline for intercultural studies. Given the specific demands in certain cross-cultural areas, the model could vary in order to fit their needs. In the fields of international IRs and HRM, cultural conflicts may emerge at the universal, national, organizational and interpersonal levels. Modules are therefore necessary to meet the needs of international IRs and HRM.

Furthermore, the macro layer of culture corresponds more to the universal, national and organizational levels of cultural comparisons, while the micro layer of culture corresponds more to the intrapersonal and interpersonal levels. The micro culture at inter- and intra-personal level is visible and tangible communication, while macro cultural encounters at universal, national, and organizational level are invisible and intangible, but literally exist as illustrated in Figure 10.1.

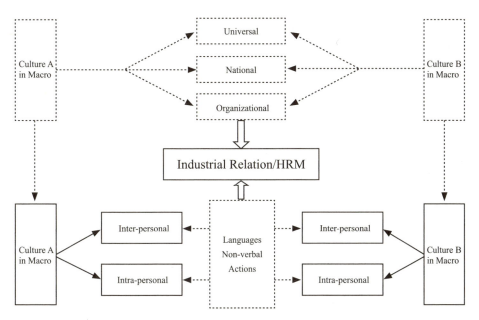

**Figure 10.1.  Cross-cultural communication in the Macro and Micro layers in the context of International IRs/HRM**

This figure shows that, in the context of international IRs and HRM, communication between people of different cultures who proceed without consideration of their macro-cultural characteristics might easily lead to misunderstanding and to the forming of barriers on account of ambiguities of language and non-verbal actions.

This figure reminds researchers some basic outlines in the comparative cultural studies. Firstly, it is necessary and compulsory to take two cultures into considerations independently from both macro and micro levels. Secondly, sorting out the similarities and differences after the comparison are the key points in helping designs for questionnaires and interview preparations. Thirdly, Macro level culture gaps are mostly invisible and can be performed indirectly by visible factors, such as language speaking or non-verbal expressions in micro level. Fourthly, almost all visible actions relating IRs and HRM activities are performed through language or non-verbal actions which are an easy way to explore its mechanism and impacts.

The evidence from the research and literature review show, both positive and limitative, that the hypotheses are tested and show off.This research has done some contributions to the knowledge in culture and language barriers in IRs/HRM in the context of Anglo-Saxon based MNCs in China which has been rarely explored by scholars before. To approach the success of the study, the author has made some efforts in all possible ways.

A model of analysis culture and language barriers from macro and micro level has been created and applied into the case studies and empirical research which being proved positive and effective (Figure 10.1.).

Hypothesis regarding to the IRs structure, culture conflicts, language strategies, differences in cultural dimensions, and corporate culture have been verified and analyzed.

The research objective proposed in Chapter one has been verified and explored item by item. The China's industrial relations and HR, in the economic transition period, has presented rich forms of performance. Generally speaking, IR and HR conflicts evolve to a more unstable and unpredictable situation, but most of time, it stops at a dynamic balance with a strong Chinese characteristic cultural feature. No matter it is the state-owned enterprises, or MNCs, traditional culture value such as in-group collectivism, face concept and personnel networking played important role in direct or indirect ways.

Enterprises from the west, which mainly refers to the MNCs coming from Anglo-Saxon based cultural heritage, has obvious unique characteristics. The culture of commercialism, respects to the law and regulations, equalitarian philosophy, Christianity heritage are completely different from the one of harmony oriented personnel network, hierarchical behaviour, Buddhism and Confucianism based philosophy which has been explicitly analyzed in the previous chapters.

## 10.2. Harmony Industrial Relations Construction

As what the study found from previous research, harmony IR and HRM philosophy has been a strategy for China government to advocate in both public and private enterprises. This research has proposed some methods to approach the harmony situation from the perspective of cross-cultural management.

### 10.2.1. Basic Strategies of Cross-cultural IRs Management

This study has found that cultural diversity makes multinational IRs management becomes more complex and difficult. However, cross-cultural management and new-type corporate culture development can effectively reduce or avoid conflicts of industrial relations caused by the cultural factors, which can tap businesses potential to the fullest extent to maximize value. The new-type corporate culture is not a combination of various cultures, but a synthesis of conflict and coexistence formed by their collisions and absorption. Subsequently, Enterprise managers need to face these cultural differences, and on this basis select the appropriate management strategies.

### 10.2.2. Recognition of Cultural Differences to Develop Cultural Identity

To correctly identify and deal with cultural differences is the precondition and base of eliminating corporate culture conflict and building harmonious industrial relations. Chinese and foreign sides should continue to strengthen exchanges and dialogue in working life to understand each other's cultural identity, and face objective difference in values, behaviours and customs. This study suggests two ways to tolerate and fully understand the different cultures: first, to forgive and understand the nation and the enterprise culture. Due to individual differences in cognitive ability, their understanding of their own culture is not the same. Only with the full understanding of their own cultural identity can the common points of different cultures be found. Second, to forgive and understand other cultures; by contrast, the second way is much more difficult to be done than the first one. As a manager, he/she should get rid of their own culture, think about and solve problems in consideration of other cultures. Moreover, he/she should find integrating points of various cultures through analysis and comparison of the different levels of cultures, so as to take effective measures to promote exchange and integration and increase employees' acceptance of different cultures. However, every culture has its excellent content and relative limitation. Managers should objectively look at the cultural differences and effectively use such cultural differences. As cultural differences for any multinational corporation may cause dysfunction type of conflict and also functioning type of conflict, which turn out to hinder or boost the businesses development. On the one hand, the objective existence of cultural differences may cause contradictions and conflicts of subjects of industrial relations, which will result in business difficulties. On the other hand, cultural diversity can offer a broader scope for thinking to produce more unique solutions and suggestions, and improve enterprises' adaptability to external environment. It is, thus, necessary to respect and give full understanding to the differences between different cultures, work hard to develop cultural identity in order to take full advantage of the positive impact of cultural differences.

### 10.2.3. Focus on Communication to Build Integration Platform

Poor communication is an important cause for cross-cultural industrial relations conflict. Good cross-cultural communication contributes to a better understanding of cultural differences, so as to achieve the respect and understanding of different cultures. In the process of building corporate culture, enterprises must mutually establish effective communication and exchange mechanism to produce mutual understanding and trust, thus promoting cultural integration, and taking full play to diverse cultures. This mainly involves two aspects: one is to overcome communication barriers; second is to establish communication and feedback mechanisms. Depending on the features of communication barriers, we usually divided them into non-verbal communication barriers and language barriers. Needless to say, language is the most direct and basic means to communicate. As the most important carrier of culture, it contains a very rich cultural content, thus blocking people of different cultural backgrounds to communicate effectively, and easily producing contradiction and conflict due to misunderstanding of different cultures. Two aspects should be emphasized to overcome communication barriers: first, use a unified language, simplify communication process to reduce the possibility of communication misunderstanding because of poor language learning and translation discomfort; second, use simple language to improve comprehension.; third, actively listen; it can prevent information omission, and easily form benign interaction, thereby improving communication efficiency and accuracy of communication. There are two ways to overcome language barriers: firstly, use sparingly non-verbal expression, such as facial expressions and movements in the communication process; secondly, strengthen cross-cultural training to understand the meaning of different expressions and actions in different cultures.

In addition, two-way communication channels should be established to improve the feedback mechanisms. Channels of communication within the organization is comprehensive three-dimensional. Cross-cultural communication channel of corporate management should not simply imitate and follow certain one-way cultural communication, but establish two-way communication channels in favor of different cultures. In this channel, there are no ill feelings between staffs who can make exchanges and communication equally and friendly, gradually reduce their sense of their own family in the participation of corporate governance affairs to form harmonious industrial relations based on same interest goal. To establish two-way communication channels, we should focus on the following work: first, highlight the importance of cross-cultural communication; cross-cultural communication should be in the crucial position in the enterprise cross-cultural management; business managers should be actively involved in ensuring communication channels open; second, find suitable communication media. Form of communication should be diversified and communication network can be constructed through interviews, telephone communication group meeting, festival celebrations and other means; third, establish feedback mechanisms; purpose of communication is to fully understand and receive the contents of the other party, which requires communicators in the communication process can respond positively and timely feedback; fourth, effectively use informal communication; information transfer of informal channels is often based on personal relationships, with more real information and a harmonious communication atmosphere, and easier access to achieve effective communication.

### 10.2.4. Implementation of Cross-cultural Integration

In order to achieve effective integration of different cultures and establish a new-type enterprise culture, multinational corporations select the appropriate cultural integration mode with the combination of the degree of influence and the proportion of different cultures within the enterprise. By eclectic manner, it takes full advantage of the enabling parts of different cultures, reduces cultural superiority and lays a solid foundation for building harmonious industrial relations.

The so-called cultural integration refers to the integration process of cultures of different characteristics through contact, exchange, mutual absorption and penetration. Cultural integration, in fact, aims to shorten the cultural distance, which by way of a compromise, so that different cultures can coordinate with each other with mutual adaptation, and the dominant culture in the amendment process not only lose some traits, but absorb some new characteristics, thus shortening the distance between different cultures. In addition, cross-cultural integration is a systematic project; enterprises should treat it as a long-term task to encourage all employees to participate in this great project. It should be emphasized that the integration process should focus on the common understanding and recognition of all the members of the corporate values, so as to ultimately realize cultural integration of values, organizational structure and employee accomplishment. On the one hand, new culture can be created to realize cultural innovation through cross-cultural integration; on the other hand, cross-cultural integration can eliminate communication barriers, reduce communication costs and cultivate a sense of understanding of mutual trust and cooperation of employees of different cultural backgrounds.

In fact, there are many factors that affect cultural integration, such as business goals, management diversity, cultural identity and staffs' cognition degree, which requires enterprises can not blindly copy some formulas in integration. It must combine with the actual situation and act according to circumstances for cultural integration with their own development model. The mode of cultural integration mainly includes cultural transplanting mode, multi-directional cross-cultural mode, cultural compatibility mode and cultural infiltration mode, and each mode has its own applicable conditions. Enterprises should carefully consider the specific choice.

Cultural transplanting mode refers to take the original culture of the home country as the main body of new culture, but absorbing key cultural elements from the host country. The advantage of this model is that taking into account the balance between both cultures, while the disadvantage is difficult implement, higher requirements for their own cultural identity. Multi-directional cross-cultural mode refers to the use of management with cross-cultural background to implement integration activities. This model is to achieve cultural integration through the integration of human resource policies with less resistance of integration. And this model is commonly used by multinational corporations. Cultural compatibility mode refers to the independence maintenance of various cultures without dominance of any culture and with complementation and independent operation of cultures, which can give full play to the cross-cultural advantages. Cultural infiltration mode refers to not contribute to the local employees to accept home country host culture in a short time, but to have a subtle influence on local staff to gradually accept and adapt through cultural infiltration approaches. Such a model is also commonly used by multinationals. Overall, multinational enterprises, according to their actual situation, should give full consideration to the cultural elements of their integration and select the appropriate modes of cultural integration to establish a new corporate culture suited for China's national conditions in a planned and orderly way.

### 10.2.5. Establishing Common Values

Any organization has its common core values. As an important part of corporate culture, it is an important basis for people to determine human behaviour and communication guidelines and to distinguish right from wrong, good from bad, love from hate. Managers engaged into transnational business activities must fully understand the cultural identity of the host and respect the objective differences in different cultures in order to promote exchanges and cultural integration with equal and friendly attitude. At the same time, he/she should carefully analyzes the similarities and differences between different cultures to extract shared values suited for local enterprises, and integrate it into the new corporate culture to improve inclusiveness and plasticity of corporate culture. There are two ways for establishing common values for reference: first, integration method. By refining the different cultural values, based on the integration principle of their own set values, the integrated values can reflect the characteristics of single values, improve into a strong elasticity, which is consistent with the core values of business development; second, the integrated approach, to refine the values of different cultures, and ultimately choose values shared by a majority of employees and gradually make other employees to accept these common values by cultural infiltration.

Establish common values is a gradual process, enterprises employees need to participate in and make tireless efforts, and only by reaching full consensus can the values be effectively implemented to the business management. Managers should lead by example, listen to the views of the majority of employees, create an open and positive communication environment, optimize communication channels to ensure that information can be transmitted efficiently, in order to promote common values recognized by all staff; moreover, they should guide each employee to combine their thinking and behaviours. By establishing common values, they can give full play to the advantages of multi-cultural potential to create harmonious and stable industrial relations.

### 10.2.6. Optimization of Human Resources Deployment and Development

As an important means to build harmonious industrial relations, cross-cultural HRM is to overcome cultural differences. Based on characteristics of the cultural differences, cross-cultural HRM is the effective management of human resources, which can greatly reduce labour costs and maintain competitive advantage while improve the human resource allocation and efficiency.

### 10.2.6.1. HRM Localization

Localization of human resources is an important strategy of overseas business management. In the early stage of transnational business, multinational enterprises often choose a number of outstanding management personnel from home country to go to the host country in management activities. In the short term this method is very effective. But with the development of enterprises, the drawbacks of this personnel policy gradually reveal, such as dampening the enthusiasm of local managers, bringing cultural prejudices, increasing operational costs. This requires multinational enterprises to adjust manpower policies to achieve localization of human resources. This strategy, on the one hand, can eliminate at a large extent the language barriers and improve the effectiveness of communication; on the other hand, create fair opportunities for staff, greatly improve staff polar plot, improve the cohesion of local staff and obtain powerful support of local human resources. In the process of specific implementation, it is necessary for multinational enterprises managers reach consensus of the importance of human resource localization; second, it is necessary to take reasonable and effective strategies to develop, attract and retain talents, such as absorbing local college graduates, with favourable treatment attracting Chinese management personnel, planning for employee with their long-term career development plans .

### 10.2.6.2. Selection of High-Quality Management Personnel

The effective implementation of cross-cultural management lies in a high-quality cross-cultural management team. The selection of HR officials should focus on the following three points: first, capable to understand and implement the parent company strategic decisions; second, professional knowledge and strong competence; third, a rich multi-cultural management experience. HR officials should be able to withstand the impact of different cultures, and have strong adaptability and coordination to different cultures. Specifically speaking, there are three selection channels for HR official: sending abroad from the mother nation; from the host country or third nation selection. Each way has its own advantages, disadvantages and applicability. Enterprises should combine their cultural identity, and make targeted selection.

### 10.2.6.3. Cross-cultural training of human resources

In multinational enterprises, there are different characteristics of cultures that seem very different; in fact, there is still a core part of many similarities, so cultural differences are not insurmountable, still can continue to promote exchanges and understanding through education and learn to achieve cultural integration. Cross-cultural training should focus on cultural adaptation and the content should be designed to scientifically and systematically which can be able to increase employee awareness of culture differences, alleviate psychological reactions caused by cultural discomfort.

The main contents of cross-cultural training include sensitivity training, language learning, lifestyle, cross-cultural communication. For the choice of training institute, enterprises should combine their strength of training, either internal training organization or external professional training institutions, such as universities, consultative service enterprises. Regardless of any routes taken, it is necessary to highlight the trainees into contact communication and interaction of different cultures in the training process, let the trainees feel the cultural difference, and through proactive communication to understand and respect this difference. Specific training methods should be diversified, such as education, cultural studies, field trips, environmental simulation, situational dialogues and role-play, etc. Cross-cultural training can strengthen the staff's understanding and recognition of different cultures, cultivate a spirit of unity and cooperation between employees and create comfortable and harmonious industrial relations environment to promote stable and healthy development of enterprises.

### 10.2.6.4. Create an attractive remuneration policy

People of different cultural backgrounds hold different views towards money, work and life. In some cultures, people attach great importance to material rewards; they are willing to get more rewards at the expense of rest and continue to work overtime during the rest time of the other employees. For these employees, the salary is an important reference standard for their careers and satisfaction. In some cultures, people who do not so value material rewards pay more attention to the sense of accomplishment brought by the work; they both work hard and attach great importance to the life quality, and strive to achieve a balance in between, and sometimes even give up work to enjoy life.

Due to this difference, enterprise managers can not copy some pattern in the design of salary structures and welfare systems, which should be designed with the combination of staffs' different values, so as to achieve overall satisfaction. For example, for those employees who emphasize substance reward, it can increase the gap between the different levels of remuneration, such as the implementation of broadband salary, which can greatly stimulate their enthusiasm for work. Meanwhile, employee vacation can be set flexibly within the extent permitted by law, to give them the opportunity to work overtime to provide more substantial overtime pay, so that they can feel satisfied through personal effort to obtain substance. In contrast, for those employees who value the quality of life, the former approach is not desirable. They need a more perfect vacation system and focuses on alleviating their workload, which enable them to have chances to enjoy personal life. For the design of the salaries and benefits, managers can use more non-material rewards, such as job promotion, good development opportunities.

### 10.2.7. Security Conditions for Cross-cultural Industrial Relations Management
### 10.2.7.1. Design rational organization

A rational organizational structure can make positive impact on the establishment of cross-cultural communication channels and organizational efficiency. Influenced by Chinese traditional culture, organizational structure of enterprises tends to be centralized power controlled by a small number of managers. The organization is generally short of distinctive responsibilities and overlapping functions due to the complicated stratification and vague accountability. In contrast, the organizational structures under the ASC tend to be decentralization. The established structure focus on the work process rather than departmental functions with less hierarchically stratification and clearer work division, which reflects the organizational structure of the flattening development trend. In the modern competitive environment, horizontal organization is the innovation and development of organizational structure. By implementing a flat organizational structure, compressing management level and increasing span of control are in favour of rapid transfer of information within the organization, enabling organizations to shorten the chain of command and delegate decision-making to lower level gradually, thus greatly improving the flexibility of management command and operating efficiency of organization. Therefore, in the design of multinational organization structure, it is necessary to fully consider the characteristics of the culture in a planned and orderly way to complete flat-organizational-structure-oriented design, to build a smooth communication channels and enhance horizontal collaboration between departments, and avoid conflict caused by cultural differences and poor design of organizational structure.

### 10.2.7.2. Establish and Improve Trade Unions for Building Enterprise Culture

Good corporate culture is the cornerstone in creating harmonious industrial relations, and its construction work is a long-term task, even in a short time it may not turn out immediate positive results. Unlike some corporates in setting up a special administrative office for the corporate culture construction, trade union may play to this function instead. Not only can it save a lot of manpower, material and financial resources, but also may trade union take the corporate culture construction as one of its own work. This is due to the functions of trade unions to safeguard the vital interests and legitimate rights and interests of the masses, which is consistent with the long-term goal of enterprise culture development.

Enterprises work with trade unions, extract corporate cultures and integrate employee values and corporate core culture values to inspire and mobilize staff enthusiasm for work to the largest extent, and create equal and friendly work environment for more harmonious and stable industrial relations.

### 10.2.8. Mechanisms Guarantee for Cross-cultural IRs Management

### 10.2.8.1. Management Mechanism for Employee Participation

This study suggests that employee participation in management is an important channel to stabilize the industrial relations. The new industrial relations no longer take employees as simple workers, but as the main role of partnership. Enterprises should provide employees with the opportunity to express their opinions and suggestions, thereby affecting the policies and decisions of enterprises, which is the main manifestation of labour cooperation. One of the effective ways for employee participation in management is workers' congress at corporate level.

It is recommended that MNCs should actively promote the workers' congress system, and make timely adjustment according to different cultures within enterprises to improve channels of employee communication, listen carefully to the needs and suggestions of them. The introduction of employee participation in management can enhance employees' sense of ownership on the one hand, and enable them to have a strong sense of responsibility and accomplishment, thus proactively thinking for enterprises and contributing their talents, and also reflecting timely the contradictions and problems in IRs management; on the other hand, the mechanisms can allow managers to detect and resolve these contradictions and problems, to reduce unnecessary friction and disputes and enhance trust between staff and managers to promote more harmonious and stable IRs.

### 10.2.8.2. Tripartite Coordination Mechanism

As mentioned in the chapter four, the tripartite coordination mechanism refers to the approach of eliminating misunderstandings and reaching consensus through government-employers-workers consultation about policy-making and labour dispute handling. Current tripartite coordination mechanism has become the valuble practice to adjust the IRs in some countries, while it has not been fully promoted, especially at the enterprise level in China. For MNCs, attention should be paid to the establishment of a tripartite coordination mechanism, and make appropriate adjustments based on the characteristics of corporate culture to highlight consultation and handle equality of industrial relations. Only focusing on building harmonious IRs and improving organizational performance goals, multinational corporations should scientifically design and optimize the existing organization systems and operation mechanism, and effectively exert the functions of tripartite coordination mechanisms, thus ultimately achieving the smooth transition of labour-management relations from competitive relations to cooperative relations and building harmonious and stable industrial relations.

### 10.2.8.3. Early Warning Mechanism for Industrial Relations

Early warning mechanism for IRs is a working mechanism for timely prevention and treatment of various contradictions and conflicts and effective protection of employees' rights by the use of communication, coordination and prediction and prevention and timely identifying conflicts and problems in cross-cultural industrial relations. As a scientific coordination mechanism, enterprises play a central role in the whole process. Enterprises need to coordinate and organize the HRM department, trade unions and other departments to strengthen cooperation and cooperation to jointly exerting systematic early warning function. Meanwhile, enterprises need to establish and improve relevant systems to assist the effective implementation of early warning system, such as contract management system, labour dispute system, and restrain and regulate industrial relations early warning mechanism through the construction of institutional system. This approach can greatly improve the early warning validity. Overall, the factors of disharmony and problems that may exist in industrial relations may be constrained in the first time through the establishment of early warning mechanism, which can avoid conflict of industrial relations, enhance their psychological sense of security to build harmonious and stable industrial relations.

### 10.2.9. Personnel Security of Cross-cultural IRs Management
### 10.2.9.1. Create Cross-cultural Management Team

To resolve problems of cross-cultural IRs management, the primary task is to establish a high-quality cross-cultural IRs management team. The selection of team members should particularly consider their positions in the enterprise. Priority should be given to senior management staff, such as general manager, president, and department head. This is because they have the dual characteristics in business management; on the one hand, they are the core management personnel of enterprise who are responsible for some key position, such as establishing the development strategies of enterprises, and managing operations; on the other hand, as an important intermediary of enterprise's management layer, they assume the role of coordinating cross-cultural adaptability and solving the conflict of industrial relations. Through their tireless efforts, gradually create equal and friendly work environment, so that employees from different cultural backgrounds can live in harmony and work together for the future development of enterprises. In addition to duties, the cross-cultural management team composed also should consider the level of education team size, team members, and other professional background and experience in cross-cultural management, while the members of the selection should be through multiple cultures, languages, management, etc. training. Taking team size for example, team size depends on two aspects: first, the scale of business organizations; second, the proportion of multicultural organization within the enterprise. If enterprises with large scale and unfocused internal multicultural organization, it is necessary to appropriately expand the scale of management team; if enterprises of moderate proportion of multicultural organization and large population of foreign employees, it is necessary to appropriately adjust the ratio of managers of different nationalities within the team, appoint or recruit managers of other nationalities to join the management team, so as to facilitate the communication and understanding between employees of different cultures, thus achieving effective cross-cultural management of industrial relations.

### 10.2.9.2. Recruitment Based on Agreed Corporate Values for Employee Integration

Recruitment is an important part of HRM. The recruited staffs also have a significant impact on industrial relations. When MNCs conduct recruitment, in addition to considering the candidate's qualifications, ability, work experience, they should also focus on whether their values and behavioural habits can match that of the enterprise. By considering these points, the enterprise can greatly reduce the culture discomfort with corporate values of staff after recruitment, and can avoid conflict of industrial relations, reduce employee turnover rate and protect the stability of the existing workforce. Meanwhile, in order to enable enterprises to continue to maintain youth and vigour and achieve a virtuous cycle of talent flow, efforts should also be made to recruit local talents and provide opportunities for them to participate in the management, develop their cross-cultural perspective. Managers trained through such channels offer some management concepts which are often more likely to be accepted by employees. Moreover, it is particularly important to integrate employees of different cultural backgrounds, which is also ignored by managers; because they consider too much about how to integrate assets, technology, markets, and other intangible assets. Through integration, on the one hand, the relationship between the executives and employees can be properly handled; on the other hand, enterprises can achieve the optimal allocation of staff so that they can leverage their maximum capacity and greatly enhance the international competitiveness of enterprises.

### 10.3. Statement of original research questions

This research has clearly identified a number of research areas, which are for understanding culture and language barriers. The research aimed at investigating cultural barriers in selected aspects of Chinese industry and those areas which had contact for MNCs, with Anglo-Saxon companies as defined in the text.

The evidence illustrates that, in the era of globalization, every country is looking for solutions to improve its competitiveness. There are many different ways of approaching this target, and one effective and remarkable phenomenon is the rapid expansion of thriving multinational companies, which may be regarded as a most effective way of promoting a nation's competitive advantage.

In the course of a MNC's evolution, strategies and methods of management may have changed along with the changes in the world's economy, political systems and the development of new technology. More importantly, the changes of emphasis on human rights demand changes to company accountabilities. The ten developing trends of MNCs explained in Chapter One demonstrate the irreplaceable position of MNCs in the world economy when stepping into the 21$^{st}$ century. MNCs have become complex in talent mobility, hi-tech transmission, capital reconstruction and social governance.

MNCs are the driving force for industrial reconstruction. In most parts of the world, capital and technology tend to move from developed countries or regions to the developing areas, where mass cheap labour resources and comparatively slack policies in the host countries motivate the MNCs to expand globally.

This internal and indirect connection of culture/language and IR/HRM is significant in the context of the globalizing tide and China's rising economy as well as its growing influence in the global community. The models acquired from China's IR and HRM practices and its theoretical frameworks may provide valuable references for MNCs' practice and guidance for policy-makers.

## 10.4. Conclusions to empirical study

The following conclusions can be drawn from the study of selected MNCs located in the different areas of China. With regard to language:

- In China, there are no fixed and changeless language strategies for MNCs management in the fields of industrial relations and human resources management. MNCs may employ adaptive methods when handling the changes to IR and HR situations. A mono-language strategy is not recommended in MNCs' operation.
- Skilled cross-cultural competence (CCC) is not formed without any practice

or systematic training. For managers engaged in IRs and HR management, it is recommended that MNCs need to organize some special training classes to improve people's communicative skills.

• Various academic criteria can be used to test individuals' competence in a foreign language. However, for those working in MNCs, competence in a foreign language is not just a matter of whether one could use this language in everyday speaking, listening, reading or writing. A more crucial perspective is to see if one can communicate successfully with other people in this foreign language.

• There is no fixed language strategy for MNCs in China. Research has demonstrated that a successful MNC has its own features of language strategies. Most of them have mandatory requirements of English proficiency for middle level managers/ staff, but for ordinary employees, foreign language is not considered at all, and furthermore, most of the employees working in MNCs are migrant workers from different parts of China who can only speak fluent dialects. Few can speak standard Mandarin, but it seems that this does not have much influence on industrial relations and human resources management.

• A variety of factors influence corporate IRs and HRM, but some are remarkable, such as the importance of personal networks (*guan xi*), the concept of face (*mian zi*)[1], collectivism behaviour, hierarchy and stereotypes.

• The research has demonstrated that traditional cultural factors could have both a positive and a negative influence on IRs and HRM practice. The interview findings revealed that MNCs can take good advantage of some traditional customs, such as the collectivist orientation and trade union leaders (who are sometimes also the leaders of the 'townsmen's association'), which can have a powerful influence in the MNCs. For those in which there is no trade union organization, the townsmen's association – the underground trade union – may

---

[1] **Face/*mian zi***, idiomatically refers to one's own sense of dignity or prestige in social contexts. For instance, in the English-speaking world, the term "To save face" describes the lengths to which an individual may go in order to preserve their established position in society—in other words, taking action to ensure that one is not thought badly of by one's peers. It is a fundamental concept in the fields of sociology, sociolinguistics, semantics, politeness theory, psychology, political science, communication, and Face Negotiation Theory, and translates at least somewhat equivalently into many world languages, both Germanic and otherwise. (source: Dong, et Lee,2007)

take the position of employees' representative.

- This study has also revealed that non-verbal actions are another factor that could be easily ignored but which actually play important roles in everyday management. As a manager in IRs or HR, it is necessary to pay attention to the emotional changes in the people with whom one is in contact, such as greetings, facial reflection of conversations, movement of fingers and hands, and even different ways of smiling.

## 10.5. Further Research Recommendations

### 10.5.1. Cultural risk

Different cultures contain different values, ethics, customs, and ways of thinking and behaving, all of which make management more complicated and bring various types of culture risks. These risks are:

- Ethnocentrism risk. Misjudge and be superior to other cultures with one's own "prejudice" and "prescience" formed in one's own cultural environment.
- Management risk, the risk that managers' management ideas, habits, methods, etc. cannot be effectively applied into a new cultural environment.
- Communication risk, the risk that a communication failure results from cultural misunderstanding created by wrong style of explaining verbal or nonverbal information.
- Business practice risk, the risk that a transaction will fail if the existing business operation practice and business negotiation style cannot adapt to the new cultural environment.
- Perceptual knowledge risk. Different values and primary standards of different cultures lead to different perceptual knowledge, and it is fairly difficult to change the different perceptual knowledge formed by differences in basic values

### 10.5.2. Cultural Difference Brings Competitive Edge

Instead of merely bringing negative effects on a firm, cultural difference can also provide competitive edges, add more flexibility and optimize the overall system for an intercultural firm. As a consequence, 1+1>2 can be achieved.

- Market. Cultural difference increases a firm's flexibility and adaptability toward the cultural preference of the target market. Companies work for a match between the makeup of their employees and important customers or customer groups from different cultural background, so as to be close to customers and establish close ties with them. For example, to run a Chinese firm with Chinese employees in order to exploit Chinese market. This localization strategy enables the company to make full use of advantages localization brings.

- Cost. A company usually pays high wages for expatriate staff along with expenses including transportation cost and subsidy. It costs a lot to send a large number of expatriate workers to the host country. Meanwhile, under the market conditions where the cultural connotation of product and consultation are increasingly demanding, the human resource with one single cultural model in the company is hard to meet the demand. However, to employ local workers can not only enhance an enterprise's adaptability to the market but also save costs.

- Problem-solving. Every culture has a unique way of thinking. Cultural difference can provide a broader perspective for problem-solving and reduce stereotyped thinking, so that new ideas and methods to solve a problem can be inspired.

### 10.5.3. Further Research

It is always difficult to attain perfection in research. There is still ample scope for further study and amelioration.

Firstly, the sample size for this study was limited. Only about two hundred questionnaires were returned, which was lower than the expectation. Furthermore, the sample was not equally distributed across different groups: for example, the number of managers was far lower than the number of staff members, and there were fewer foreign staff than Chinese employees. Secondly, a wider range of research methods could be adopted in future studies; thirdly, the interpretation of internal connections of the findings from quantitative and qualitative research requires further explanation.

Nevertheless, it is hoped that this initial research will provide conceptual and research process foundations upon which later scholars can build in efforts to learn more about the mechanism of interference between culture/language factors and IRs/HR management. Attention to what is happening today in China will contribute to achieving a better life for all of us in this global village.

## 10.6. Research model and method limitations & strengthens

To facilitate this investigation, a research model was developed from consideration of theoretical work in cultural spreading over various fields in multi-disciplinary fashion from anthropology to linguistics, to cross-cultural studies in management and other related areas. The methods of investigate focus on the quantitative and qualitative approach, and focused on case study and a questionnaire survey which was conducted both by written questionnaires and partly for the use of website. The limitation of this were clear that selected industries with particularly in the country like China's dimension very small, and every interview conducted in the open-ended interviews, and only 30 respondents to be interviewed. However it does give indications, particularly it linked to the existing literature in the field. There is a gap about comprehensive understanding of China in particular, and its culture barriers.

The model designed by author came from the contributions of previous researchers and scholars engaging in the relevant research areas, and the reason is, after times of comparing the current model with the actual situation of culture/language barriers in China's context, that it is hard to simply use indiscriminately the previous model invented by other scholars. For example, the Hofstede's cultural dimension, there have been critiques on the shortage and misleading of his theoretical frameworks (McSweeney, 2002, 2015, 2016; Kuipers, 2012; Venaik. et Brewer, 2012; Vaiman. et Bewster, 2015), but it can give the researcher a quantitative and measurable direction to follow up only if some improper factors being amended and rectified.

Limitation for the research is another unavoidable factor to face due to various reasons. It was not easy to earn the trust from the people in the first meeting; personnel networking may sometimes give a limited selection in research subject confirmation. Time is another crucial factor and not all the people can find vacant moment and accept the interview.

Samples collected from questionnaires may exist some kind of bias as well. It is not completely collected randomly but from the people introduced by researcher's graduates and relatives. The duration of research has been lasting for nearly 2 years long, and more case studies were supplemented in the recent time, which may lead to some kind of incoherency.

Nevertheless, the empirical study did find some useful information and present a number of valuable references and clues for further research which the author shall propose in the next section.

Again, this study explored the possible connection between culture/language and IRs/HRM. Definitions of culture vary depending on the special interests of each different research object. In Chapter Two, this paper collected some typical definitions and illustrations of culture and its features, from which value systems are regarded as key parts of culture connotation.

Of these findings from culture research, Hofstede's theory of four cultural dimensions represents a practical approach to the empirical study of cultural impact on MNCs. Further theoretical findings on culture and its impacts from a number of scholars (Hall, 1959; Kluckhohn, 1951; Trompenaars, 1997; Earley and Ang, 2003; Triandis, 1990) have become resources for a new model of the connections of culture/language and IRs/HRM

As regards language theories, findings from the fields of applied linguistics (Grice, 1989; Leech, 1983) and cross-cultural communications (Sapir, 1958; Whorf, 1940; Samovar, 1998) offered references for this research's theoretical structure. Language, including non-verbal action, is the material carrier of culture and value systems. Most of the time, the argument, bargaining and administration of IRs and HRM issues have to rely on parole communications. Research on the principles of verbal and non-verbal communications shall turn a new page for exploring effective and positive IRs and HR relations.

Regarding the role of language in business, previous research (Feely, 2004) has revealed that language is engaged in almost all of the different stages of business life, and that the research into language functioning in IRs/HRM is just a small part of business studies (Figure 11.1).

In regard to the features of Chinese cultural characteristics, Chinese culture has been sustained by three important periods of Chinese history: five thousand years of traditional culture legacy, the communist ideology since the 1920s, and more directly the impact of ideas generated after China's economic reforms since 1978. But, in the operational stage, the cultural characteristics may present diversities in accordance

with the regions and territories. For example, Personal Networking (*guan xi*) is an important Chinese cultural feature impacting people's lives, but it has various

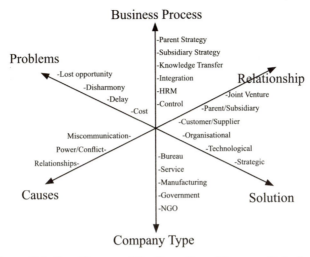

**Figure 11.1.  Star diagram of the dimensions of language in business**
*Source: by Feely, J.A., 2004*

formats, rituals and unspoken rules (*qian gui ze*)[①] in different regions. That is why the conflicts of IRs and HRM may present corresponding managerial styles. Culture at the macro level labels us as unique in terms of geographic location, beliefs, religions and value systems, which are hiding beyond our outward appearance; while at the micro level, culture creates magic artefacts, cuisine and languages which bring distinctive manifestations.

## 10.7. Suggestions for future research
As a tentative exploratory study applying Hofstede's cultural dimensions as well as

---

① Unspoken rules are behavioral constraints imposed in organizations or societies that are not voiced or written down. They usually exist in unspoken and unwritten format because they form a part of the logical argument or course of action implied by tacit assumptions. Examples involving unspoken rules include unwritten and unofficial organizational hierarchies, organizational culture, and acceptable behavioral norms governing interactions between organizational members. In the workplace, unspoken rules can have a significant impact on one's job satisfaction, advancement opportunities, and career trajectory. For example, research conducted in the United States by the Level Playing Field Institute and the Center for Survey Research and Analysis at the University of Connecticut revealed that 36% of white women, 37% of women of color, and 33% of men of color identified the fact that only certain people are part of important social groups at work as the greatest obstacle to fairness in their workplaces.(source: wikipedia:2014. *http://en..org/wiki/Unspoken_rule*)

theoretical frameworks from other scholars in cross-cultural studies, this research has attempted to set up some references to guide the practice of IRs and HR management in China. While there are more issues waiting to be explored in the course of further research, which are not limited by the research patterns defined in this programme, new problems keep emerging along with the changes to the internal and external situations for MNCs. For instance, the following topics of study are worthy of continuing research in the future.

### 10.7.1. Project One

**Research on the function of non-verbal action in MNCs' IRs and HR management.**

Non-verbal communication (NVC) is not just relating to psychological analysis, but also relies on theories of communication, sociology and management. When interviewing ordinary employees, it was noticed that most of the time, true information could be acquired from their instant emotional changes, which was more reliable than simple 'yes' or 'no' answers from the questionnaire. Further, NVC varies with different cultural backgrounds: for example, people from different provinces of China may present different ways of thinking, greeting, and politeness. NVC is an important issue for IRs and should not be ignored.

### Steps for applying NVC IRs and HRM

The first step is to categorize NVC features by searching the literature and examining findings from previous empirical studies. In addition, NVC presents multi-dimensional characteristics, so it is necessary to develop a model that is applicable to the context of MNCs with a Chinese cultural background.

In the next step, researchers will categorise the research subjects and the types of MNCs' NVC cultural background in both the guest and home countries. Due to the distinct features of China's seven cultural regions, MNCs located in the North, East and South of China may demonstrate localized cultural features in NVC.

The selection of appropriate companies and interviewees for the case study will be a challenge. The researcher should have a good understanding of the cultural groups of the employee working in the MNCs. This suggests that a comparative study of NVC from the North, East and South regions will make this study more interesting and instructive. Conversations with the employees will require researchers to have a good understanding of local NVC connotations. Qualitative research such as joining in with the process of bargaining, negotiation and other IRs activities are encouraged.

## 10.7.2. Project Two

### Impact of migrant workers on China's MNCs

Migrant workers (*nong min gong*) are a unique and remarkable phenomenon in the process of China's industrialization. Statistics reveal that there are more than 200 million migrant workers spread throughout all types of companies in China, drawing much attention not just from the Chinese government (each year, there are additional regulations or red-seal documents focusing on the issues of migrant workers), but also from scholars and from society. In 2009, only 9.9% of labour workers had higher education experience, while more than 80 million migrant workers joined the trade unions (People's Daily, 2010) .

Unlike the traditional labour workers, who have been living in the city for generations and have no land of their own in the countryside, migrant workers present some extraordinary features. They work periodically in the city, but own land in the countryside, while their wives and children, or sometimes just children and older parents, stay and look after their homes and land. In the city, they are like strangers, limited by China's household registration system (*hu kou*)[1], losing many rights in employability, education for children and medical treatment. As for the negative influence of government, the tide of migrant workers has also led to much social instability such as crime and the degeneration of social morality.

In other words, China's migrant workers themselves are typical cultural representatives in a special historical period in the course of China's industrialization. Successful management of migrant workers in the MNCs requires success in cross-cultural management.

---

[1] **hukou** is a record in the system of household registration required by law in the People's Republic of China (mainland China). The system itself is more properly called "*huji*", and has origins in ancient China. A household registration record officially identifies a person as a resident of an area and includes identifying information such as name, parents, spouse, and date of birth. A *hukou* can also refer to a family register in many contexts, since the household registration record is issued per family, and usually includes the births, deaths, marriages, divorces, and moves, of all members in the family. (Source: Liu et Kuang, 2012)

Common features of migrant workers shall be the first step to address. With reference to previous studies on culture and language differences, this continuing research plans to select some typical areas in China where most of the workers are migrants working in the MNCs. Cross-cultural encounters may elicit various conflicts and clashes, which require a suitable research method to follow up.

The findings on migrant workers' cross-cultural adaptation will be a perfect complement to the current research.

### 10.7.3. Project Three

**Harmony or Conflict: developing trends of Chinese MNCs in other countries**

With the improving competitive advantages of China's products, more and more Chinese companies have been attempting extension of their business on a global scale. Recently Alibaba, a Chinese e-commerce company,① set an unprecedented record by selling its initial public offering (IPO) for up to 25 billion US dollars in the New York Stock Exchange in September of 2014. More such Chinese companies have started to go abroad, taking not just their products and services, but also their culture.

Reports of the cultural conflicts in the course of Chinese companies' offshore expansion have come to the press more often in recent years. This is partly because of

---

① **Alibaba Group** (NYSE: BABA) is a Chinese Internet-based e-commerce company, including business-to-business online web portals, online retail and payment services, a shopping search engine and data-centric cloud computing services. The group began in 1999 when Jack Ma founded the website Alibaba.com, a business-to-business portal, to connect Chinese manufacturers with overseas buyers. In 2012, two of Alibaba's portals handled 1.1 trillion yuan ($170 billion) in sales. The company primarily operates in the People's Republic of China (PRC), and at closing time on the date of its historic initial public offering (IPO), 19 September 2014, Alibaba's market value was measured as US$231 billion. In September 2013, the company sought an IPO in the United States after a deal could not be reached with Hong Kong regulators. Planning occurred over 12 months before the company's market debut in September 2014. The Alibaba ticker symbol is "BABA. N", while the pricing of the IPO initially raised US$21.8 billion, which later increased to US$25 billion, making it the largest IPO in history. However, buyers weren't purchasing actual shares in the group, since China forbids foreign ownership, but rather just shares in a Cayman Islands shell corporation. Alibaba's consumer-to-consumer portal Taobao, similar to eBay.com, features nearly a billion products and is one of the twenty most-visited websites globally. The Group's websites accounted for over 60% of the parcels delivered in China by March 2013, and 80% of the nation's online sales by September 2014. Alipay, an online payment escrow service, accounts for roughly half of all online payment transactions within China. Alibaba is planning to enter India and was in talks with Snapdeal in September 2014. (Source: McClay,2017)

the poor awareness at the top managerial level of the importance of cultural clashes, partly because of the background of these companies, which lack preliminary training in improving cross-cultural communication skills and do not understand foreign local cultural features and legitimated systems in terms of IRs and HR.

To offer a key to unlock the cultural barriers of Chinese MNCs' overseas development, this research is planning to undertake case studies of famous Chinese brands, such as Geely Auto in the automobile industry, Huawei in the telecommunication technology, Haire in household appliances, Shanghai Baosteel Group in the steel industry and the Alibaba Group in E-commerce. Those Chinese companies have had excellent records of output and earned great success in mainland China, but sometimes attract negative feedback on their overseas marketing. One hypothesis is that these setbacks are due to cultural conflicts, which makes this research very significant.

A systematic cross-cultural theory and research framework have been developed from previous studies. More challenging for future research is the need to collect cases from the above companies, even though the researcher may benefit from good *guan xi* (personal network) when approaching the middle and higher managers. Generally, big companies place more emphasis on data protection and social reputation: thus, it is vital to earn the trust of the managerial group.

This planned study involves one to two years of investigation of the above Chinese companies, focusing on collecting typical failure cases in cross-cultural communications. Solutions to defuse these cultural barriers and conflicts will be presented to help policy makers and scholars.

# Bibliography

Adler, J. N. Campbell N., Laurent A. 1989. In search of appropriate methodology: from outside the people's republic of China looking in, *Journal of International Business Studies*, Vol. 20 (I) 1, pp. 61-74.

Adler,N.J., Doktor, R. and Redding, G.S. 1986 'From the Atlantic to the Pacific Century: Cross-cultural Management Reviewed', *Journal of Management* (Yearly Review), 12: 295-318.

Ainsworth, J. 2013. Business language for intercultural and international business communication: a Canadian case study. *Business Communication Quarterly.* 76(1): 28-50.

Allen, R. 1979. Organizational Politics: Tactics and Characteristics of Its Actors. *California Management Review.* 22 (1).

Azumi,K. 1974, *Japanese Society: A Sociological Review*. In Tiedemann, A.E. ed. An Introduction to Japanese Civilization. New York: Columbia University Press.

Almond, P., Edwards, T .Colling, T. Ferner, A, Gunningle, P., Muller-Carmen, M.,Qunitanilla, J. & Wachter,H. 2005, 'Unraveling Home and Host Country Effects: an Investigation of HR Policies of American Multinationals in Four European Countries', Industrial Relation 44, 2, 276-306.

Aid, Christian.*Trade for Life: Making Trade Work for the Poor* (2001), p. 114, citing Sarah

Amason,A.C. 1996. Distinguishing the effect of functional and dysfunctional conflict on strategic decision making: resolving a paradox for top management teams. Academy of Management Journal. 39:123-148.

Anderson and John Cavanagh, "Top 200: The rise of corporate global power", Institute for Policy Studies, Washington, 2000, p. 1.

Barnevik, P. and Taylor, W. 1991, The logic of global business, *Harvard Business Review*, March/April, pp.91-105.

Barna, L. 2000 Stumbling Blocks in intercultural communication. *International Communication a Reader*. R. Porter. Belmont CA, Wadsworth.

Barner-Rasmussen, W. and Bjorkman, I. 2005. Surmounting interunit barriers: factors associated with interunit communication intensity in the multinational corporation, *International Studies of Management and Organization*, Vol. 35 No.1. pp. 28-46.

Bartlett, C. and Ghoshal, S. 1990. the Multinational Corporation as an Interorganizational Network. *Academy of Management Review*, Vol. 15, No.4, pp.603-625.

Bass, B.M. 1965 Organizational Psychology, Boston, MA:Allyn & Bacon.

Bi, Jiewan. 1999. Nonverbal Communication, In A Dictionary of British and American Culture, ed. By Hu Wenzhong et al. Beijing: Foreign Language Teaching and Research Press.

Bordia, S.,& Bordia, P. 2015. Employee's willingness to adopt a foreign functional language in multinational organizations: the role of linguistic identity. *Journal of Internaitonal Business Studies* pp. 415-428.

Butollo,Florian. 2013. Moving beyond cheap labour? Industrial and social upgrading in the garment and LED industries of Pear River Delta. in: Journal of Current Chinese Affairs. 42.4. pp. 139-140.

Bhagat, R.S. and McQuaid, S.J. 1982 'Role of Subjective Culture in Organizations: A Review and Directions for Future Research', *Journal of Applied Psychology*, 67:653-85.

Bhagat,R.S.,and Prein,K.O.1996. Cross-cultural training in organizational context, in *Handbook of Human Intercultural Training* (vol. 2), eds. G.R. Ferris and K.M. Rowland, Greenwich, CT:JAI press.

Black B. 2005 Comparative industrial relations theory: the role of national culture, *International Journal of Human Resource Management*, Rutledge 16:7 1137-1158.

Black,J.S. and Mendenhall,M.E. 1990. Cross-cultural training effectiveness: a review and theoretical framework, *Academy of Management Review*, 15(1), pp. 113-136.

Black,J.S. and Gregersen,H.B. 1991. Antecedents to cross-cultural adjustment for expatriates in Pacific rim assignments. *Human Relations*, 44, pp. 497-515.

Bloom, A.H. 1986. *The linguistic shape of thought: a study of the impact of language on thinking in the west*. Hillsdale, New Jersey. Erlbaum.

Bolton, K.2002. Chinese Englishes: From Canton Jargon to Global English. *World Englishes* 21(2):181-199.

Braithwaite, V.A., & Law, H.G. 1985. Structure of human values: testing the adequacy of the Rokeach Value Survey, *Journal of Personality and Social Psychology*, 49, 250-263.

Braun, W. and Warner,M. 2002, Strategic Human Resource Management in Western Multinationals in China, *Strategic Human Resource Management*, Vol. 31 No.5, 2002, pp.553-579.

Brewer,P. & Venaik,S. 2012. On the misuse of national culture dimensions. *International Marketing Review,*29(6):673-683.

Bright William 1976. *Variation Change in Language*. Stanford University Press

Bridges, G. 2002. "Grounding Globalization: The Prospects and Perils of Linking Economic Processes of Globalization to Environmental Outcomes". *Economic Geography* 78 (3): 361–386.

Bond, M.H. 1981. *The psychology of the Chinese mind*, London: Oxford University Press.

Brown, P., and Levinson, C.S., 1978. *Politeness: some universals in language use*, London, CUP.

Buckley, P.J. Carter, M.J.Clegg, J. and Tan, H. 2005. Language and social knowledge in foreign knowledge transfer to China, *International Studies of Management and Organization,* Vol.35 No.1, pp. 47-64.

Buller,P.F.&Kohls,J.J.&Anderson,K.S. 2000. When ethnics collide: managing conflicts across culture, Organizational Dynamcs, 28(4):52-66.

Björkman, I. and Lu, Y.2001. Institutionalization and bargaining power explanations of HRM practices in international joint-ventures: the case of Chinese-western joint ventures, *Organization Studies*, 22:3,491-512.

Braveman, Hary. 1974. Labour and Monopoly Capital: the Degradation of Work in the Twentieth Century. New York: Monthly Review Press.

BjÖrkman,Ingmar et Fan, Xiucheng. 2002. Human resource management of Western firms in China, the International Journal of Human Resource Management, 13:6,853-864.

Blyton,P. and Turnball,P.1994. The Dynamics of Employee Relations. London: Macmillan.

*Contemporary Chinese Dictionary*, 2016. The Commercial Press.

Chang, Kai. 2005. Industrial Relations, *laodongguanxixue*, Press of China Labour Social Securities, *Zhongguo laodong shehui baozhang chubanshe*.

Chan, K. C.C. 2010. The Challenge of Labour in China: Strikes and the Changing Labour Regime in Global Factories. London: Routledge.

Chiang Flora, 2005. A critical examination of Hofstede's thesis and its application to international reward management, *International Journal of Human Resource Management*. 16:9, 1545-1563.

China Industry Data 2007 http://www.cncompany.cn/ accessed in May, 2008.

China Business Information. 2017. http://www.askci.com/news/data/2015/01/21/85126s6u5.shtml

Chatterjee, R. S., and Nankervis, R. A. 2007. Asian Management in Transition Emerging Themes, Palgrave, New York: Macmillan.

Child, J. 1981 'Culture, Contingency and Capitalism in the Cross-ntrional Study of Organization'. In Cummings, L.L. and Staw, B.M. (eds*) Research in Organization Behaviour,* Vol.3. Greenwich, CT:JAI Press, pp. 303-56.

Child, J. and Warner M. 2003, *Culture and Management in China,* University of Cambridge, the Judge Institute of Management.

Choi, Y. 2008. Aligning labour disputes with institutional, cultural and rational approach: evidence from East Asian-invested enterprises in China. *The International Journal of Human Resource Management*. Vol. 19 (10), pp. 1929-1961.

Chinese Culture Connection. 1987. Chinese Values and the search for culture free dimensions of culture. *Journal of Cross-Cultural Psychology,*18(2),143-164.

Clark et al, 1999 'Running on the spot? A review of twenty years of research on the management of human resources in comparative and international perspective', *International Journal of Human Resources Management*, 10:3 520-544.

Clarke S, et al. 2004 Collective Consultation and Industrial Relations in China, London, *British Journal of Industrial Relations*. Vol. 42, No. 2, pp. 235-254.

Cooke, F.L. 2002. Ownership change and reshaping of employment relations in China: a study of two manufacturing companies, *the Journal of Industrial Relations*, Vol. 44 No. 1, 19-39.

Cooney,S. Biddulph,S. & Zhu, Y. 2013. *Law and Fair Work in China*, Routledge, Abingdon.

Collings, D. G., & Wood, G. 2009. Human resource management: A critical approach. In

D. G. Collings & G. Wood (Eds.), Human resource management: A critical approach (pp. 1-16). London: Routledge.

Cooke, F.L. 2008. *Competition, Strategy and Management in China*, Palgrave Macmillan, New York.

Confucius, 2008, *Lun Yu, The Analects,* Hunan People's Press.

Cyr J. D. and Scheider S. 1996, Implication for Learning: Human Resource Management in East-West Joint Ventures, *Organization Studies*, 17/2 207-226.

Chang, Kai. 1988. Compendium of Trade Union Science, *LilunGonghuixueGailun.* Beijing: Economic Management Press.

Chang, Kai. 2005. Labour Relations Science (*laodong guanxi xue*) Press of China Labour Social Securities (*Zhongguo laodong guanxi baozhang chubanshe*).

Cheng, Yanyuan. 2002. Industrial Relations (*laodong guanxi*) Press of China People's University (*Zhongguo renmin daxue chubanshe*).

Caramani, Daniele. 2008. Comparative Politics. Oxford University Press. London

Child,J. 1994. *Management in China during the Age of Reform*, Cambridge University Press, Cambridge.

Clegg,H.1954. The System of Industrial Relations in Great Britain. Oxford: Basil Blackwell.

China Xinhua News Agency. http://finance.sina.com.cn/china/ 20130411/ 153215117440. shtml http://www.publications.parliament.uk/pa/ld200203/ldselect/ldeconaf /5/507.htm - n74

Darlington, G. 1996. Culture, a Theoretical Review. in: Joynt and Wasner (1996), pp.33-55.

De Cenzo,D.A. & Robbins,S.P. 2001. Human Resource Management, 6th Ed., NY: John Wiley and Sons,INc.

De Vaus, D. 2002. *Surveys in Social Research*. 5th Eds. London. Routledge.

Deutsch, M. 1949. A theory of cooperation and competition. Human relations. 2:129-151.

Deutsch, M. 1990. Sixty years of conflict. International Journal of Conflict Management. 1:237-263.

Ding, Z.D.et al. 2002. The impact of economic reform on the role of trade unions in Chinese enterprises, *International Journal of Human Resources Management*, Vol. 13:3 431-449.

Ding,Z.D. et al. 2001. A new form of Chinese human resource management: Personnel and labour-management relations in Chinese township and village enterprises: a case study approach, *Industrial Relations Journal*, 32:4.

Dickens, P., 2007. *Global Shift*, 5th Eds, Sage, London.

Dunlop, John. 1958. Industrial Relations Systems. New York: Entry Holt.

Drucker, F. P. 2006, the practices of management, Collins Business, Reissue.

Earl of Cromer, 2006. Political and Literary Essays, Read Books.London

Earley, P.C. and Mosakowski, E. 2004. Cultural intelligence, *Harvard Business Review*, October, pp. 139-146.

Economist. 2011. Multinational companies and China: what future. the Economist Intelligence Unite Limited 2011.

Edwards, P. 1995.The Employment Relationship. In P.Edwards (eds), Industrial Relations: Theory & Practice in Britain. London: Blackwell,pp.3-26.

Ethington, P. 1996.Toward Some Borderlands Schools for American Urban Ethnic Studies? American Quarterly 48:348.

Fang T. 2003.A critique of Hofstede's fifth national culture dimension, International *Journal of Cross Cultural Management*, Vol 3(3): 347-368.

Fairbank, J.K. 1987. *The Great Chinese Revolution 1800-1985*. London: Chatto and Windus.

Fei Xiaotong 2008. *Xiang Tu Zhong Guo*, (China's Countryside), Beijing, People's Press.

Feely , A. 2003. Communication across language boundaries. *Theory and Practice in International Management*. M. Tayeb. Harlow, Pearson Education Limited.

Feely,A.J. and Harzing, A.W. 2003. Language Management in Multinational Companies, *Cross Cultural Management*, Vol.10 (2), pp. 37-52.

Feely, F. A., 2004. the Impact of the Language Barrier on the Management of Multinational Companies. British Library. London.

Feng, You-lan. 1997. a Short History of Chinese Philosophy. the Free Press. USA

Fan,X. Che., Ingmar, Bjorkman. 2003. Human recourse management and the performance of foreign invested enterprises in China, *Journal of Management Sciences in China*. Vol.6 No. 2, 54 – 59.

Frazier W.M., 2006. *The Making of the Chinese Industrial Workplace*, Cambridge University Press, Cambridge.

Flanders,A.1965. Industrial Relations: What is Wrong with the System? An Essay on its Theory and Future. London: Faber and Faber.

Fan, gang, ed. 1994, Toward Market (1978-1993: an Analysis of the Economy of China, *Zhouxiangshichang (1978-1993):zhongguojingjifenxi.* Shanghai People's Press:Shanghai

Feton-O'Creevy,M., Gooderham,P. & Nordhaug,O. 2007. 'HRM in US Subsidiaries in Europe and Australia', Journal of International Business Studies.

Financial Times, 2011 ( *http://www.ftchinese.com/story/001037460/ce)*

Flanders,A., 1965. Industrial Relations- What's Wrong with the System, London, Faber.

Fleming, Robin. 2004. Kings and lords in Conquest England. Vol. 15. Cambridge University Press.

Fox, Alan. 1975. Collective Bargaining, Flanders, and the Webbs. *British Journal of Industrial relations,* Vol. 13; 151-174.

Giles, H. and Johnson, P. 1981. The role of language in ethnic group relations, in Turner, J.C.and Giles, H. (eds), *Intergroup Behaviour*, Blackwell, Oxford, pp. 99-243.

Goodall, K. & Warner, M. 1997. Human resources in Sino-foreign joint-venture: selected case studies in Shanghai, compared with Beijing, *the International Journal of Human Resources Management,* 8:5 pp.569-594.

Godden, Malcolm. 1994 "Apocalypse and Invasion in Late Anglo-Saxon England," in From Anglo-Saxon to Early Middle English: Studies Presented to E. G. Stanley, ed. Malcolm Godden, Douglas Gray, and Terry Hoad. Oxford: Clarendon Press.

Gamble.J., 2000. Localizing management in foreign-invested enterprises in China: practical, cultural, and strategic perspective. *International Journal of Human Resource Management.* Vol. 11(5), pp. 883-903.

GLOBE 1996. *The development of cross-cultural validation of scales measuring societal culture, organizational culture, and prototypical leader attributes.* Wharton School, PA, in review.

Gao Ai-di, et al. 2008, A History of China Labour Movement,Zhongguo gong renyun dong shi, Press of China Labour and Social Security, Beijing

Gerring, John.2007. Case study research: principles and practices. Cambridge, UK: Cambridge University Press.

Global Economics, 2012. China: For many expats. It's not worth it.

Godard,J. and Delaney,J.2000. Reflection on the High Performance Paradigm's Implications for Industrial Relations as a Field.*Industrial and Labour Relations Review*, 53:482-502.

Godden, Malcolm. 1994. "Apocalypse and invasion in late Anglo-Saxon England." In From Anglo-Saxon to Early Middle English: Studies Presented to EG Stanley, pp. 130-62. Oxford: Clarendon Press.

Greer, Jed. And Singh, Kavaljit. 2000. A Brief History of Transnational Corporations. Global Policy Forum. (http://www.globalpolicy.org/component/content/article/221-transnational-corporations/47068.html)

Grice P. 1989. *Studies in the Way of Words*, Harvard, London.

Guest,D.1990. Human Resource Management and the American Dream.The Journal of Management Studies. 27(4):377-98.

Guest, David. 1987. Human Resource Management and Industrial Relations, *Journal of Management Studies*. 24:5,503 – 521.

Gunderson, Morley, 1995, Union Management in Canada, 3rd Ed, Addison-Wesley Publish Limited.

Gupta,V.et Hanges,P.J. 2004. 'Regional and climate clustering of societal cultures', in R.J.House, P.J.Hanges,M.Javidan, P.W. Dorfman and V.Gupta (Eds) Culture, Leadership and Organizations: the GLOBE study of 62 societies, 178-218. Thousand Oaks,VA:Sage.

Harrod, J.W. 2000. Multinational Corporations. Global Transformations and World Future: Knowledge, Economy, and Society. Vol.1.

Harari,Y.N. 2014. Sapiens: a Brief History of Humankind,Vintage Books, London

Harzing A. and Feely A. 2008. the Language Barrier and its Implications for HQ-subsidiary Relationships, *International Journal of Cross Culture Management*, Vol. 15 No.1 pp. 49-61.

Harzing A, 2001, an Analysis of Functions of International Transfer of Managers in MNCs, *Employee Relations*, Vol. 23, No.6 pp. 581-598.

Harzing, A.W., Koster, K., & Magner, U. 2011. Babel in business: the language barrier and its solution in the HQ-subsidiary relationship. *Jorunal of World business* 279-287.

Harzing, A.W.,& P M. 2013. Language competencies, policies and practices in multinational corporations: a comprehensive review and comparision of Anglophone, Asian, Continental European and Nordic MNCs. *Journal of World Business* 87-97.

Hall T. Edward. 1976. *Beyond Culture*, Garden City, Doubleday, New York.

Hall T. Edward. 1969. *The Hidden Dimension*, Doubleday, New York.

Hall T. Edward. 1959. *The Silent Language*, Doubleday, New York.

Hall, E. and Hall, M. 1990. Understanding Cultural Differences, Boston, MA., London: Intercultural Press.

Hall, P. & Soskice,D. 2001. Varieties of Capitalism, Oxford University Press, Oxford.

Henderson, J.K. 2005. Language diversity in international management teams, *International Studies of Management and Organization*, Vol.35 No.1. pp.75-127.

Hei, qiming. 2004, Scientific definition of ten essential categories in the research of industrial relations, *laodong guanxi yanjiu shida jiben fanchou de kexue jieding*, Theory and Modernization, *lilun yu xiandaihua.*

Hill B. and Ide S., et al. 1986. Universal of linguistics politeness: Quantitative evidence from Japanese and American English. *Journal of Pragmatics*, 10, pp. 347-371.

Higham, Nicholas,et. Martin J. Ryan. 2013.The Anglo-Saxon World. Yale University Press,

Hills, S.1995.Employment Relations and the Social Sciences. Columbia, SC: University of South Carolina Press.

H, G. 1991. Culture Tales: a Narrative Approach to Thinking, Cross-cultural Psychology and Psychotherapy. *American Psychologist*, 46, 187-197.

Hofstede, G. *Culture's Consequences: International Differences in Work-Related Values,* Beverly Hill, CA, 1980.

Hofstede, G. & Bond, M.H. 1988. The Confucius connection: From cultural roots to economic growth. *Organizational Dynamics*, 16(4):4-21.

Hofstede, G. & Minkov, M.2010. Cultures and organizations: Software of the mind (3rd ed.) New York: McGraw-Hill

Holden, Nigel. 2002. Cross-cultural Management: a Knowledge Management Approach. Harlow: Prentice Hall - Financial Times.

Holden, N. 1987. The Treatment of Language and Linguistic Issues in the Current English language Management Literature, *Multilingua*, Vol. 6 No.3 pp. 233-46.

Holden, J. Nigel, 2002. Cross-cultural Management: a Knowledge Management Perspective. Prentice Hall. London.

Holden R. 2001. Managing people's values and perceptions in multi-cultural organizations: the experience of an HR director. *Journal of Employee Relations*. Vol.23 No.6 614-626.

Holton RH (1990) Human Resource Management in the People's Republic of China, *Management International Review* 30: 121-136.

House, R.J. 1993. *GLOBE prospectus,* internal publication. Philadephia: Wharton School of Management.

House,R.J., Hanges. P., & Agar, M. 1995. *GLOBE prospectus* (updated). Internal publication, Philadelphia: Wharton School of Management.

Huang H.T., and Zhao J.J., 2007. *Economic Globalization and Reconstruction of Industrial Relations in China,* Social Sciences Academic Press (China), Beijing.

Hui, E.S. & Chan, C. K. 2015. Beyond the Union-centred approcah: a critical evaluation of recent trade union elections in China. British Journal of Industrial Relations. 53:3, pp.601-627.

Hu, Wenzhong, 1993. A Cross-culture Research in Foreign Language teaching, shi lun wai yu jiao xue zhong de kua wen hua yan jiu, *Journal of Foreign Language and Teaching*, Beijing,

Hu.X. B. et Xi, J. 2013. Towards a more appropriate university English curriculum in China in the context of English as an international language. *Changing English.* 20(4)388-394

Huntingtong, S.P. 1996. The Clash of Civilizations and the Remaking of World Order, Simon & Schuster, New York. NY.

Hymes, H.Dell, 1971. Competence and performance in linguistic theory. In *Language Acquisition: Models and Methods*, (Eds) Huxley,H. and Ingram,E. New York: Academic Press, pp. 3-28.

Hyman,R. 1975. Industrial Relations: A Marxist Introduction. London: Macmillan.

Jabbour, C.J.C. 2013. Environment training in organizations: From a literature review to a framework for future research. Resources, Conservation and Recycling, 74, 144-155. doi:10.1016/j.resconrec.2012.12.017.

Janssens,M. J.,Lambert, and C. Steyaert. 2004. Developing language strategies for international companies: the contribution of translation studies. *Journal of World Business.* 39 pp.414-43.

Jonges, R.A., et al. 1978. System of values and their multidimensional representations, *Multivariate Behavioural Research*, 13, 255-270.

Jiang, Kaiven. 1996. The Conflicts between trade union and the Party-state: the reform of Chinese trade unions in the 1980s. *Gonghuiyu dang-guojia de chongtu: bashiniandaiyilai de zhongguogonghuigaige.*Hong Kong Journal of Social Sciences. 8:121-58.

*John Donne, 1624. Devotions upon Emergent Occasions: Together With Death's Duel.*
*Createspace Independent Publishing Platform. London*

Kaufman E.B., 2008. Paradigms in industrial relations: original, modern and versions in-between, *British journal of Industrial Relations*. 46:2, pp. 314-339.

Kay, P. and W. Kempton, 1984. What is the Sapir-Whorf Hypothesis? *American Anthropologist* 86(1): 65-79.

Kealey,D.J. and Protheroe, D.R. 1996. The effectiveness of cross-cultural training for expatriates: an assessment of the literature on the issue, *International Journal of Intercultural Relations*, vol. 20 (2), pp 141-165.

Keynes, Simon. 2001 "Mercia and Wessex in the ninth century." Mercia. An Anglo-Saxon Kingdom in Europe, ed. Michelle P. Brown/Carol Ann Farr. p310-328. London

Kim Uichol. et al. 1994. *Individualism and Collectivism: Theory, method, and applications,* London, Sage Publications.

Klerck, G. 2009. "Industrial relations and human resource management". In D. G. Collings & G. Wood (Eds.), Human resource management: A critical approach (pp. 238-259). London: Routledge.

Kim, M.S. 1994. Cross-cultural comparison of the perceived importance of interactive constraints. *Human Communication Research*, 21, pp. 128-51.

Kluckhohn, C. 1951. Values and Value-orientations in the theory of action: an exploration in definition and classification. In T. Parsons & E. Shils (Eds.), *Toward a general theory of action.* Cambridge, MA: Harvard University Press.

Kochan, Thomas A. & Katz, C. H, & McKersie, R. B. 1986. The Transformation of American Industrial Relations. Basic Books, Inc. Publishers, New York

Kogut,B. and Zander,U. 1992. Knowledge of the firm, combinative capabilities, and the replicational technology. *Organization Science.* 3(3). pp. 383-397.

KPMG.2012. the Future of MNCs in China: a KPMG Study, Swiss. www.kpmg.com.cn

Krugman. P. at el. 2008. *International Economics: Theory and Policy.* 8th eds. Pearson Education.

Ke, Huangrui, 1988. Labour Law and Regulations in Economic Zone, *jingjitequlaodongfaluzhidu,* Journal of Ganshu Institute of Political Science and Law, Vol. 2, 1988.

Kaufman,B,2004. The Evolution of Industrial Relations: Events, Ideas and the ILRA. Geneva: International Labour Organization.

Kaufman, B, 2008. Paradigms in Industrial Relations: Original, Modern and Versions In-between. British Journal of Industrial Relationship.46:2 June. pp. 314-339.

Kuang, Kuang. 1984. Working Class in China. *ZhongguoGongrenJieji*. Changchun: Jinlin People's Press.

Katz,H.1988. Collective Bargaining and Industrial Relations, 2$^{nd}$ ed. Homewood, IL: Irwin.

Kelly,G.1955. The Psychology of Personal Constructs (Vols.1 &2), New York: Norton.

Knight, J. & De Wit, H. 1997. Internationalization of higher education in Asia Pacific countries. Amsterdam, Netherlands: European association for International Education.

Kochan, T. 2000.On the Paradigm Guiding Industrial Relations Theory and Research: Comment on John Godard and John T. Delaney, "Reflections on the High Performance Paradigm's Implications for Industrial Relations as a Field". Industrial and Labour Relations Review, 53(4):704-11.

Kuipers, G.M.M. 2013. "The rise and decline of national habitus: Dutch cycling culture and the shaping of national similarity", *European Journal of Social Theory,* Vol.16 No.1, pp.17-35.

Larson, D. et Smalley, W. 1972, Becoming Bilingual: A Guide to Language Learning, University Press of America.

Lachman, R., Nedd, A. and Hinings, B. 1994 Analyzing Cross-national Management and Organizatyion: A Theoretical Framework', *Management Science*, 40:40-55.

Laurent Andre, 1981. Matrix Organizations and Latin cultures: a note on the use of comparative-research data in management education, *International studies of management & organization,* Vol. X, No. 4, pp. 101-114.

Laurent Andre, 1983. The Cultural diversity of western conceptions of management, *International studies of management & organization*, Vol. XIII, No. 1-2, pp. 75-96.

Leech. G. 1983. *Principles of Pragmatics*, Longman, New York.

Lee.Hyo-Soo, 1996. Theory construction in industrial relations: A synthesis of PDR systems, The Korean Review, New Series, (12): 199-218.

Liang, Shuminh. 2011. *zhongguowenhuayaolue, the Outline of Chinese Culture,* Shanghai People's Press

Liang, Qichao. 2016. *kongziyurujiazhexue, Confucius and the Confucius Phlosophy,* Zhonghua Book Company.

Lincoln R.J and Kerbo. R. H et al, 1995, Japanese Companies in Germany: A Case Study in Cross-Cultural Management, *Industrial Relations*, Vol. 34, No.3

Lockett, M. 1988. *Culture and the problem of Chinese management.* Organization Studies, 9:475-96.

Longman. 1992. Longman Dictionary of English Language and culture, Longman Group UK Limited.

Lovelave,K.,Shapiro,D.L. & weingart,L.R. 2001. Maximizing crossfunctional new product teams' innovativeness and constraint adherence: A conflict communications perspective. The Academy of Management Journal, 44(4):479-493.

Luo,Y. and Chenkar,O.2006. The multinational corporation as a multilingual community: language and organization in a global context, *Journal of International Business Studies,* Vol.37 No.3, pp.321-40.

LIU, Yufang. 2001. On the Changes Occurred Within the Structure of Working Class. *Qia ntangongrenjiejiduiwuneibujiegoubianhua.*Workers' Daliy. 26 December 2001:(3).

Liu Mingkui, 1985. Historical Situation of China Working Class,*ZhongGuo Gong Ren JieJi Li SHi Zhuang Kuang*, China Communist History Press, Beijing.

Li, Zongfu, 2012. Review Deng's Conversation in South of China, Firmly Develop the Opening Reform Policies, *ChongwenDengxiaopingNanfangTanhua, JiandingBuyiTuijin Gaige Kaifang*, Qunyan, Vol.2, 2012.

Lu,Xiaobo. 1997. Minor Public Economy: the Revolutionary Origins of the *Danwei. In Xiaobo Lu and Elizabeth J. Perry (Eds).Danwei: the Changing Chinese Workplace in Historical and Comparative Perspective.*Armonk:M.E.Sharpe.

Li,S. and Nesbit,P . 2013. An exploration of the HRM values of Chinese managers working in Western multinational enterprises in China: implications for HR practice. The International Journal of Human Resource Management.25:11,1529-1546.

Liu, Chongxiao.2010.Working language situation and strategy in the context of globalized MNCs. *Quanqiuhuabeijingxiakuaguo gong si gong zuoyuyanzhuangkuangji dui ce.*Journal of Jianghan University. Vol. 29, No.6, 77-80.

Luo, Xiuyun.2011. *Second largest poor group in China: the Lay-off Workers.*http:// www.360doc.com/content/11/0306/11/5177773_98574464.shtml

Magala, S.J. 2005, Cross-cultural Competence, Routledge, Abingdon and New Tork, NY.

Marschan-Piekkari, R., et al. 1997. Language: the forgotten factor in multinational management. *European Management Journal.* Vol. 15 (5), pp.591-598.

Marschan Rebecca, Welch D. and L., 1996 Control in Less-hierarchical Multinationals:

the Role of Personal Networks and Informal Communication, *International Business Review*. Vol.5. No.2. pp.137-150.

Markus,H.R. & Kitayama, S. 1991. Culture and the self: implications for cognition, emotion, and motivation. *Psychological Review.* 98, pp. 224-253.

Markit, 2015, retrieved from https://www.markiteconomics.com/Survey/PressRelease.mv c/19b9a30401ff4330bf91d11ad2b92019

McSweeney,B. 2002. Hofstede's model of national cultural differences and their consequences: A triumph of faith – a failure of analysis. *Human Relations.* Vol.55 (1) pp 89-118.

McSweeney, B. 2015. "GLOBE, Hall, Hofstede, Huntington, Trompenaars: common foundations common flaws", in Sanchez, Y. and Bruhwiler, C.F. (Eds), Transculturalism and Business in the BRIC State: A Handbook, Aldershot Gower, Farnham, pp. 13-58.

McSweeney, B. 2016. Collective cultural mind programming: escaping from the cage, *Journal of Organizational Change Management,* Vol. 29, No.1.

Merkle, Judith A. 2010.Management and Ideology. University of California Press.

Meltz, N.M. 1993 'Industrial Relations Systems as a Framework for Organizing Contributions to Industrial Relations Theory'. In Adams, R. and Meltz, N.(eds) *Industrial Relations Theory*, Metuchan, NJ: Institute of Management and Labour Relations Press.

Mencius, 2016. *the works of Mencius*, Zhongzhou Ancient Books Publishing House. Zhengzhou

Minkov,M.& Hofstede, G. 2011. The evolution of Hofstede's doctrine, *Cross Cultural Management: An International Journal,* Vol.18 No.1. pp.10-20.

Minkov,M.& Hofstede, G. 2012. Hofstede's fifth dimension: New evidence from the World Values Survey. Journal of Cross Cultural Psychology, 43, 3-14.

Ministry of Commerce People's Republic of China, 2016, retrieved from http://www.saic. gov.cn/zwgk/tjzl/zhtj/xxzx/201604/t20160421_168124.html

Morrison, A.J. 2000. Developing a global leadership model. *Human Resources Management Journal*, 39, 2&3, 117-131.

MOE, 2017, China Ministry of Education,   http://www.moe.edu.cn/jyb_xwfb/ s5147/201703/t20170302_297870.html

McGraw,P. 2004. 'Influence on HRM Practices in MNCs: a Qualitative Study in the

Australia Context', International Journal of Manpower 25.6.

Ming, Jie. 2012.TradeUion has the Power, *Gonghui You Liliang*, China Newsweek, Vol. 566. June. 2012

Milsom, S.F.C.1981.Historical Foundations of the Common Law. 2nd ed.. London.

Mursell, Gordon. 1997. The Wisdom of the Anglo-Saxon. Oxford: Lion Publishing.

Manzella,Pietro. 2012. Analyzing corporate discourse in globalized markets: the case of FIAT. Lap Lambert Academic Publishing GmbH &Co.KG

MOE official website. 2014. www.crs.jsj.edu.cn/index.php/default/index/sort/1006

NBSC, 2016. Natioanl Bureau of Statistics of China, http://www.stats.gov.cn/tjsj/ndsj/2016/indexch.htm

NBSC, 2003. National Bureau of Statistic of China, http://www.stats.gov.cn/ accessed in June, 2009

Negandhi, A.R. 1974 'Cross-cultural Management Studies: Too Many Conclusions Not Enough Conceptualization', *Management International Review*, 14:59-72.

Naughton, B. 1997, '*Danwei: The Changing Chinese Workplace in Historical and Comparative Perspective*, London: M.E. Sharpe.

National Bureau of Statistics of China, 2003, Report of China Statistics, *Zhongguo tong jizaiyao*, Press of China Statistics,: Beijing

Oberg, K. 1960. 'Cultural shock, adjustment to new cultural environments. Practical Anthropology, 177-182.

Oliver, N. & Wilkinson, B. 1988. The Japanization of British Industry, Oxford: Basil Blackwell.

O'Leary, G, 1998. 'The making of the Chinese working class' in O'Leary, G. (ed) *Adjusting to Capitalism*, London: M.E. Sharpe.

O'Neill. Jim. 2001. *Building Better Global Economic BRICs*, Global Economics. Paper No: 66. Goldman Sachs.

Patel,Taran. 2014. Cross-cultural Management: a Transactional Approach, Routledge, London and New York.

Park Hoon, et al., 1996 sources and Consequences of Communication Problems in Foreign Subsidiaries: the Case of United States Firms in South Korea, *International Business Review* Vol.5, No. 1. pp 79-98.

Phoenix News, 2011, http://fo.ifeng.com/news/detail_2011_08/25/8671934_0.shtml

Piekkari,.R., 2005. Preface: language and communication in international management.

*International Studies of Management & Organization.* Vol.35(1) pp.3-9.

Poole, M. 1986 *Industrial Relations: Origins and Patterns of National Diversity.* London Routledge & Kegan Paul.

Poole,M. 1993 Industrial Relations: Theorizing for a Global Perspective'. In Adams, R. and Meltze, N. (eds) *Industrial Relations Theory*, Metuchan, NJ: Institute of Management and Labor Relations Press.

Porter M. 1998. *the Competitive Advantage of Nations*, Macmillan.

Puck, F.J., et al. 2008. Does it really work: Re-assessing the impact of pre-departure cross-cultural training on expatriate adjustment, *International Journal of Human Resources Management,* Vol.19(12) pp.2182-2197.

Putnam,L.L. & Wilson, S. R. 1982. Communicative strategies in organizational conflict: Reliability and validity of management scale. Baverly Hills, California: Sage.

Piore, Michael J. & Charles F. Sabel. 1984. The Second Industrial Divide. New York : Basic Books, 182.

Patel, Taran. 2014. Cross-Cultural Management: a Transactional Approach. Routledge. London

People'sTribune.2014.http://paper.people.com.cn/rmlt/html/2014-09/01/content_1476503.htm

Pruitt, D. 1981.Negotiation Behaviour. NY: Academic Press,

Qin, Liuqing, 1995. Improving the Strengthens of State-owned Enterprises by Properly Managing the in-depth Conflicts, *Chuli hao guoyouqiye shengcengci de maodun, zengqiang guoyouqiye huoli*, Lingnan Journal, Canton

Reeves, N., and C. Wright. 1996. *Linguistic Auditing: A Guide to Identifying Foreign Language Needs in Corporations.* Clevedon, UK: Multilingual Matters.

Redpath, L. and Nielsen, M.O. 1997 A Comparison of Native Culture, Non-native Culture and New Management Ideology, *Canadian Journal of Administrative Science* 14(3):327-39.

Redding, S.G. 1994, 'Comparative Management Theory: Jungle, Zoo or Fossil Bed?', *Organization Studies*, 15:323-59.

Renwick, D.., Redman, T. & Maguire, S. 2013. Green human resource management: A review and research agenda. International Journal of Management Reviews, 15(1), 1-14.

Ritzer, G. 2011, The McDonaldization of Society, 6th ed. Pine Forge Press, Thousand

Oaks, CA, London and New Delhi.

Robock, S.H. & Simmonds, K. 1989. *International Business and Multinational Enterprises.* Homewood,IL:Irwin.

Robert Murphy. *Culture and Social Anthropology: An Overture.* 2nd ed. Englewood Cliffs, NJ: Prentice Hall, 1986: 14

Robert, K.H. 1970 'On Looking at an Elephant: An Evolution of Cross-cultural Research Related to Organizations', *Psychological Bulletin,* 74:327-50.

Robinson, Gail. 1985, Computer-assisted-instruction in foreign language education: a comparison of the effectiveness of different mythologies and different forms of error correction. U.S. Department of Education, National Institute of Educational Resources Information Centre (ERIC), Mills College, Oakland, CA. 94613.USA

Rogers .E; et al. 2002. Edward T. Hall and the history of Intercultural Communication: the United States and Japan, *Keio Communication Review* No. 24

Rogers Priscilla & Tan Joo-Seng, 2008. *Fifty Years of Intercultural Study: a Continuum of Perspectives for Research and Teaching,* Ross School of Business Working Paper Series, University of Michigan.

Ruan, Chongwu. 1996. Speech at the national conference of directors of labour bureaus, (*Zaiquanguolaodongtijuzhanghuiyi de jianghua*), 15 December 1992, In Jianxin Wan (ed). China Labour Yearbook:1992-1994. China Labour Press: Beijing

Regulations of PRC on Chinese-Foreign Cooperation in Running Schools. 2003, http://www.crs.jsj.edu.cn/index.php/default/news/index/3

SanAntonio, P.M. 1988, Social mobility and language use in an American company in Japan, in Gudykunst, W.B. (ed), *Language and Ethnic Identity, Multilingual Matters,* Clevedon.

Sandver. M. H. 1987. Labour Relations: Process and Outcomes. Boston: Little, Brown and Company, 26-34.

Sapir, E. 1929: 'The Status of Linguistics as a Science'. In E. Sapir (1958), *Culture, Language and Personality* (ed. D. G. Mandelbaum). Berkeley, CA: University of California Press.

Salamon M.. 2000. *Industrial Relations: theory and practice,* 4th eds. Prentice Hall, FT, London.

Schwartz, H.S. & Bilshy W. 1987. Toward a universal psychological structure of human values, *Journal of Personality and Social Psychology.* Vol. 53. No.3. pp. 550-562.

Schneider C.S. & Barsoux J.L. 2003. *Managing Across Cultures*, (2nd Ed), Prentice Hall, London.

Schneider, S.C. 1988. National vs. corporate culture: implications for HRM. Human Resource Management. 27(2): 231-246.

Shay, Scott . 2008. The history of English: a linguistic introduction. Wardja Press. p. 86.

Subramanian, et al., 2016. Green competence framework: evidence from China. the International Journal of Human Resources Management. Vol. 27, No.2, 151 - 172.

Sung, C.C. Mathew. 2013. Learning English as an L2 in the Global Context: Changing English, Changing Motivation. *Changing English*. Vol.29. No.4, 377-387. Routledge

Schein, E. 2004. *Organizational culture and leadership*, (3rd ed) San Francisco: Jossey-Bass

Schramm,W. 1971. Notes on case studies of instructional media projects. Working paper for academy for Educational Development, Washington D.C., cited in Yin,K. 2003. *Case Study Research*. 3$^{rd}$ Eds. London. Sage

Sekaran, U. 1983 'Methodological and Theoretical Issues and Advancements in Cross-cultural Research', *Journal of International Business Studies*, 14:61-73.

Scollon,R. & Wong Scollon,S. 1995. *Intercultural communication: a discourse approach*, Cambridge: Blackwell.

Shaffer ,M.A., Harrison, D., & Gillery, K. 1999.Dimensions, determinants, and differences in the expatriate adjustment process. *Journal of International Business Studies*. 30, 557 - 581.

Shenkar, O. & Ronen,S. 1987. the cultural context of negotiations: the implications of Chinese interpersonal norms. *The Journal of Applied Behavioural Science*, 23: 263-75

Singh,A.,& Vlatas,D.A. 1991. Using conflict management for better decision making. Journal of Management in Engineering, 7(1):70-82.

Smircich, Linda, 1983. Concepts of Culture and Organizational Analysis. *Administrative Science Quarterly,* Sep83, Vol. 28 Issue 3, p339-358, 20p.

Smithson,M. and Verkuilen, J. 2006. *Fuzzy Set Theory: Applications in the Social Sciences*. London, Sage

Sondergaard, M. 2001 Book Review. Geert Hofstede, Culture's Consquences: Comparing Values, Behaviors, and Organizations across Nations', International *Journal of Cross Culture Management* 1(2):243-6.

Salamon, M. 2000. 4th Ed. Industrial Relations: Theory and Practice. Prentice Hall,

London.

Seawright, J. etGerring,J. 2008. Case selection techniques in case study research: a menu of qualitative and quantitative options, *Political Research Quarterly*. Vol.6 No.2, 294-308.

Sil, Rudra.1997. The Russian 'Village in the City' and the Stalinist System of Enterprise Management: the Origins of Worker Alienation in Soviet State System. In Xiaobo Lu and Elizabeth J. Perry (Eds).*Danwei: the Changing Chinese Workplace in Historical and Comparative Perspective*. Armonk: M. E. Sharpe.

Shenkar, O. &Ronen,S. 1987. the cultural context of negotiations: the implications of Chinese interpersonal norms. The journal of applied behavioural science, 23: 263-75.

S.J. Wood, A. Wagner, E.G.A.Armstrong, J.F.B. Goodman and J.E.Davis, The industrial relations system concept as a basis for theory in industrial relations, British Journal of Industrial Relations, vol. 13, 1975.

Strauss. G.2001. HRM in the USA: Correcting Some British Impressions. International Journal of Human Resource Management. 12(6):873-97.

Tabb, W K. 2007. *"Globalization."* Microsoft® Student [DVD]. Redmond, WA: Microsoft Corporation.

Tan, B.C., & Lau, T.C. 2010. Attitude towards the environment and green products: Consumers' perspective. Management Science and Engineering, 4, 27-39.

Taylor, B. 2001. The management of labour in Japanese manufacturing plants in China. *International Journal of Human Resources Management*, 12(4) 601-620.

Tajfel, H. 1978. Social categorization, social identity, and social comparison, in

Tajfel, H. 1982. *Social Identity and Intergroup Relations*. Cambridge, Cambridge University Press

Tayeb, M.H. 1994 Organizations and National Culture: Methodology Considered, *Organization Studies* 15:429-46.

The World Bank, 2014, retrieved from http://data.worldbank.org/indicator/BX.KLT. DINV.CD.WD

Tenzer,H.,Pudelko,M., & Harzing, A.W., 2013. The impact of language barriers on trust formation in multinational teams. *Journal of International Business Studies* 508-535

Ting-Toomey, S. 1988. *Intercultural Conflicts styles: A face negotiation theory. Theories in Intercultural Communication*. W.B. Gudykunst. Newbury Park CA Sage.

Tjosvold,D. 1988. Cooperative and competitive interdependence: Collaboration between department to serve customers. Group and Organization Studies. 13(3):274-289.

Tjosvold, D., Law,K.S. & Sun,H. 2006. Effectiveness of Chinese teams: the role of conflict types and conflict management approaches. Management and organization review, 2(2):231-252.

Touburg, G. 2016. National habitus: an antidote to the resilience of Hofstede's "national culture"? Journal of Organizational Change Management, Vol.29 No. 1 pp.81-92.

Triandis C.H. et al. 1990 Multi-method Probes of Individualism and Collectivism, *Journal of Personality and Social Psychology*, Vol. 59. No.5 1006-1020.

Triandis C.H. 1995. *Individualism and collectivism*. Boulder, Co: Westview Press.

Trompenaars. F. and Hampden Turner, C. 1997. *Riding the Waves of Culture: Understanding Cultural Diversity in Business.* 2(Eds). London. Nicholas Brealey.

Trompenaars. F et al. 2004. *Managing People Across Cultures.* England Capstone.

Taylor, W.K.Bill, Kai. Chang, et al. 2003. Industrial Relations in China, Edward Elgar Publishing, Inc. USA

Tyler,E.B. 1871. Primitive Culture. Quoted in: Encyclopaedia Britannica (2000)

Tang, Shurong, Xi, Ongsheng. (eds) 1994. A Complete Works of Application of Labour Law. (*Laodongfashiwuquanshu*). China Workers Press: Beijing

UNCTAD. 1995. World Investment Report 1995. Transnational Corporations and Competitiveness. Geneva: United Nations.

Verburg, M. R., et al. 1999. Managing human resources across cultures: a comparative analysis of practise in industrial enterprises in China and the Netherlands. *The International Journal of Human Resources Management*. Vol. 10 (3), pp.391-410.

Weihrich,E.U. & Koontz,H., 1993. Management: A Global Perspective, 10th Edition,. McGraw-Hill.

Warner, M. 1993. Human Resource Management 'with Chinese Characteristics', *International Journal of Human Resources Management,* Vol. 4 (1),pp. 45-65.

Warner M, 1994, Japanese Culture, Western Management: Taylorism and Human Resource in Japan, *Organization Studies*, 14/4 509-533.

Warner, M. 2003. *The Future of Chinese Management,* Frank Cass, London.

Wang, Jing. 2008. Research on the cross-cultural management of Chinese transnational corporations. Hunan University of Industry. China

Wang, Yongxi. 1992. History of Chinese Trade Union, (*Zhongguogongyunshi*). Dangshi Publishing House: Beijing.

Wang, Yuqin. 2010 Positive Research on the Effects of Transactive Memory System on Team Effectiveness. Postgraduate paper from Didian University, China

Welch.D., Welch. L., Piekkari.,R., 2005. Speaking in tongues: the importance of language in international management processes. *International Studies of Management & Organization.* Vol.35(1).pp.10-27.

Whorf, B.L., 1940. Science and Linguistics, *Technology Review*, 42(2) 229-31, 247-8.

Whorf B. L. 1956. *Language Thought and Reality*. J. Carroll (Ed). Cambridge, MA MIT Press.

Wang, Lifeng and Zhu, Jinwei. 2013. A Survey on the Languages of Transnational Corporations in China. Applied Linguistics. No.1, P80 -88.

Wagner, Augusta. 1938, Labour Legislation in China. Peking, cited in Chen Guo-jun, 1960, Labour Legislation, *(lao gong li faxinlun)*, Zhengzhong Publishing House, Taipei.

Wen, Jiabao, 2010, Government Gazette, http://finance.ifeng.com/a/20100306/1895727_0.shtml

Wood, S.J., et al. 1975. 'The Industrial Relations System' Concept as a Basis for Theory in Industrial Relations, vol.13, p295

Wikipedia.2014. http://en.wikipedia.org/wiki/Developed_nation

Wikipedia.2014. http://en.wikipedia.org/wiki/Globalization

Wikipedia. 2011. Wukan Protests. http://en.wikipedia.org/wiki/Wukan_protests

Wikipedia.2017. https://en.wikipedia.org/wiki/Taoism

Wikipedia.2017. https://en.wikipedia.org/wiki/Anglo-Saxons#Culture

Whitley, R. 2001. 'How and Why are International Firms Different? The Consequences of Cross-border Managerial Coordination for Firm Characteristics and Behaviour' in Morgan, G. Kristensen, P.H. & Whitley, R. (Eds), the Multinational Firm: Organizing Across Institutional and National Divides, Oxford: Oxford University Press.

Wright, Patrick. 2011. The 2011 CHRO Challenge: Building Organizational, Functional, and Personal Talent". Cornell Centre for Advanced Human Resource Studies (CAHRS).

Xi,Jinping, 2014, Xi Jinping: the Governance of China, Foreign Language Press, Beijing

Xie, Fusheng. 2007 Capitalist Labour Process: the Transition from Fordism to Post-Fordism. *Journal of Remmin University of China.*No.2. Beijing

Xie, D.M. 2012. *Behavioural Experiment on Cross-cultural Decision-making Conflict Management by Communication between Chinese and Germen.* PhD Dissertation from Southwest Jiaotong University.

Xinhua News, 2013 *http://news.xinhuanet.com/fortune/2013-02/12/c_124343194.htm*

Xinhua News, 2012  http://news.xinhuanet.com/2012-05/25/c_112036687.htm

Yao,Shihua, 2007, *Study on HRM of Shenzhen Companies with FDI*, PhD dissertation, Xiamen University.

Yeb, R.S. and Lawrence, J.J. 1995 Individualism and Confucian Dynamism: A Note on Hofstede's Cultural Root to Economic Growth, *Journal of International Business Studies* 26(3):655-69.

Yin, K. R. 2003. *Case Study Research*. 3rd Eds. London, Sage.

Xu, L.2004. Intercultural communication in English. Shanghai Foreign Language Education Press. Shanghai.

Shen, Xu. 2013. The dictionary of words (*Shuo wen jie zhi*), Zhonghua Book Company. Beijing

Yeh, Wenshin. 1997. republican Origins of the *Danwei*: the Case of Shanghai's Bank of China.In Xiaobo Lu and Elizabeth J. Perry (Eds).*Danwei: the Changing Chinese Workplace in Historical and Comparative Perspective.* Armonk: M. E. Sharpe.

Zander L., 2005. Communication and country clusters: a study of language and leadership preferences. *International Studies of Management & Organization*. Vol.35(1) pp.83-103.

Zhang, L, E, & Peltokorpi, V, 2016. Multifaceted effects of host country language proficiency in expatriates cross-cultural adjustment: A qualitative study in China. *the International Journal of Human Resources Management*. Vol. 27, No. 13, 1449-1469.

Zhang, E.L., & Harzing, A.W. 2016. From dilemmatic struggle to legitimized indifference: expatriates' host country language learning and its impact on the expatriates - HCE relationship. Journal of World Business. 774-786.

# Appendix 1. Trompenaars and Hampden-Turner's seven cultural dimensions

| | |
|---|---|
| Universalism versus Particularism | Universalistic societies believe that laws are written for everyone and must be respected by everyone at all times. In particularistic societies, the nature of a particular relationship takes precedence over the details of the situation. Some researchers have claimed that this dimension is a potential source of conflict in cross-border partnerships since mutual trust can be difficult to establish between partners from universalistic and particularistic cultures (Adier 1997, Child and Faulkner 1998). |
| Individualism versus Communitarianism | This dimension is the same as Hofstede's individualism versus collectivism dimension and refers to the degree of an individual's orientation towards themselves rather than towards common goals and objectives (Child and Faulkner 1998). |
| Affective Versus Neutral | This dimension explains the degree to which a society allows its members to express their emotions. In a neutral culture, people control and subdue their feelings effectively, whereas, in affective cultures, people express their feelings openly. |
| Specific versus Diffuse | This dimension explains whether people engage others in specific areas of their life and personality or diffusely in multiple areas of their life and personality at the same time. |
| Achievement versus Ascription | In an achievement-oriented society, status is attributed to people based on their achievements; it reflects 'doing'. On the other hand, in an ascription-oriented society, status is ascribed based on age, class, education, gender, etc., and it reflects 'being'. |
| Sequential versus Synchronic perception of time | In a sequential culture, time is considered as a series of passing events. In contrast, according to the synchronic approach, the past, present and the future are interrelated. |
| Internal versus External locus of control | This last dimension addresses societal orientations towards nature. If society dictates that individuals can and should control nature by imposing their will upon it, then this reveals an internal locus of control. On the other hand, if society supports that individuals are part of nature and should follow its laws, directions and forces, then this indicates and external locus of control. |

*Source: Trompenaars and Hampden-Turner:1997*

# Appendix 2.
# The Chinese Value

1. 孝（服从父母，尊敬父母，尊崇祖先，赡养父母）Filial piety (Obedience to parents, respect for parents, honoring of ancestors, financial support of parents).

2. 勤劳 Industry (Working hard).

3. 容忍 Tolerance of others.

4. 随和 Harmony with others.

5. 谦虚 Humbleness.

6. 忠于上司 Loyalty to superiors.

7. 礼仪 Observation of rites and social rituals.

8. 礼尚往来 Reciprocation of greetings, favours, and gifts.

9. 仁爱（恕，人情）Kindness (Forgiveness, compassion).

10. 学识（教育）Knowledge (Education).

11. 团结 Solidarity with others.

12. 中庸之道 Moderation, following the middle way.

13. 修养 Self–cultivation

14. 尊卑有序 Ordering relationship by status and observing this order.

15. 正义感 Sense of righteousness.

16. 恩威并施 Benevolent authority.

17. 不重竞争 Non–competitiveness.

18. 稳重 Personal steadiness and stability.

19. 廉洁 Resistance to corruption.

20. 爱国 Patriotism.

21. 诚恳 Sincerity.

22. 清高 Keeping oneself disinterested and pure.

23. 俭 Thrift.

24. 耐力（毅力）Persistence (perseverance).

25. 耐心 Patience.

26. 报恩与报仇 Repayment of both the good or the evil that another person has caused you.

27. 文化优越感 A sense of cultural superiority.

28. 适应环境 Adaptability.

29. 小心（慎）Prudence (Carefulness).

30. 信用 Trustworthiness.

31. 知耻 Having a sense of shame.

32. 有礼貌 Courtesy.

33. 安分守己 Contentedness with one's position in life.

34. 保守 Being conservative.

35. 要面子 Protecting your "face".

36. 知己之交 A close, intimate friend.

37. 贞洁 Chastity in women.

38. 寡欲 Having few desires.

39. 尊敬传统 Respect for tradition.

40. 财富 Wealth.

# Appendix 3. The nine societal culture dimensions proposed by GLOBE scholars

| Cultural dimension proposed by GLOBE Scholars | Past frameworks that have influenced the emergence of GLOBE cultural dimension |
|---|---|
| 1. Uncertainly avoidance: the text to which members of an organization or society try to avoid uncertainty by relying on social norms, rituals and bureaucratic practices. | This dimension is similar to Hofstede's(1980) uncertainty avoidance versus risk-taking dimension. |
| 2. Power distance: the degree to which members of an organization or society agree with a power differential between people(i.e. People at higher levels of an organization or the government hold more power). | This dimension is similar to Hofstede's(1980) high- versus low-power distance dimension. |
| 3. Collectivism I (Institutional collectivism): the degree to which organizations and societies reward collective distribution of resources and collective action. | In Hofstede's(1980) framework, these two dimensions are treated as one dimension, namely, individualism versus collectivism. |
| 4. Collectivism II (In-group collectivism): the degree to which individuals express pride, loyalty and cohesiveness in their organization or families. | |
| 5. Gender egalitarianism: the extent to which a society minimized differences and promotes equality between genders. | These two dimension draw on Hofstede's(1980) dimension of masculinity versus femininity. |
| 6. Assertiveness: the degree to which individuals in organizations or societies are assertive, confrontational and aggressive in social relationships. | |
| 7. Future orientation: the degree to which individuals in organizations and societies plan and invest in the future and the extent to which they are comfortable with delayed gratification. | This dimension is similar to the future-orientation component of Hofstede's fifth dimension - Confucian dynamism (Hofstede and Bond 1988). |
| 8. Performance orientation: the extent to which an organization or society rewards members for performance improvement and excellence. | This dimension is influenced by McClelland's(1985) 'need for achievement'. |
| 9. Humane orientation: the degree to which individuals in organizations or societies encourage their members to be fair, altruistic, friendly, generous, caring and kind to others. | This dimension is influenced by Kluckhohn and Strodtbeck's(1961) dimension 'human nature as good' versus 'human nature as bad', Putnam's(1993) work on civic society and McClelland's(1985) concept of the affiliative motive. |

*(Source: House, Quigley and de Luque, 2010)*

# Appendix 4

COMPANY:_____

## Questionnaire on Cross-Cultural Communication Barriers for Companies in China

This research project focuses on cultural differences in the companies employing Chinese and Non-Chinese staff. We would be very grateful if you could fill in the questionnaire. **All respondent and answers will be strictly anonymous.**

Researcher:

Prof. Gean Xi

China Three Gorges University
No. 8 Daxue Road, Yichang 443002
Hubei Prov. China

### Part I: Background Information

1. Gender _____ 2. Age _____ 3. Nationality_____ 4. Education _____

5. Country of Origin_____ 6. Overseas Education _____

7. Chinese Language Proficiency _____

8. Position in the Company_____ 9. Years of service _____

### Part II: THE COMPANY

**Please read the following statements carefully, and then answer them as best as you can: 1, I strongly agree; 2, I agree; 3, I neither agree nor disagree; 4, I disagree; 5, I strongly disagree**

| | 1 | 2 | 3 | 4 | 5 |
|---|---|---|---|---|---|
| 10、Compared with foreign-owned enterprises, Chinese native enterprises have more efficient management systems and communication. | | | | | |
| 11、Chinese native companies have a better working environment than foreign-owned companies. | | | | | |
| 12、Your company has provided employees with a sound working environment and promotion opportunities. | | | | | |
| 13、Adaptation to the working environment in China is not difficult. | | | | | |
| 14、The enterprise culture of this company is not very different from similar companies in foreign countries. | | | | | |
| 15、During company meetings, communications can be problematic. | | | | | |
| 16、There have been significant changes in management/employment relations during my time in the country. | | | | | |

# Appendix 5

Please read the following statements carefully, and then answer them as best as you can:1, I strongly agree; 2, I agree; 3, I neither agree nor disagree; 4, I disagree; 5, I strongly disagree

| | | | | | |
|---|---|---|---|---|---|
| 17. Decision making processes in the company are similar to companies outside China. | 1 | 2 | 3 | 4 | 5 |
| 18. There is a marked difference between my values and perceptions from the Chinese employees. | 1 | 2 | 3 | 4 | 5 |
| 19. Chinese employees advocate mutual cooperation and trust between people more than myself. | 1 | 2 | 3 | 4 | 5 |
| 20. Some of my ideas of doing things are influenced by Chinese colleagues. | 1 | 2 | 3 | 4 | 5 |
| 21. Individualism is advocated more than collectivism. | 1 | 2 | 3 | 4 | 5 |
| 22. Chinese employees favour clear authority structures in a company. | 1 | 2 | 3 | 4 | 5 |
| 23. Chinese employees have a stronger risk–taking tendency than myself. | 1 | 2 | 3 | 4 | 5 |
| 24. Chinese employees prefer detailed instructions. | 1 | 2 | 3 | 4 | 5 |
| 25. Traditional Chinese cultural values are very important. | 1 | 2 | 3 | 4 | 5 |
| 26. Communication with Chinese colleagues is more effective with a knowledge of Chinese culture and customs. | 1 | 2 | 3 | 4 | 5 |
| 27. When communicating with Chinese colleagues, sometimes it is difficult to find the right expression. | 1 | 2 | 3 | 4 | 5 |
| 28. The way to solve communication problems is by language and culture training. | 1 | 2 | 3 | 4 | 5 |
| 29. When communication misunderstandings happen, you are willing to seek help from a third party. | 1 | 2 | 3 | 4 | 5 |
| 30. I work more effectively at work with colleagues who are culturally near to my own culture. | 1 | 2 | 3 | 4 | 5 |
| 31. I have frequent contact with Chinese colleagues outside work. | 1 | 2 | 3 | 4 | 5 |
| 32. Trade Union has been playing an important role in my company | 1 | 2 | 3 | 4 | 5 |
| 33. There are different understanding of the function of trade union between Chinese and foreign employees | 1 | 2 | 3 | 4 | 5 |

We thank you for your cooperation. It you wish to receive the research result, please leave your telephone or email address. The questionnaire is confidential and anonymous. Thank you for your support!

# Appendix 6

公司名称:_____

# 在华企业中跨文化沟通障碍调查问卷

尊敬的员工:

　　您好！该问卷旨在研究外企中国员工和外籍员工跨文化沟通中所遇见的障碍问题。对于您支持并填写该调查问卷，我们将不胜感激，同时我们将对您填写的所有信息进行保密，请放心参与！再次感谢您的积极配合及参与。

调研人员：席敬制教授

三峡大学

中国湖北省宜昌市大学路8号，443002

**第一部分：背景知识**

1.性别：○男　　○女　　　2.年龄：_____　　　3.籍贯：_____　　　4.学历：_____

5.常驻工作地：_____　　　　　　6.是否有海外教育经历：是○　否○

7.外语水平：○公四 ○公六 ○专四 ○专八 ○其他（请在横线处具体标明）_____

8.职位：_____　　　　　　9.工龄：_____

**第二部分：主体部分**

请仔细阅读以下陈述，并选出最佳选项：1.完全赞同；2.赞同；3.既不赞同也不反对；4.反对；5.强烈反对。

| | 1 | 2 | 3 | 4 | 5 |
|---|---|---|---|---|---|
| 10、较国企而言，外企拥有更高效的管理体制和沟通机制。 | | | | | |
| 11、就工作环境而言，国企比外企更加优越。 | | | | | |
| 12、您所在的公司为员工提供了良好的工作环境以及公平的晋升机会。 | | | | | |
| 13、就我而言，适应外企的工作环境和氛围并不困难。 | | | | | |
| 14、我所在外企的企业文化与国企并无太大不同。 | | | | | |
| 15、公司例会上，沟通成为一大障碍。 | | | | | |
| 16、在您任职期间，公司管理和雇佣关系发生了重大变化。 | | | | | |

# Appendix 7

请仔细阅读以下陈述，并选出最佳选项：1. 完全赞同；2. 赞同；3. 既不赞同也不反对；4. 反对；5. 强烈反对。

| | 1 | 2 | 3 | 4 | 5 |
|---|---|---|---|---|---|
| 17、公司决策过程与国外公司类似。 | | | | | |
| 18、我的价值观和认知观念和外国员工有明显不同。 | | | | | |
| 19、外籍员工更注重相互合作和信任。 | | | | | |
| 20、我的一些做事思维和方法受到外籍同事的影响。 | | | | | |
| 21、集体主义比个人主义更值得推崇。 | | | | | |
| 22、中国员工更喜欢明确的权威和等级制度。 | | | | | |
| 23、外籍员工比我更具有冒险意识。 | | | | | |
| 24、外籍员工更喜欢细节性的指导和要求。 | | | | | |
| 25、传统的中国文化价值很重要。 | | | | | |
| 26、在与外籍同事交流过程中，了解他们的文化和习俗，让我在沟通过程中更轻松。 | | | | | |
| 27、在与外籍同事交流过程中，有时候很难找到正确的表达方式。 | | | | | |
| 28、解决沟通障碍的方法是语言和文化培训。 | | | | | |
| 29、当沟通障碍发生时，您愿意需求第三方帮助。 | | | | | |
| 30、我在和文化背景相近的同事共事时，工作效率更高。 | | | | | |
| 31、工作之余，我经常和外籍同事联系。 | | | | | |
| 32、工会在我的单位作用很重要 | | | | | |
| 33、外籍员工对工会的理解和我们不一样 | | | | | |

感谢您耐心填写问卷。如果您希望收到我们的调查研究结果，请您留下您的电话或者邮箱地址。问卷所有信息将为您保密。再次，感谢您的支持。

电话：＿＿＿＿＿＿＿＿        邮箱：＿＿＿＿＿＿＿＿

# Appendix 8

## Brief introduction of Interviewees' Companies

### 1. Company A1 Garment

The parent company of Company A1 is one of the Fortune Global 500, which is located in UK. Over the years, the group has always been the largest manufacturer and supplier of industrial sewing thread and zip. In the year of 2004, the group invested 500m yuan in establishing Company A1. Up to now Company A1 has boasted a team of 800 people and 10 foreign staff included.

### 2. Company A2 Life-science

A2, founded in 1851 in the US, is one of the world top 500 MNCs, and has a close cooperation with China over 25 years. Today, A2 has owned 8 manufacturing factories, 3000 staff with more than 3 billion dollars investment in the grand China area. The most recently founded subsidiary, A6 Shanghai Financial Service and Management, Ltd. was unveiled on the 28th of October in 2005. One of A6's subsidiaries engaged in life-science industry in Shu Zhou, a city near Shanghai, was defined as the research subjective where there are about 300 staff including 2 positions for expatriates.

### 3. Company A3 Tourism and Hospitality

A3 belongs to a global company founded in 1777 with 9 hotel brands. With over 4,700 hotels and nearly 674,000 rooms in almost 100 countries around the world. It is one of the greatest companies in the world by creating Great Hotels Guests Love. A3's corporate culture is a commitment to act responsibly in everything they do.

A3 is located in the city of Yichang, Hubei Province, centre of China. The city is famous for its close location of world biggest hydro-electric project, Three Gorges Dam site, thus, a booming industry for tourism and hospitality as well. Being one of the city's few five-star hotel, there are 200 working staff including 1 expatriate position who is in their shift in almost every three years.

### 4.Company A4 Education

A4 is a subsidiary of American based MNC in the city of Wuhan, capital of Hubei Province with nearly 1.6 million populations. It is a new transnational company founded by American Chinese in 2007, but has thriving business in the mainland China. Native English speakers coming from Britian, the US, and Australia were hired by the company and lectures in different cities. Nearly 600 staff in full or part time working in A4 with contract based employment relations. But foreign staff coming just work for short time.

### 5.Company A5 Pharmaceutics

A5 is the third biggest company of pharmacy, biology and health products located in London. It is also one of the earliest foreign pharmacy companies which established joint venture enterprises in China. In the first two decades of entering China, A5 had set up seven registered companies, including five joint-venture enterprises, with 230 million US dollars registered assets. A5, having established offices in 32 principal cities, including Hong Kong, in China, employing more than 2500 staff, is rich in qualified business management talents and technique personnel.

### 6. Company A6 Automobile

A6 automobile, founded on June 12, 1997, is the first Sino-foreign joint venture for auto design and development established by Chinese and American companies in half-half share. Aiming at "becoming a whole-car designing and developing company facing future, leading domestic market, competitive in international market", A6 combined the advanced technology and professional management of American technology and the deep-level understanding and insights into Chinese market. A6 is providing professional automobile engineering service for its parent company and other car manufacturers.

A6 links the company development closely with the individual development. Presently, there are more than 1700 staff, among whom, 3% are with doctoral degree, 35% with master's degree and 51% with bachelor's degree.

### 7. Company A7 Agriculture

A7 has set up production bases and sales offices in Australia, New Zealand, the America, Europe and Asia. There are more than 2,600 employee worldwide working together to provide high quality products and first-class pesticide and marketing technical support for farmers and distributors. Currently, A7 has registered globally about more than 2100 pesticide products, and is selling which to more than 100 countries.

A7 entered Chinese market in 1990s', along with which, there are many famous products marketed successfully in China. In order to further improve the service system and business development in the Chinese market, A7 officially registered a wholly-owned subsidiary in Shanghai Waigaoqiao Tax-protected Zone in September 2005.

## 8. Company A8 Shipping

A8 is a global engineering, technical and business services organization wholly owned by a UK charity dedicated to research and education in science and engineering. Founded in 1760 as a marine classification society, A8 now operates across many industry sectors, with over 9,000 employees based in 78 countries.

A8 has 700 employees working in China office involving business in ship registry, quality control, consultancy. A8 is a foreign director investment company in China.

# Appendix 9

# 访谈提纲（中文版）

访谈号：

日　期：

公司（组织）名称：

## Ⅰ 受访人信息

### 1.1 请选择下面最合适的选项

| 年龄区域 | 20–29 岁 | 30–39 岁 | 40–49 岁 | 50–59 岁 | 60–69 岁 |
|---|---|---|---|---|---|
| | | | | | |

性别：男　　女

### 1.2 请注明您参加工作的时间以及您目前的工作地点

| 基本情况 | 开始工作时间 | 职位 | 所在国家 |
|---|---|---|---|
| | | | |

## Ⅱ 贵公司的劳动关系以及人力资源管理

| 2.1 您如何评价下面有关贵公司劳动关系的表述 | |
|---|---|
| a) | 雇员之间的关系 | |
| b) | 员工与领导之间的关系 | |
| c) | 员工与人事部门的关系 | |
| d) | 员工与经理层的关系 | |
| e) | 工会代表与工会会员的关系 | |
| f) | 工会代表与人事部经理的关系 | |
| g) | 工会代表与公司高层的关系 | |
| h) | 在公司的不同层面，是否有员工（员工代表）参与决策的机会？如果有的话，是在什么方面？ | |

### Ⅲ 文化障碍

| | | |
|---|---|---|
| 3.1 | 盎格鲁．萨克森文化与中国文化最明显和最有影响力的因素是什么? | |
| a) | 贵单位的企业文化特点是什么? | |
| b) | 您对盎格鲁．萨克森文化了解多少? | |
| c) | 您对中国的传统文化了解多少? | |
| d) | 文化的差异是否在公司的工会以及管理等不同的层级带来一些问题? | |
| e) | 文化的差异会给您与外国同行的交流带来问题吗? 如果是, 有哪些问题? | |
| f) | 你是如何理解和谐劳动关系的概念? | |
| g) | 您认为从传统文化的角度考虑, 是否有必要成立工会? | |
| h) | 您公司的有关劳动法规执行的情况如何? | |

### Ⅳ 语言障碍以及非言语沟通障碍

| | | |
|---|---|---|
| 4.1 | 贵公司是否有语言策略政策? | |
| a) | 语言表达差异在词法的层面的表现 | |
| b) | 语言表达的差异在语用层面的表现 | |
| c) | 语言表达的差异在话语分析层面的表现 | |
| d) | 是否有来自非言语表达的障碍? 比如: 面部表情, 体态, 手势, 眼光身体碰触, 人际距离等等。 | |

### Ⅴ 跨文化能力, 跨文化智慧和跨文化能力培训

| | | |
|---|---|---|
| 5.1 | 跨文化能力培训是否对劳动关系和人力资源管理有效? 如果有效, 如何开展此类培训。 | |
| a) | 您是如何看待跨文化能力? | |
| b) | 您的公司有组织过跨文化能力培训的项目吗? | |
| c) | 您认为跨文化能力与劳动关系和人力资源管理的提升是否有关联? | |
| d) | 贵公司提倡企业文化吗? 如果是, 企业文化是如何帮助构建和谐劳动关系的? | |
| e) | 您对贵公司的企业文化是否满意? 对贵公司的劳动关系是否满意? | |

# Appendix 10

# Semi-structured interview (English version)

Interview number:

Date:

Company (organization):

## I  Information about the respondent

1.1 Please specify the categories to which you belong:

|  | 20-29years | 30-39years | 40-49years | 50-59years | 60-69years |
|---|---|---|---|---|---|
| Age group |  |  |  |  |  |

**Sex:** Male      Female

1.2 Please specify the year when you started to work with the company where are you working now.

|  | Starting date (year) | Position | Country |
|---|---|---|---|
| General information |  |  |  |

## II  IR and HRM in your company

| | 2.1 How would you assess the following employment relations in your organization | |
|---|---|---|
| a) | Relations among employees | |
| b) | Relations between employee and supervisor | |
| c) | Relations between employee and personnel manager | |
| d) | Relations between employee and manager | |
| e) | Relations between union representatives and union members | |
| f) | Relation between union representatives and the personnel/HR managers | |
| g) | Relation between union representatives and the top level management | |
| h) | Is there any type of employee participation (direct or through their representatives) in the decision-making process at the workplace or company level? If the answer is yes, in which areas? | |

## III  Culture barriers

| | | |
|---|---|---|
| 3.1 What are the most distinctive and influence factors of Anglo-Saxon and Chinese culture | | |
| a) | What are the characteristics of your corporate culture? | |
| b) | How much do you know Anglo-Saxon culture? | |
| c) | How much do you know Chinese traditional Culture? | |
| d) | Do cultural differences make any problems between trade union and managers at different levels? | |
| e) | Do you agree that culture barriers create problems for your communications with Chinese peers and government? if so, how | |
| f) | How do you understand Chinese term of Harmony Employment Relations? | |
| g) | Do you think that it is necessary to organize trade union in your company from the cultural tradition? | |
| h) | How is labour legislation being implemented in your company? | |

## IV  Language and non-verbal communicating barriers

| | | |
|---|---|---|
| 4.1 Are there any language strategies in your company? | | |
| a) | Different language expression at lexical level. | |
| b) | Different language expression at pragmatics level. | |
| c) | Different language expression at discourse analysis level. | |
| d) | Any barriers coming from non-verbal actions? Facial expression, posture, gesture, eye contact,Touching, distance | |

## V  Cross-cultural competence (CCC), intelligence and training

| | | |
|---|---|---|
| 5.1 Does the CCC training programme work effectively in IR and HR management? If so, how to conduct it? | | |
| a) | How do you think of CCC? | |
| b) | Are there any CCC training programme organized by the company? | |
| c) | Is the CCC correlated with the improvement of IRs and HRM? | |
| d) | Has the corporate culture been advocated by the company? If so, how does it help with the harmonious IRs and HRM? | |
| e) | Are you happy with your corporate culture and with the IRs and HRM in your company? | |

# Appendix 11

**Table1**     **Demographics of interviewees 2010-2013**

| No. | Participant Identifier | Nationality | Ethnicity | Age | Gender | Industry | MNC tenure | Expatriation Duration | Job function/position |
|---|---|---|---|---|---|---|---|---|---|
| 1 | A1 | US | US | 31-40 | Male | Life-science | 10 | 4 | CEO |
| 2 | A2 | MAS | MAS | 41-50 | Male | Life-science | 15 | 5 | General Manager |
| 3 | A3 | CN | CN | 31-40 | Female | Life-science | 10 | -- | Division manager |
| 4 | A4 | US | US | 31-40 | Male | Life-science | 8 | 1 | Project manager |
| 5 | A5 | US | US | 20-30 | Male | Life-science | 5 | 0.5 | Engineer |
| 6 | A6 | Taiwan | Taiwan | 41-50 | Male | Life-science | 10 | 2 | Projector manager |
| 7 | A7 | CN | CN | 41-50 | Male | Life-science | 15 | 10 | HR manager |
| 8 | B1 | AU | AU | 41-50 | Male | Agriculture | 10 | 2 | Department Manager |
| 9 | B2 | AU | AU | 31-40 | Male | Tourism | 5 | 2 | Quality Supervisor |
| 10 | B3 | AU | AU | 31-40 | Female | Tourism | 3 | 1 | Department Manager |
| 11 | B4 | AU | CN | 31-40 | Female | Tourism | 2 | 1 | Director Assistant |
| 12 | B5 | AU | AU | 31-40 | Female | Education | 2 | 1 | Quality Control |
| 13 | B6 | CN | CN | 21-30 | Male | Agriculture | 3 | - | Projector Manager |
| 14 | B7 | CN | CN | 21-30 | Male | Agriculture | 2 | - | Sales Manager |
| 15 | B8 | AU | IND | 31-40 | Male | Agriculture | 5 | 2 | Maintenance Director |
| 16 | C1 | IND | IND | 31-40 | Male | Pharmaceutics | 5 | 2 | Head of Team |
| 17 | C2 | UK | UK | 31-40 | Male | Pharmaceutics | 8 | 2 | Quality Manager |
| 18 | C3 | UK | UK | 31-40 | Male | Pharmaceutics | 6 | 1 | Project Manager |

*Note: AU=Australia; CN = China; IND=India; NZ=New Zealand ;MAS = Malaysia; US = the United States; UK=the United Kingdom*

269

# Appendix 12

**Table2**      **Demographics of interviewees 2010-2013**

| No. | Participant Identifier | Nationality | Ethnicity | Age | Gender | Industry | MNC tenure | Expatriation Duration | Job function/position |
|---|---|---|---|---|---|---|---|---|---|
| 19 | C4 | UK | UK | 31-40 | Female | Garment | 3 | 1 | Director of Quality Control |
| 20 | C5 | CN | CN | 21-30 | Female | Garment | 2 | -- | Employee |
| 21 | C6 | UK | UK | 31-40 | Male | Garment | 5 | 2 | Department Manager |
| 22 | C7 | UK | CN | 31-40 | Female | Ship Manufacture | 4 | 2 | Engineering Department |
| 23 | C8 | UK | UK | 41-50 | Male | Ship Manufacture | 8 | 1 | Quality Department director |
| 24 | D1 | US | US | 41-50 | Male | Automobile | 6 | 1 | Product Manager |
| 25 | D2 | US | CN | 41-50 | Male | Automobile | 10 | 2 | Project Manager |
| 26 | D3 | CN | CN | 21-30 | Male | Automobile | 2.5 | -- | Sale support |
| 27 | D4 | CN | CN | 21-30 | Male | Automobile | 3 | -- | Sale manager |
| 28 | D5 | CN | CN | 41-50 | Female | Automobile | 10 | -- | Account Manager |
| 29 | D6 | CN | CN | 31-40 | Male | Automobile | 8 | -- | Production Manager |
| 30 | D7 | CN | CN | 31-40 | Male | Automobile | 9 | -- | HR Department |

*Note: AU=Australia; CN=China; IND=India; NZ=New Zealand ;MAS=Malaysia; US=the United States; UK=the United Kingdom*

# Appendix 13

# Appendix 14

## Questionnaire on Cross-Cultural Communication Barriers for Companies in China

This research project focuses on cultural differences in the companies employing Chinese and Non-Chinese staff. We would be very grateful if you could fill in the questionnaire. **All respondent and answers will be strictly anonymous.**

Researcher:

Prof. Gean Xi
China Three Gorges University
No. 8 Daxue Road, Yichang 443002
Hubei Prov. China

### Part I: Background Information

Gender    ○ Male  ● Female

Age

Nationality

Country of Origin